Henry James
and the French Novel

In the same series

Stendhal Michael Wood
Thomas Hardy: The Poetic Structure Jean R. Brooks
The Nouveau Roman: A Study in the Practice of Writing
    Stephen Heath
Aldous Huxley Keith May

In preparation

Kafka Franz Kuna
Flaubert Jonathan Culler
Melville Robert Lee

Novelists and Their World
General Editor: Graham Hough
Professor of English at the University of Cambridge

Henry James and the French Novel

A study in inspiration

Philip Grover

Paul Elek London

First published in Great Britain
1973 by
Elek Books Limited
54-58 Caledonian Road
London N1 9RN

ISBN 0 236 17681 1

Printed in Great Britain at
St Ann's Press, Park Road,
Altrincham, Cheshire.

Contents

Acknowledgements

A work like this is naturally indebted to numerous scholars and critics. Those works that have been most useful to me I have tried to indicate in my notes. A few of the others that I have found stimulating and useful are given in my Suggested Further Reading. A work I have not there mentioned, however, is the indispensable bibliography produced by Leon Edel and Dan Laurence. All students of James are in their eternal debt for this work. Without such a guide many of James's articles on French literature, some of which still lie in nineteenth-century periodicals, would have gone unremarked and I should have been without many essential clues and references.

Many people have been very helpful in the preparation of this book. For giving me the chance to undertake the necessary initial research I am very grateful to Mr Philip Mosedale, former Head of the Department of English and General Studies at the Cambridgeshire College of Arts and Technology, and to the Principal and Governors of the College as well as the Cambridgeshire County Council I am indebted for their generously arranging the necessary leave of absence. To Darwin College, Cambridge, I am extremely grateful for providing such a delightful and stimulating atmosphere in which to carry on my researches. The Librarian of the Brotherton Collection at the University of Leeds generously permitted me to consult their collection of letters of Henry James to Edmund Gosse. Mrs Marian Childe typed a most difficult original manuscript and to her patience and meticulous care I owe a great debt. Mr Peter Gurney-Davey read the original manuscript and I am most grateful for his scrupulous assistance. But my greatest debt of all is to Professor Graham Hough. He encouraged me in my first faltering steps and without his constant support and criticism over the years it has taken to get this book finally prepared I could never have completed it. I only wish the final product were more worthy of him. More than the usual formal apology is meant to suggest, I am aware how much the remaining errors are alone my responsibility.

Chapter 5 originally appeared in a slightly different form in *The Modern Language Review*, Vol. 66 (October 1971), and I wish to thank the editors and the Modern Humanities Research Association for their permission to reprint it here.

Preface

A great deal has been written about Henry James. Yet no one has hitherto undertaken a serious examination of the abiding interest that James had in French literature and examined the important effect his constant reading and re-reading of French novelists had on his own development as a writer. Certain studies have dealt with part of this subject, especially with regard to James's early works. Cornelia Kelley's important book *The Early Development of Henry James* (1930, revised edition 1965) rightly emphasizes the importance of Mérimée's influence on James's early short stories, the example of Balzac for *Roderick Hudson*, and the value of Gautier for the development of James's early travel descriptions. But she has limited her analysis to the period up to the writing of *The Portrait of a Lady* (1881). It is my conviction, however, that many of James's later techniques and concerns as a novelist have their origin in his attempts at emulating Balzac and in his reflections on Balzac's manner of solving certain problems faced by all novelists. Nor has anyone taken seriously James's lasting affiliation with what was valuable in the 'L'Art pour L'Art' movement as it was developed by the followers of Gautier: Flaubert, the brothers Goncourt and Daudet. I have attempted to make certain stylistic comparisons between Flaubert and James because I believe that James's search for a unified language—one in which there is no distinctive break between narration, description, dialogue and interior monologue—is Flaubertian in origin. But these are not the only important links that James had with French nineteenth-century writers. James's interest in French literature never lapsed—he did not 'turn English all over' to the point of neglecting the important and interesting developments in representation that continued to take place after the death of Flaubert (1880). His articles on Zola, Pierre Loti, the Goncourts and above all Alphonse Daudet are sufficient evidence of this. I believe that the practice of the Goncourts and of Daudet, particularly the latter, was of great importance for the way James developed his own methods of presenting the visible world in his later novels.

In the present book I try then to deal broadly with these three areas: the lesson of Balzac, the importance of Flaubert and the significance of the 'L'Art pour l'Art' movement for James. In doing so I shall at times discuss how James borrowed and used the themes, situations, plots or characters suggested to him by other authors. Of course the comparison is often of interest because James greatly changed the original work to fit his own purposes, but the 'germ' of a story or interesting situation often came to him as he reflected on what he might do with material first handled by someone else. The degree of relationship between the Jamesian work and the corresponding French work is not always the same. For example the relationship between 'The Madonna of the Future' (1873) and Balzac's *Le Chef d'Oeuvre inconnu* is very close. But that between *The Princess Casamassima* and *L'Education sentimentale* is much looser. Both these works deal with a subject of much interest to many nineteenth-century writers—revolutionary movements. And James firmly placed himself in the realistic tradition when writing *The Princess Casamassima* and *The Bostonians*, both first serialized in 1885.

I am not very much interested in sources in the usual sense. The comparison between *Le Chef d'Oeuvre inconnu* and 'The Madonna of the Future' is the one most like that form of study. In the rest of the section on Balzac I am more concerned with technique, structure, composition and style, as indeed I am throughout this work. It is these formal elements that James above all appreciated in French literature. He never failed to emphasize how, to his mind, the French had a superior sense of form and how, in comparison, both American and English literature were sadly lacking. In such considerations it is never —or at most only rarely—a question of straightforward borrowing, but rather one of the adaptation and modification of a suggestion or inspiration derived from another writer's work.

In the case of Balzac we have much evidence from James's own writings that he felt that Balzac had solved problems that he had failed to solve in some of his early works and that to Balzac he had a debt that he could but repay in instalments. However, he did not simply imitate Balzac; rather he felt inspired, I believe, by his example to seek his own, but often analogous, solutions to similar problems of fictional presentation.

In discussing Flaubert and James I am principally interested in how they handled similar subjects and how James evolved a style of his own in order to achieve certain objectives which Flaubert had also set himself. The study becomes consequently not one of sources or specific influences but a comparative study of two major novelists evolving different techniques to solve similar problems. Nevertheless some of these techniques, in James's case, I think were developed in emulation of Flaubert's achievement. I am, of course, more interested in James than Flaubert for the purposes of this work, and my main emphasis therefore falls on him. The comparisons however I feel not to be without interest.

It seems to me that James came to desire ends similar to those pursued by Flaubert and hence developed a style that, in its own way, is parallel to Flaubert's without in any way being an imitation of it. This I think was partly due to his own experience which brought him closer to the position of certain writers associated with or in important ways influenced by the 'L'Art pour l'Art' movement. These affinities and comparisons I explore in the last section of this book. James showed great interest in the visible world, and the ways of presenting it evolved by such writers as Daudet, and a comparison of their and James's methods of presenting the pictorial side of a subject is one of the specific areas of comparison I shall make. But the whole 'L'Art pour l'Art' movement is of greater significance in the understanding of James than has hitherto been appreciated, and there are many parallels and comparisons which will illuminate James's work.

These then are some of the recurring areas of interest in the present study: James's borrowing of themes and subjects from certain French writers; his adaptation and development of some of their techniques in the composition of the novel; and his critical response to French authors and his assimilation of many of the critical ideas that were current in French thinking about the art of the novel.

Part One

The Lesson of Balzac

I
The Ideal World of Art

The life of the artist—as hero, tragic victim or the great image of imaginative and creative life, bringing the sweet waters of art to the barren lands of prosaic existence—is one of the most persistent themes in the literature of the nineteenth century.[1] Henry James constantly returned to this theme, writing a number of tales and novels in which the artist appears as either the central character or as a narrator of an action that his position as an artist—usually that of a portrait painter—gives him an opportunity to observe. The first of his tales which deal with the artistic temperament are 'The Madonna of the Future' and 'The Sweetheart of M. Briseux' (both 1873), and as Cornelia Kelley first pointed out, both of these stories owe much to Balzac's *Le Chef d'Oeuvre inconnu* (1831).[2]

We may examine Balzac's *Le Chef d'Oeuvre inconnu* and James's 'The Madonna of the Future' together for two reasons other than this mere historical filiation. In his tale Balzac devotes much space to the discussion of the relationship of art to the external world, to the difference between copying nature and expressing it, and hence to the reality of art. And furthermore he dramatizes the conflict between the love for a woman and the love for art. For him there is an irreconcilable conflict between the demands made by art and the exigencies of the artistic vocation on the one hand and normal human passionate desires on the other. These themes find their counterparts in James's story, even if his answers to the problems may differ. But more importantly James returned to these themes in a number of later works beginning with *Roderick Hudson* (1875) and going on to the great novels and stories about artists and the artistic life of the 1880s and 1890s: 'The Lesson of the Master', *The Tragic Muse*, 'The Death of the Lion', for example. So already in this early story we can see James treating material that will become of even greater importance to him when he has absorbed more of the lessons of the 'L'Art pour l'Art' movement; already adumbrated here are some of his most prevailing themes and attitudes and his later works will show an even greater affinity, in their discussions of the conflict between art and life, with Balzac's tale than 'The Madonna' does itself.

The other major reason for discussing James's and Balzac's stories together is this. Art, as both insist, is not the mere copying of nature but an imaginative interpretation and transformation of experience by the artist. A comparison of their different artistic temperaments and sensibilities as shown in the way they handle their stories will help to bring out some of James's distinctive qualities, and to define his art and his nature as an artist. James nourished himself on French literature. A major aim of this study will be to discuss the ways he absorbed and transformed French influences into his own unique art, and no place is better to start than with Balzac.

I

In Balzac's tale *Le Chef d'Oeuvre inconnu*[3] a young aspiring painter, who turns out to be Nicolas Poussin, calls on a famous court painter, François Porbus, now living in retirement. He is preceded into the master's studio, however, by an old man of singular appearance. Porbus asks his strange guest to tell him what he thinks of a painting of his—a Marie Égyptienne—which has made some stir amongst connoisseurs. The old man equivocates and then declares that it fails to give us the illusion of life. After some lengthy discussions about the nature of art he proceeds to demonstrate his theories, and in a fit of inspiration and frantic work he transforms Porbus's painting. His adroit application of *chiaroscuro* succeeds in rendering the painting more life-like.

The picture completed, he asks the other two home with him. Here Poussin is impressed by the magnificence of his house and the superb paintings, one of which he takes to be a Giorgione but which is actually one of his strange companion's early works. Porbus now, for the first time, addresses the strange old man as Maître Frenhofer, and asks him about the painting he has been working on for the last ten years and which no one has yet seen. Frenhofer refuses to show it because he has not yet perfected it, and he is beset by doubts about the nature of painting and his own success in giving physical substance to his vision. One thing he seeks is a perfect woman who could act as his model. When he arrives back at his *grenier* Poussin broaches the subject of posing for Frenhofer to his beautiful and perfect mistress Gillette. If she will pose then he can enter Frenhofer's studio and see his painting, the 'Belle-Noiseuse'. After some painful discussion the young girl agrees but not without many misgivings as to the future of their love as a result of her sacrifice.

At first Frenhofer is not prepared to let Porbus and Poussin see his painting in return for the opportunity of having a sight of Gillette, for he defends his painting as he would his wife: no one else should look upon the woman that he loves and lives with. But when he sees Gillette his needs as an artist triumph over his hesitations as a lover. When they actually see the picture Poussin and Porbus are puzzled, for there is nothing but a mass of daubs and criss-crossing lines. Poussin lets out the truth and Frenhofer is awakened from his illusion. He realizes that he has produced nothing for his ten years of work, and falls into tears and despair. The next day when Porbus anxiously returns he finds that Frenhofer, after burning all his paintings, has died during the night.

In this tale Balzac has introduced four main themes: the nature of the artistic temperament, the relation of art to reality, the techniques of painting, and the conflict between love of art and human love.

Frenhofer exemplifies a particular concept of the artist. This comes out forcibly in Balzac's description of Frenhofer correcting Porbus's Marie Égyptienne.

Il travaillait avec une ardeur si passionnée que la sueur se perla sur son front dépouillé; il allait si rapidement par de petits movements si impatients, si saccadés, que pour le jeune Poussin il semblait qu'il y eût dans le corps de ce bizarre personnage un démon qui agissait par ses mains en les prenant fantastiquement contre le gré de l'homme. L'éclat surnaturel des yeux, les convulsions qui semblaient l'effet d'une résistance donnaient à cette idée un semblant de vérité qui devait agir sur une jeune imagination.[4]

(He worked with such passionate fervour that beads of sweat gathered upon his denuded brow; he went at it so quickly, with such impatient, such abrupt little movements, that it seemed to young Poussin as if there were a demon within the body of this singular being who worked through his hands by fantastically using them against the man's own will. The unearthly glitter of his eyes, the convulsions that seemed the result of a struggle, gave to this fancy a semblance of truth which could not but stir a young imagination.)

The story started out as a 'conte fantastique' and developed in later versions into a story about art with philosophical implications.[5] But in the strange figure of Frenhofer Balzac left qualities appropriate to a tale of fantasy when the emphasis of the story had shifted. In the later versions about one-third of the tale is taken up with Frenhofer's technical discussion of painting. His basic nature does not change, however, and hence it would appear that for Balzac the artist, particularly when inspired, is essentially a demonic creature. So that we are not tempted to think that Frenhofer is some sort of freak—an unusual person of special and perhaps impossible powers—Balzac quite clearly states that he was 'une complète image de la nature artiste'. We have too the testimony of the young Poussin whom after all we are intended to trust: his is no mere passer-by's appreciation. 'Ce vieillard était devenu [for Poussin] par une transfiguration subite, l'Art lui-même, l'art avec ses secrets, ses fougues et ses rêveries.'[6] ('This old man had become, by a sudden transfiguration, Art itself, art with all its secrets, its passions and its dreams.')

If Frenhofer is a somewhat exceptional manifestation of the artistic temperament he is not the only artist in the story. All the participants, except Gillette, are painters. This certainly helps in creating that unity of tone and interest that Balzac aimed at. (James in those early stories based on this tale does not succeed so well.) We have the young, enthusiastic but poor genius, aware of his powers and full of visions, but not yet sure of his path nor, before his meeting with Porbus and Frenhofer, of his real talents. This is Poussin. In Porbus we have the master who has created some great works but who is still striving for greater perfection. And lastly we have Frenhofer whose ability is attested in many ways but who loses himself in trying to go beyond the inevitable limitations of art. All share one important trait in common: doubt as to their own powers. Poussin's doubts arise from the fact that he has yet to prove himself, Frenhofer's from his trying to do too much, and Porbus's from the fact that he has not yet achieved a work which fully satisfies him. Their doubts as to their own abilities and accomplishments have a necessary link with their being true artists endowed with artistic sensibilities. It is because of their perceptiveness, their acuteness, their sensitiveness that they doubt, but these qualities are also essential to them as creators. To be able to doubt is to be able to create: the one is not possible without the other. An artist who before an accomplished master is not without doubts as to his own ability will always lack something in his work.

Although Gillette is not an artist her fate is intimately bound up with that of the others, and her story is as much part of the tale as Frenhofer's passion for creating a work of art to match or surpass nature itself. For Balzac here treats briefly, but profoundly, one of the central themes that puzzle writers throughout the century, not least James himself: the relation of creative activity to the experience of life. Here it takes the concrete form of the struggle between love for a woman and love for art. The beautiful woman is perhaps after all the fullest and most compelling symbol for what experience can offer to the sensual man that we all are, and not least of all artists with their power to respond to beauty. Balzac spares no pains to make Gillette the ideal embodiment of womanhood:

. . . il avait rencontré soudain une maîtresse, une de ces âmes nobles et généreuses qui viennent souffrir près d'un grand homme, en épousent les misères et s'efforçent de comprendre leurs caprices; forte pour la misère et l'amour, comme d'autres sont intrépides à porter le luxe, à faire parader leur insensibilité. Le sourire errant sur les lèvres de Gillette dorait ce grenier et rivalisait avec l'éclat du ciel. Le soleil ne brillait pas toujours, tandis qu'elle était toujours là, recueillie dans sa passion, attachée à son bonheur, à sa souffrance, consolant le génie qui débordait dans l'amour avant de s'emparer de l'art.[7]

(. . . he had unexpectedly met with a mistress, one of those noble and generous souls who choose to suffer by a great man's side, who share in his poverty and endeavour to understand his whims; as powerful in their bearing of poverty and love as other women are brazen in their display of luxury and the showing off of their insensibility. The smile that stole over Gillette's lips shed a golden light in this garret and rivalled the brilliance of the heavens. The sun, moreover, did not always shine whereas she was always there, absorbed in her passion, occupied with his happiness and his sorrow, consoling the genius who overflowed in love before possessing himself of art.)

Gillette then represents much more than physical beauty and sensuous pleasure; she is devotion, fidelity, love and all the support that a man seeks from a woman to make his life tolerable and complete in human terms. It is this woman and this love, and hence life itself and all its rewards and pleasures, all the things that most men need to live at all, that Poussin is ready to sacrifice for the sake of his art. If Gillette will pose for Frenhofer then Poussin will have an occasion to penetrate into the other's closely guarded *atelier* to see his 'Belle-Noiseuse'. The choice is clearly presented as one that involves a conflict between Poussin as an artist and as a lover, between art, fame, honour and glory on the one hand, and human love, devotion and contentment on the other. And obviously Poussin is both man and artist. So the conflict is one that involves him constantly as first one part and then the other of his self predominates.

Gillette at first resists Poussin's request to pose for Frenhofer. To expose her body to the other painter will entail a diminution of his love for her. Not only will he cease to care for and respect her, she herself will feel unworthy of him. Even to pose for him is inimical to their love, for he does not look at her in the same way when he paints her as when he admires and adores her as a woman he loves.

'Si tu désires que je pose encore devant toi comme l'autre jour,' reprit-elle d'un petit air boudeur, 'je n'y consentirai plus jamais, car, dans ces moments-là, tes yeux ne me disent plus rien. Tu ne penses plus à moi, et cependant tu me regardes.'[8]

('If you wish me to sit once more for you as I did the other day,' she rejoined with a slightly pouting air, 'I will never consent to it, because at such times your eyes say nothing at all to me. You no longer think of me even though you are looking right at me.')

The loved woman ceases to be a woman for the artist is not concerned with the individuality and personal soul of his model but with her as an object that will enable him to translate his vision into terms comprehensible to others. Experience is essential to his art, but that art consumes experience and normal human beings for its own immortal purposes and passes beyond. This is simply but instinctively realized by Gillette.[9]

At first the issue is settled by Poussin's renunciation of his art for the sake of his love. He throws himself at Gillette's feet and exclaims:

'J'aime mieux être aimé que glorieux. Pour moi, tu es plus belle que la fortune et les honneurs. Va, jette mes pinceaux, brûle ces esquisses Je me suis trompé. Ma vocation, c'est de t'aimer. *Je ne suis peintre, je suis amoureux!* Périssent et l'art et tous ses secrets!'[10] [Emphasis—P.G]

('I would rather be beloved than famous. To me you are more beautiful than riches or honours. There, throw away those brushes, burn those sketches. I was mistaken. My vocation is to love you. *I am not a painter. I am a lover!* May art and all its secrets perish.')

Such a sacrifice is extremely flattering to Gillette: she feels triumphant. But as a woman who loves intensely and completely she is prepared to sacrifice herself, and the future of her love, for the sake of the future fame and glory of the man she loves. This capacity for renunciation and self-sacrifice for the sake of love is the supreme feminine virtue—it is the quality that makes woman an ideal figure for the imagination. And this is as true for James as for Balzac. It is obviously of such fundamental ethical importance for each that there can be no question of 'influence' in the narrow sense of 'borrowing'. And Gillette acts according to a beautiful ideal—as does Isabel Archer or Milly Theale: 'Ah! me perdre pour toi. Oui, cela est bien beau! mais tu m'oublieras.'[11] ('Ah, to ruin myself for you! That is indeed fine. But you will forget me.')

Poussin struggles between his love for Gillette and his love for art, but Frenhofer has only one love: his art. He transfers all his sexual and amorous passions to his painting. He is not completely unaware of the differences between his creation and a living woman, for he claims at one point that he can make her *seem* to live. But the boundary between seeming and reality is confused, and that confusion is given dramatic expression by the manner in which Frenhofer speaks of his picture. He refers to it as '*mon épouse*'. When Porbus suggests that he show his painting to them in return for the chance of viewing Gillette he protests indignantly: 'Déchirer le voile sous lequel j'ai *chastement* couvert mon bonheur? Mais ce serait une horrible prostitution!'[12] (Emphasis—P.G.) ('Rend the veil that has chastely covered my happiness? But that would be a shameful prostitution!') This last comment gains added poignancy when we remember that precisely the same struggle has gone on between Gillette and Poussin.

When Gillette arrives at the studio the old man's eye lights up at the sight of her. Frenhofer admires her as a man and as an artist. His power as an artist in fact heightens his appreciation of her as a woman: Frenhofer, 'par une habitude de peintre, déshabilla, pour ainsi dire, cette jeune fille en–devinant ses formes les plus secrètes.'[13] ('. . . as painters do, undressed, so to speak, this young woman by divining her most secret forms.') Poussin becomes immediately jealous and wishes to withdraw. He threatens immediate death to Frenhofer if Gillette in any way cries out or protests at his behaviour.

But in each the passion for art overcomes feelings of jealousy, for when Frenhofer sees Gillette he realizes that at last he has before him the perfect model that he has sought in order to finish his paintings. So he overcomes his scruples for the sake of his art, in the same way as Poussin, in order to penetrate the secrets of Frenhofer, is prepared to sacrifice Gillette and their love and swallows his jealousy.

One of the most dramatic moments in the story is when the real and the ideal women are confronted. Gillette in fact seems to attain to that beauty which is ideal and hence impossible for any human being. As Poussin and Porbus examine the painting she is in tears and realizes that her love, as she had feared, has been destroyed. Frenhofer, in trying to equal nature and create a living woman, has not only destroyed his art but the love that was between Gillette and Poussin. The beauty of the real woman triumphs over that of the painting, which is an incoherent jumble of lines and crosses, but art has displaced life.

The true artist, Frenhofer insists, does not imitate nature, he is not 'un vil copiste'. The aim of the artist is to *express* nature. But this expression is only possible when the artist has seized upon the essence of the beautiful inherent in a number of particular instances but fully manifested in none of them. To be a *poet*—in the sense of a man of a particular mode of perception and power to understand—is to go beyond appearance to the truth of things and present the ideal. 'Nous avons à saisir l'esprit, l'âme, la physionomie des choses et des êtres.'[14]

('We must capture the spirit, the soul, the physiognomy of things and beings.') A hand or any other part of the body is a means of expressing a thought and it is this connection that must be found. The art of the portrait painter is thus nearest to that of the biographer or novelist. In Balzac's remarks on the connection between the external fact and the thought with which it is connected we have the source of both his practice of detailed specification and hence his particular kind of symbolism (to be discussed in section III of the next chapter.) 'La Forme est, dans ses figures, ce qu'elle est chez nous, un truchement pour se communiquer des idées, des sensations, une vaste poésie.'[15] ('Form is, in its figures, what it is for us all— a translator of ideas, of sensations, of great poetry'.)

But there is another sense in which the artist is not a 'vil copiste'. 'Toute figure est un monde, un portrait dont *le modèle est apparu dans* une vision sublime'.[16] (Emphasis—P.G.) ('Every face is a world, a portrait whose model has appeared in a sublime vision'.) The ideal is the poet's *vision*. It is this he reproduces, to which he tries to give concrete form, not to something *seen* by the eyes of day. James too found that the most suggestive hints are those that have the least accretion of detail and upon which therefore the imagination can most freely work.

It is stressed more than once that Frenhofer's gift is in his remarkable ability to make pictures seem to live. In this he rivals nature. He fails when he tries to do more than art can. He is the Faustus of art. His efforts are part of man's attempts— or Romantic man's—to 'saisir un infini qui échappe sans cesse à ses mains débiles'—*Les Proscrits* ('seize an infinity which continually evades his feeble hands'). The ideal, the internal vision, surpasses any realizable creation of man or nature. And what the artist can imagine is always greater than what he can accomplish. Frenhofer overreaches himself by trying to do more than human art can do, by trying for an impossible perfection where art ceases to be art and becomes creative in the way that nature herself does, producing real beings. By seeking to transcend art so that it is reabsorbed in life he destroys art. But he inspires respect for two reasons. He has created magnificent works of art. And in his desire to give forms to visions, to make his creations equal his dreams, he represents the impossible but inspiring aim of the artist. It is Porbus who indicates the necessary limitations and teaches the lesson: a painter should only meditate 'with brush in hand'. Too much thought is destructive of the creative powers, and dreams must be entertained in conjunction with the means to execute them.

II

In James's story 'The Madonna of the Future' the artist, Theobald, has a vision of the ideal Madonna, the perfection of all previous pictorial incarnations of the type, but is unable to translate his vision on to canvas. In his case he has not yet, after twenty years, painted a stroke. His canvas remains blank and cracks with age. When he is awakened from his dreams he too dies. But although it may be seen that in basic conception the story owes much to Balzac, James has not merely rewritten the story in English but has adapted it to his own purposes.

First there are differences as well as similarities in his conception of the artist. Frenhofer is rich and has painted a number of successful pictures. He is recognized as a master by competent judges. Theobald on the other hand is extremely poor, a down-and-out. He has sold no pictures, and is known for no works. He is even suspected by some of the Americans in Florence to be a mere charlatan, incapable of even drawing a decent likeness. He has talked much and done nothing. He is now neglected by most as a vain and fatuous wind-bag. This is not the attitude taken by the narrator, but that represented by one of the American colony, and there seems at first some reason to accept it. He has done one piece of good work: a drawing of a child. This he created in a burst of inspiration and work as the child was dying. Only the narrator, as one who can judge of its real value, sees it.

Theobald is first seen by moonlight in front of the statues of David and Perseus in the square in front of the Palazzo Vecchio at Florence. James in fact is here drawing upon another source for his artist: Tebaldeo in Musset's *Lorenzaccio*. James's artist gives the impression of being fantastic, unreal, and picturesque. This is much closer to Balzac's Frenhofer, without implying any demonic or diabolic powers on Theobald's part, than to Musset's artist. But both Tebaldeo and Frenhofer, and Theobald after them, believe in the ideal vocation of art. It is his inner vision that the painter tries to represent. But the result, except for a few, is a failure to create works which match the artist's imagination. Tebaldeo refers to one of his own paintings as 'a miserable sketch of a magnificent dream'. And he sums up the painter's life as an attempt to 'realize his dreams' (*Lorenzaccio*, Act II, scene 2). It is not surprising of course that Musset and Balzac should thus agree, for their ideas are common stock in Romantic theories of art. James does not essentially differ from them. He emphasizes as they do that the artist has an ideal image which he tries to translate into a concrete representation. Theobald studies Raphael's 'Madonna in the Chair', because she is a 'spotless image'. And in his enthusiasm he exclaims: 'What a master, certainly! But ah, what a *seer*!' [Emphasis—P.G.]

James too gives us his version of the discussion in Balzac about the difference between imitation and creation. The narrator suggests that Raphael perhaps had a model. That does not, says Theobald, 'diminish the miracle. He took his *hint*' from the young woman, 'but meanwhile, the painter's idea had taken wings.' [Emphasis—P.G.] 'He saw the fair form made perfect; he rose to the vision without tremor . . . That's what they call idealism; the word's vastly abused, but the thing is good.'[17] In this emphasis on idealism, in the sense of striving to incarnate an artistic vision rather than to copy the externals of nature, we can see where Musset, Balzac and James meet. But idealism is a word, as James notes, that can be abused. Or perhaps we should say that at the least it is ambiguous. Balzac's idealism tends toward the creation of ideal types: men and women who are larger than life, whose passions and actions, however based on observations and given specific forms, are more violent, permanent and dominating than those of everyday life.

For James, however, idealism also has a moral meaning, and he strives to incorporate at least one person in each of his major novels who acts from a sense of moral idealism. And this for James is also an aesthetic value. Many of his strictures on French fiction come from his feeling that this form of idealism is there neglected. If men and women do not exist as he can imagine them then so much the worse for the world. And art should incorporate them as they can be imagined. Much of this idealism is bound up with the notion of self-sacrifice—present in so many of his heroines—or acting for ends that are good in themselves but not beneficial to the agent. Life is hence transformed and improved by art.

The conflict between earthly love and love for art is central to Balzac's story. But James does not suggest that there is any direct antagonism between the two passions: his Theobald does not have to sacrifice his love for his art. Balzac however is recalled when Theobald asks the narrator: 'Can you look upon a beautiful woman with reverent eyes?'[18] Whereas Frenhofer's woman was a picture, Theobald's beautiful woman is still a woman, but she is only beautiful to him. It is his vision that has transformed her as Frenhofer's picture was transformed into a near-living creature by the power of his imagination. In Balzac's work this transformation is seen as almost a disease of the imagination; in James's, it is a beautifying vision that does no one any harm, least of all Theobald. James has furthermore eliminated any suggestion that sexual passion plays a part in Theobald's admiration for his Serafina; in Balzac's story sublimated, or not so sublimated, eroticism forms a large part of Frenhofer's feelings for his painting. Some of the terms which Theobald uses about his model recall Frenhofer's, however. His Serafina is 'a beauty with a soul' and he feels the same modesty and jealous protection towards her: 'I feel somehow . . . as if it were a sort of violation of that privacy in which I have always contemplated her beauty,' he says when he proposes to his friend to take him to her dwelling. Theobald has made a work of art out of a real woman; Frenhofer tried to make a woman out of a work of art. Serafina is a common, even vulgar woman, once beautiful, who has allowed herself to be seduced when young. Theobald's passion for his art transmutes any amorous or sexual passion he might have had into a pure aesthetic contemplation of a beauty out of nature. His love for Serafina is purely platonic and we are told more than once that he lives as a monk or saint. Here is another way in which James interprets idealism and which differs from Balzac's portrayal of types.

Theobald's transformation of his common Serafina into a young and radiant Madonna is linked with his failure as Frenhofer's dream is the cause of his. Theobald has failed to notice what is happening to his model. And he has failed to notice that she is growing old because he continues to live in his vision waiting for the time when he can translate it on to his canvas. Theobald as a 'poet' transforms reality into more pleasing and harmonious illusions: he repairs nature's faults and blemishes by an act of the imagination. His desire for perfection however is as self-defeating as Frenhofer's. His error is to spend his time 'forever preparing for a work forever deferred'.

Here James rejoins Balzac. For both their artists have visions that are too great for any realization. But the power to have visions is part of the creative process. Art is forever an attack upon the inarticulate—because it cannot be expressed. For both there is the same gap between aspiration and performance. In Theobald's case it paralyses him, and he doesn't even try. This is related in James's story to a theme of his own: the poverty of art in America and the American artist's sense of his overwhelming task. James uses this situation, however, to urge production as the only way to establish art.

Theobald, as he himself recognizes, is half a genius. He has dreams in full measure, but lacks the power of execution. His complement is provided in the vulgar little maker and marketer of near-pornographic figures of cats and monkeys which satirize and caricature human attitudes. His attitude is cynical; in them, he says, is all human life. They are, James remarks, 'at once very perfect cats and monkeys and very natural men and women . . . Their *imitative* felicity was revolting.' (Emphasis— P.G.) His art lacks vision and idealism, and consequently degrades men and women to the status of animals. This is a frequent charge of the idealistic French critics of the time against Flaubert and the 'Realists'. This character expresses his 'philosophy' in these terms: 'Truly, I don't know whether the cats and monkeys imitate us, or whether it's we who imitate them.' James, through this figure, is making a satirical caricature of realism. And Theobald's refusal to make money, his purity of motive and his devotion to the ideal are enhanced by the contrast, although we are made not to forget that it takes both the vision and the hand to make a work of art.

Theobald, we have already noted, is conscious of his failure. He meditates upon it and draws the moral for himself.

'I waited and waited to be worthier to begin, and wasted my life in preparation . . . I've taken it all too hard! Michael Angelo didn't when he went at the Lorenzo! He did his best at a venture, and his venture is immortal. *That's* mine!'[19]

And he points to his empty canvas. His tragedy is more than personal for he represents those 'talents that can't act, that can't do nor dare'. His power to analyse his failures and to accept them consciously makes him a truly Jamesian figure and sets him apart from Balzac's Frenhofer who is driven by his passions and who never recognizes *why* he has failed. Balzac's universe is Hobbesian; men and women are driven on by one desire after another, struggling for power, wealth, honour, titles, love—but all dominated by powerful and insatiable passions. James's world is Kantian and idealistic, where men assume their full significance only in conscious moral choices.

2
The Art of the Novel:
'The Costly Charm of Composition'

In his essay 'The Lesson of Balzac' (1905) James paid Balzac
the tribute of calling him 'the father of us all'. He wrote: 'I
speak of him, and can only speak, as a man of his craft, an
emulous fellow-worker, who has learned from him more of the
lessons of the engaging mystery of fiction than from any one
else, and who is conscious of so large a debt to repay that it
has positively to be discharged in instalments.'[1] He goes on
to indicate some of the lessons that Balzac provides for any
novelist. One of these is quantity and intensity: quantity of
life of all types and in all its manifestations, and intensity of
representation. Since it is the novelist's task to create as intense
an illusion of life as possible, Balzac's overwhelming specification of all the possible details of the virtues and vices, the
inward and outward lives of his characters makes him the model
for all. James praises Balzac for presenting to us the 'constituted
consciousness' of his characters. James and Balzac have in
common the adding of one detail upon another, the seeking
out of the illustrative action, word, gesture or, in James's case,
the specific tone of thought or feeling. As James observed in
the preface to *The American*: 'Since no "rendering" of any
object and no painting of any picture can take effect without
some form of reference and control, these guarantees could
but reside in a high probity of observation.'[2] This view has
its roots in James's study of Balzac's practice.

In 'The Lesson of Balzac' James observed other characteristics of Balzac's method which are of permanent importance
to the novelist's practice. James speaks of the 'costly charm of
composition'. There are many ways in which the elements
of a novel may be organized and fused. Important for both
James and Balzac seems to be the use they made of antithesis.
Another of Balzac's great merits is his ability to foreshorten
the representation of the passage of time: to present all the
sense without all the surface. Balzac's ability to make vivid to

us all the conditions—social, moral, economic and personal—of his characters is a very complex subject, and we shall here explore only the way in which James and Balzac use description, not only to 'render' conditions but also to play an important part in the overall structure and meaning of their novels.

I

Few authors have made as consistent a use of contrast as Balzac. With him it is not an occasional device for emphasis or for the heightening of an effect. It is an essential principle of composition, round which sometimes a whole novel is built and articulated.[3] Furthermore, one scene is often set sharply against another, so that juxtaposition, a well-tried dramatic device, is combined with contrast. (James speaks of alternation rather than of juxtaposition.) In such a category come the death-bed scenes of Mme Grandet and of old Grandet. The latter makes us think of the former and is set off by it. In Balzac the use of contrast has a deep source and one that gives it its full value aesthetically: for the contrast or antithesis is a means of giving intensity and vividness to the basic dramatic conflict which is the source of so many of his novels. *La Rabouilleuse, La Vieille Fille, Le Cabinet des Antiques, Le Curé de Tours* are all based on struggles for an inheritance, a room, a bride, etc. in which two people or two groups of people are in conflict. But they are not in conflict merely as individuals. In Balzac the struggles are most often between people who represent social classes or cultural groups that are opposed to each other. But before examining Balzac further, let us consider a relevant passage in the preface to *Roderick Hudson*. James is excusing himself for having introduced the town of Northampton, Mass. by name, and then for having failed to 'do' it in the way Balzac 'did' Angoulême, Guérande or Saumur. He explains then what he wanted from his town:

Could I verily, by the terms of my little plan, have 'gone in' for it at the best, and even though one of these terms was the projection, for my fable, at the outset, of some more or less vivid *antithesis* [emphasis —P.G.] to a state of civilization providing for 'art'? What I wanted, in essence, was the image of some perfectly humane community which was yet all incapable of providing for it, and I had to take what my scant experience furnished me.[4]

This is not the only reference to antithesis that James makes in this preface. For he goes on to discuss the presence of Mary Garland, who in retrospect does not seem to him to have been made vivid enough for the office she is asked to fulfil, that of a young lady who could inspire an instant passion in both Roderick and Rowland. Her way of casting a spell on Rowland, he says, does not convince us. And because she is not strong and we do not see how she has so impressed and charmed him 'the damage to verisimilitude is deep.' Her presence is explained on the same grounds as the depiction of Northampton, Mass.: 'The difficulty has been from the first that I required my antithesis—my antithesis to Christina Light, one of the main terms of the subject.'[5]

The above quoted passages make it clear that James is concerned with at least two different types of contrast or antithesis: that of place and that of character. Both have a vital part in the 'constructional game'—James's phrase for the intriguing technical problems of novel-writing which he uses in the preface to *Roderick Hudson*. The importance of the antithesis of Paris and the provinces in one Balzacian novel after another is clear. It is a major theme in *Illusions perdues*. Angoulême indeed has more than one point in common with Northampton, Mass. These are the provincial towns that do not provide for art, whatever other human values they may represent. From them Lucien de Rubempré and Roderick Hudson feel that they must escape in order to fulfil themselves as artists.

A basic antithesis, such as that between Paris and the provinces, may be employed structurally and dramatically in a number of ways. The values and standards of the one place, the expectations they have given rise to, may be played off against those that are prevalent in the other, so that the significance of the differences is enhanced. Both places at once may be presented to the mind of the reader. Such a 'double view' may be accomplished in various ways. A scene, or a series of short illustrative scenes, in which the central character himself feels the differences between the two places represents one powerful way.

For then the act of comparison taking place in the central character's mind may bring about some fundamental change in his attitude or values, so that the comparison is a vital part of the character's progress and development, and the objects compared are integrated into the story because of the effect they have on him. This technique is close to James's use of a 'centre' and of making everything tell for that central consciousness. Balzac gives us such a scene and such a technique in the first section ('Les Prémices de Paris') of the second part ('Un Grand Homme de Province à Paris') of *Illusions perdues* (1834-43).

Lucien de Rubempré is wandering in the streets of Paris on his second day after arriving there with Mme de Bargeton. The night before, the comparison between him, the young, naïve, ridiculously dressed, poor and awkward poet and the mature, suave, sophisticated, elegant, man-of-the-world Sixte de Châtelet has already been made by Mme de Bargeton, and to Lucien's disadvantage. Now Lucien begins to compare himself to others, Angoulême and the provinces to Paris, and Mme de Bargeton to *Parisiennes*. In each case the comparison is to the disadvantage of what is not of Paris. At first he notices things more than people. Then the presence of so many people acts upon his imagination. He feels diminished. And this is related to his changed residence:

Les personnes qui jouissent en province d'une considération quelconque, et qui y rencontrent à chaque pas une preuve de leur importance, ne s'accoutument point à cette perte totale et subite de leur valeur. Être quelque chose dans son pays et n'être rien à Paris, sont deux états qui veulent des transitions.[6]

(People who in the provinces enjoy some sort of consideration and who encounter at each step proof of their importance do not at all accustom themselves to this sudden and total loss of their value. To be somebody in one's native place and to be nothing in Paris are two conditions which call for some transitional stages.)

If Lucien is the young man of imagination and talent who finds that he is nothing in Paris, the Baron de Châtelet on the other hand is the old dandy who is perfectly at home in the Parisian world. He grows larger and his power and importance are more obvious in Paris. Both characters are more fully revealed by the way they understand and are received by Parisian society. Lucien's evening at the theatre, however, is a great step forward in his education and in his losing his provincial tastes and attitudes. And one of these significant steps is his comparing Mme de Bargeton to the elegant Parisian ladies that surround them. 'En province il n'y a ni choix ni comparaison à faire' but the same woman judged beautiful in the provinces 'transportée à Paris' becomes commonplace. As Balzac notes: 'Il se préparait chez madame de Bargeton et chez Lucien un désenchantement sur eux-mêmes dont la cause était Paris.'[7] ('In Mme de Bargeton and in Lucien a process of disenchantment was at work; Paris was the cause.') Their previous provincial life and its values are constantly referred to and implicitly used for comparison with those of Paris, which in most spheres sets the true standards of value and appreciation.

If Châtelet, the Parisian dandy, has set the standard by which Mme de Bargeton judges Lucien, Mme d'Espard sets the standard of feminine Parisian elegance by which Lucien later judges Mme de Bargeton. The Marquise d'Espard is the Mme de Bargeton of Paris and she brings out the imperfections of the lady from Angoulême. Lucien at last sees his mistress as she really is, and that is the way the people of Paris see her. What Lucien hasn't yet perceived is what she will look like when she is properly dressed—as she can learn to be with the help and guidance of her elegant cousin, the Marquise d'Espard.

Balzac has another way of drawing our attention to the contrast between the two societies which form the poles of his novelistic world. So far we have seen him compare the two societies in general considerations of the differences in manners, dress and customs. But in his farewell letter to Mme de Bargeton Lucien refers not so much to what the provinces are like in these details but to the type of life, and what it meant, that they led there, and what that life seemed then to promise in love and hope. 'Après les belles espérances que votre doigt m'a montrées dans le ciel, j'aperçois les réalités de la misère dans la boue de Paris,' he writes.[8] ('After the great expectations which your finger showed me in the heavens, I perceive the realities of poverty in the mud of Paris.') And this letter leads to an even more important comparison between the two lives and the two places; it leads to Lucien recalling vividly the room he lived in at Angoulême and his family with their love and the sacrifices they made for him.

Lucien se reporta par la pensée au milieu de sa famille: il revit le joli appartement que David lui avait décoré en y sacrifiant une partie de sa fortune, il eut une vision des joies tranquilles, modestes, bourgeoises qu'il avait goûtées; les ombres de sa mère, de sa soeur, de David vinrent autour de lui, il entendit de nouveau les larmes qu'ils avaient versées au moment de son départ et il pleura lui-même, car il était seul dans Paris, sans amis, sans protecteurs.[9]

(Lucien's thoughts went back to his family circle. He saw again the pretty rooms which David, by sacrificing part of his own fortune, had decorated for him. He had a vision of those quiet, simple and bourgeois pleasures which he had enjoyed. The shades of his mother, his sister and of David came about him; he heard anew their sobs at the moment of his leave-taking and he cried himself for he was alone in Paris, without either friend or patron.)

In the midst of his Parisian despair appears the tranquil life which he led in the provinces as the cherished child of the family, and this is made present in a vivid and concrete image. The two lives, the past and the present, are juxtaposed in one compelling vision.

As Paris is the centre for French writers in *Illusions perdues*, Rome is the capital for American sculptors in *Roderick Hudson* (1875). The contrast between a society that embodies certain humane virtues but does not provide for 'art' and one that, whatever its other dangers, does so provide is at the heart of this novel as it is at that of *Illusions perdues*. Therefore we have an attempt, however incomplete, to present the 'local type', to portray the provincial society that is intellectually and spiritually infertile for the artist. Rome may be destructive to Roderick, although it is not so much Rome as his own weaknesses. But if he stays in Northampton there is no chance for development at all. Cecilia, Rowland's cousin, presents the case succinctly:

The flame is smouldering, but it is never fanned by the breath of criticism. He sees nothing, hears nothing, to help to self-knowledge. . . . Then his mother, as she one day confessed to me, has a holy horror of a profession which consists exclusively as she supposes in making figures of people without their clothes on. Sculpture to her mind is an insidious form of immorality.[10]

In both James's and Balzac's novels the domestic virtues are represented by the people of the provincial town: Ève and David

Séchard and Mme Chardon (Lucien's mother) in Angoulême, and Mrs Hudson and Mary Garland in Northampton. The people in Balzac's novel are both worse and better than those in James's. The Parisians are more egoistic and treacherous than any of the Romans or Europeanized Americans Roderick meets. On the other hand Ève and David Séchard ruin themselves for Lucien in a way that Mary Garland and even Mrs Hudson would find unthinkable. Nevertheless the contrast between the security of family life and the domestic virtues on the one hand, and a need for the artist to find a centre where art is nourished on the other, is made. To make this contrast clear James has a scene that in its technique essentially resembles the scene of Lucien recalling, after he has written his letter to Mme de Bargeton, his former room in Angoulême. Rowland in Northampton is debating about the wisdom of his interfering in Roderick's life and taking him off to Rome.

As he looked up and down the long vista, and saw the clear white houses glancing here and there in the broken moonshine, he could almost have believed that the happiest lot for any man was to make the most of life in some such tranquil spot as that. Here were kindness, comfort, safety, the warning voice of duty, the perfect absence of temptation.[11]

And as he so muses Roderick passes him singing of 'castle walls and snowy summits old in story'—of those things that America does not have and which both he and Rowland assume are part of the great artistic accumulation of Europe that make a rich soil for the aspiring artist. Through these contrasting images James brings both societies and what they represent before us at the same time.

America seemed to James to lack those diversities of human behaviour essential to the observer of life: without elaborate institutions and social forms, of a historical past that created complicated and mysterious human beings, living its life in the open, without obscurities, America was a poor soil for the growth of art and for the types of human beings with their forms and customs that he desired to depict. An elaborate social network existed in Europe for a non-European writer to exploit, but a new interest, a new artistic value was to be gained by the introduction of Americans to the European scene. Already in *Roderick Hudson* the antithesis between the provincial society that is all humane but does not make for art and a 'capital' city which does is a further contrast between America and Europe, between Northampton, Mass. and Rome. If it were too much to say that the international theme grew out of the technique of contrast and antithesis, this technique at least provided a means of properly exploiting it.

In *Illusions perdues* Balzac does more than merely take his hero from the provinces to Paris. That contrast is an active one in his consciousness and is part of his developing experience of life in Paris. It is by the contrasts, as he feels and sees them, that Paris makes the decisive impact on his life, his feelings, his standards of taste and judgement and ultimately on his morals as well as his manners. The presence of the provincial consciousness, as well as provincial dress and behaviour, in the person of Lucien or Mme de Bargeton is essential to the full meaning of the things seen and experienced. Without the presence of the provincial the significance of Paris is lost. Something very similar to this takes place in James's long story 'A London Life' (1888). Here Laura Wing, an American girl of intense moral probity, finds her married sister, Selina Berrington, leading a life of intrigue and adultery. She sees her sister heading for a scandalous divorce. Her pain and disapprobation arise from a mixture of horror at her sister's action and an overpowering sense of shame at being connected to such a public exposure. Her sister will smear her honour as much as her own.

In his preface to the New York edition of *The Spoils of Poynton* (where 'A London Life' also appears) James remarks that he no longer understands fully why he thought that he had to make his characters Americans. 'There was enough of the general human and social sort for them without it; poor young Wendover in especial, I think, fails on any such ground to attest himself—I needn't, surely, have been at costs to bring him all the way from New York.'[12] Laura Wing too figures as a touching creature who would have suffered and acted as she did regardless of the land of her birth. Later however in the same preface James does go some way to providing an answer for the Americanness of these two characters. Laura Wing's repulsion is based upon her American innocence and her awareness of another, simpler social order across the seas. Throughout this preface in fact James speaks of the 'conflict of manners', of 'the pictorial value of the general opposition', and of finding the right oppositions in his subject; Laura Wing is an American because 'the impression was always there that no one so much as the candid outsider, caught up and involved in the sweep of the machine, could measure the values revealed.'[13] Her Americanness is an artistic value, permitting certain distinct effects by the force of contrast. And this is the reason, although James does not say so, why Wendover is an American too. He does not understand English modes of behaviour, their customs and their taboos. He is even more of an innocent, or at least more ignorant of the ways of the country, than is Laura. It is essential for the story that he should be. It is because they are both Americans that James can get certain effects. Essential to the progress of the story is the fact that Laura *believes* she knows certain of the customs and manners of the country. If she is shocked at the *dérèglement* of her sister's morals she is aware of the conventions that surround her as an unmarried girl in England and that these conventions are not the same as those that prevail in New York. James plays off these opposing manners in the tale, as Wendover tries to understand the expected thing in England whilst the two of them, Laura and himself, enjoy acting, at times, in the way that their being Americans permits them.

Within this story in fact James is able to play off oppositions and contrasts with some subtlety. There is the American who has been corrupted by Europe, Selina Berrington, although it must be confessed that there is little reason for accepting her as an American except James's designating her as such. Laura Wing has an intense, nearly barbarous, moral probity, and in the *Notebook* entries this is seen, if not emphatically, at least clearly, as an American trait—a trait applicable to certain American types. Wendover has little in himself that is American, but he is so in his ignorance of English customs and his assumptions about possible behaviour, his innocence as to what constitutes an offence to a girl in English society. (In his original notes James made him a young clerk at the Foreign Office.) Lionel Berrington is a young Englishman who enjoys himself in sport and other amusements and has neither the intelligence, tact nor moral authority to control his wayward and wanton wife. His children are healthy, robust, unconscious English children destined, we are led to infer, to an unintelligent and unquestioning life in the Guards or Rifles. Lady Davenant, Laura's friend and adviser, takes to her and appreciates her, but is aware of her intensity, her almost morbid concern with her sister's shame and dishonour. She provides a reference point as to what English society will really think about both Laura and her sister. In this way we get the measure of Laura's exaggerated sensitivity without finding her 'impossible'.

Wendover's ignorance and innocence in face of the facts of London social customs is woven into the story in much the same way and there are effects of contrast and opposition similar to Lucien's growing awareness of the differences between Paris and Angoulême in *Illusions perdues*. But James derives a greater richness from his contrasts. For Laura is at times refreshed by Wendover's being an American and then at times aware of the immense distance between them that her experience in London has created, a distance of which he is entirely unconscious. When they first meet it is in the London house of her sister, Mrs Berrington. They leave the house together, after she has expressed the desire 'as an American girl does in such a case, that they should see him again.'

She hoped he would ask her leave to go with her the way she was going—and this not on particular but on general grounds. It would be American, it would remind her of old times; she should like him to be as American as that. There was no reason for her taking so quick an interest in his nature, inasmuch as she had not fallen under his spell; but there were moments when she felt a whimsical desire to be reminded of the way people felt and acted at home. Mr Wendover did not disappoint her, and the bright chocolate-coloured vista of the Fifth Avenue seemed to surge before her as he said, 'May I have the pleasure of making my direction the same as yours?'[14]

The full force of this passage comes with the implied contrast between the simple habits of America and the debased and corrupted world that Laura has found her sister Selina living in. She hopes to breathe a fresher, purer air, to recapture something of the simplicity and innocence of American habits, a chance to free herself, even if only momentarily, from the atmosphere of adultery and scandal that seems to hang over her sister's house and her 'set'. We notice how the physical appearance of the other place, Fifth Avenue, bursts in on the scene, as Angoulême becomes suddenly present to Lucien in a similar moment of moral suffering. Laura's sense of the differences between English and American society is however very different from that of her companion. He inquires in the artless and serious fashion of a traveller taking notes, and his good faith is stupendous. In her view there are certain differences that one feels but which cannot be expressed, and those that one can express are not very important. Therefore most of his questions seem to her to be importunate or irrelevant. 'They were talking about totally different things: English society, as he asked her judgement upon it and she had happened to see it, was an affair that he didn't suspect.'[15]

Some of the differences between English and American customs are exploited for their ironic and comic effects, for the opportunity they give to James to make witty comments, usually at the expense of American habits. But the differences are used much more centrally and dramatically in the scene at the opera. Here the different ways that Laura and Mr Wendover appreciate her being left alone with him after Selina excuses herself from their box are essential to Laura's actions and the outcome of the story. Wendover sees Selina's flight as wounding him. Laura perceives this but is also very conscious of the affront it is to her to be left alone in public with a young man. He seems to welcome the chance to be alone with her and is not conscious of any impropriety. She realizes that Selina wants to make her look 'fast', to disparage her in the eyes of all London. Appearances would be slightly improved if Mr Wendover's friend who accompanied Selina to her other friends in the house returned. When Laura asks why he doesn't return he replies, 'Oh, there's plenty of time—we are very comfortable.'[16] Wendover's replies are ambiguous. They are mere politeness and gallantry on his part, but because of Laura's position and because of her sense of both what is proper and the impropriety of her being alone with him, she takes his words to mean more than they do. The crisis comes when she is about to leave the theatre. She has sent Mr Wendover off to see what has become of her sister. He returns to tell her that he has found Mr Booker who had been enjoined by Selina *not* to return to their box. As to where she is Mr Booker has no idea.

39

Laura asks to be put into a cab. 'Ah, you won't see the rest?' he asks. 'Do stay—what difference does it make?' For Laura such words could well seem to be leading to a serious declaration or proposal. His attentions and his desire not to let her go home would be consistent with such an interpretation, particularly if he were as aware as she is of the falsity of her position in being there alone with him. This consciousness is possible to her because of her absorption in English standards and ways. But these thoughts do not come to him because he is still acting as a simple and open American unaware of what the 'done thing' is in English society. So when she asks him what his attentions have meant, and declares herself in effect ready to accede to a proposal, he is startled. His frequent visits have been no more than the 'American way'. They really indicate nothing at all. (This difference in courting customs is also used for comic purposes in 'The Point of View'.) Therefore although James could say later in his preface that there was no reason why Laura Wing and Wendover had to be Americans, in the actual composition of this story he had been well aware of the structural uses he could make of their nationality for the purposes of antithesis.

II

No one begins, to my sense, to handle the time-element and produce the time-effect with the authority of Balzac in his amplest sweeps— by which I am far from meaning in his longest passages. That study of the foreshortened image, of the neglect of which I suggest the ill consequence, is precisely the enemy of the tiresome procession of would-be narrative items, seen all in profile, like rail-heads of a fence; a substitute for the baser device of accounting for the time-quantity by mere quantity of statement.   ('The Lesson of Balzac')

One of the main criticisms that James himself made of *Roderick Hudson* in his preface for the New York Edition was 'that the time-scheme of the story is quite inadequate'. Roderick's disintegration was to have been a gradual process spread over two years, yet in the presentation of the story we do not feel the passage of so much time, but rather we have the sense that the whole thing happens in a few weeks or months. He falls apart too fast and with too little cause. James's great problem, he confessed, was how to boil down the many facts and events so that the reader would feel their presence and force and yet confine the narrative to a short space—to give the sense of a relatively long passage of time without unduly drawing out the story. He wanted 'intensity, lucidity, brevity, beauty'— and how was he to achieve all of these? He saw his problem as not his alone but one that faces all novelists:

> To give the image and the sense of certain things while still keeping them subordinate to his plan, keeping them in relation to matters more immediate and apparent, to give all the sense, in a word, without all the substance or all the surface, and so to summarize and foreshorten, so to make values both rich and sharp, that the mere procession of items and profiles is not only, for the occasion, superseded, but is, for essential quality, almost 'compromised'— such a case of delicacy proposes itself at every turn to the painter of life who wishes both to treat his chosen subject and to confine his necessary picture . . . This eternal time question is accordingly, for the novelist, always there and always formidable; always insisting on the *effect* and the great lapse and passage, of the 'dark backward and abysm', by the terms of truth, and on the effect of compression, of composition and form, by the terms of literary arrangement.[17]

As James makes clear, time is a problem for any novelist who has passed beyond the simple narrative devices of the chronicle and the fairy-tale, the 'once upon a time', 'and so the years passed.' We need not of course believe that James learned all his narrative techniques which deal with the question of time from Balzac. All we need note here is that the techniques of 'foreshortening' developed by Balzac and James were often similar. If a technique is present in Balzac and then later in James we have the only kind of evidence that is possible in such a study as this.

Commenting on the unsatisfactory portrayal of Roderick's collapse in Rome through the sole agency of Christina Light, James suggested that Balzac would have known how to achieve the effect which he had unsuccessfully sought. There are obvious examples of the type of collapse he has in mind in the immense world of *La Comédie Humaine*. One such, a case of 'foreshortened' collapse, is that of Victurnien d'Esgrignon in *Le Cabinet des Antiques*.

Victurnien arrives in Paris from his home in Alençon and like so many of Balzac's young men he succumbs to its attractions for he is basically a man without strength of character or force of will. His father, the Marquis, is a representative of the old aristocracy and of its habits, beliefs, manners and standards of personal conduct. The d'Esgrignon house is full of old people as well as old ways—hence its name, 'Le Cabinet des Antiques'.[18] On the other hand the young Victurnien is the symbol of the possible rebirth of the aristocracy. His education and the prejudices of his family have, however, ill-equipped him to deal with the world of the Restoration of 1815. But whatever his other faults Victurnien is no fool. He soon discovers that there are important differences between the world of Alençon, where he is expected soon to receive a royal appointment, partly because of his name and ancestry and partly in return for the loyal services performed by his family to the restored monarchy, and Paris, where social and political power is not possible without immense wealth as well as a good name and important connections. Rather than drag this discovery out over a long period Balzac endows his young man with a Jamesian-like percipience: 'un seul fait lui suffit' ('a single fact sufficed for him').

This fact is composed of two juxtaposed scenes. Victurnien presents a letter of introduction from his father to the Duc de Lenoncourt. The next day he sees the same man in the street, and he compares the grandeur of the man in his magnificent ducal mansion, surrounded by aristocratic splendours, and the same man in the street, without decorations and distinctions, walking casually about with an umbrella. That, and the smile he had seen on the Duke's lips when he gave him his father's letter, reveals to Victurnien the immense distance that separates 'Le Cabinet des Antiques' from the Tuileries of 1822. Here a whole change of epoch which Balzac has before presented analytically is summed up for us in the Duke's smile. And the smile is the clue that permits Victurnien to make an immense leap in time from the past of his family to the present realities of power and influence in the Restoration monarchy. Much of the effectiveness of this image rests upon our having been told many of the facts of the case beforehand. But by suggesting a sudden flash of insight on the part of his hero Balzac permits him to become possessed of that historical analysis. This then becomes part of the lived experience of the novel. Victurnien's act of consciousness brings the past and present together and makes the past operative. Like Isabel Archer's meditations before her fire, Victurnien's understanding advances the action as much if not more than any mere incident.

By a different technique Balzac can portray an unspecified lapse of time through a series of acts of the same general kind or through the same act repeated a number of times in different circumstances. For example, Victurnien is admitted to a number of salons. That what happens in one is similar to what happens in another, and that the first is only one of a series, is implied in this phrase: 'Comme le lui dit de Marsay, le *premier* dandy qu'il trouva dans le *premier* salon où il fut introduit . . .'[19] ('As de Marsay said to him, the first dandy he found in the first salon where he was introduced.') There follows a list of names of people whom he met in a number of salons, at the opera, at embassies, '*partout* où le mena son beau nom et sa fortune apparente.' [20] (Emphasis—P.G.) ('. . . everywhere his good name and apparent fortune led him.') Our general sense of the way things happen tacitly fills in the sequence of specific events that must have occurred to bring about such an aggregate. This enumeration leads to a composite image of a number of salons: 'un nom de haute noblesse, reconnu et adopté par le faubourg St-Germain qui sait ses provinces sur le bout du doigt, est un passeport qui ouvre *les portes* les plus difficiles à tourner sur *leurs gonds*.' (Emphasis—P.G.)[21] ('. . . a name of great nobility, recognized and adopted by the Faubourg St-Germain which knows its provinces thoroughly, is a passport which opens the stiffest doors.')

Much of what Balzac achieves here depends upon his accumulation of examples, an accumulation implying a number of acts occurring over a period of time—we know that otherwise it is impossible for them all to have occurred. But furthermore, they build up into a picture of a specific way of life: in this case one that is expensive and futile. The recurring acts are a part of a life of receptions, balls, evenings in salons, gambling, expensive dinners, visits to relatives and introductions to influential people. If Victurnien gambles it is not merely in one place but in many, and Balzac reels off a list of names to prove it. Not only one duke or prince wants, after meeting Victurnien, to introduce him to the King, but many vie for the pleasure and privilege. And this introduction leads to a series of conclusions in Victurnien's thinking which are spread out in a chronological sequence for the reader: 'Victurnien vint au Tuileries . . . Il devina . . . Il comprit . . . Il s'élança donc.'[22] ('Victurnien came to the Tuileries . . . He guessed . . . He understood . . . He launched himself.') It is precisely this sense of a particular way of life, extending over a period of time and which would explain his ultimate collapse, that James failed to achieve for Roderick Hudson.

There is another general method of condensing time which Balzac uses in these chapters: he presents a desire that needs a large expense of time and money for its accomplishment, and then soon afterwards records its fulfilment. For example, Victurnien soon comes to feel the need to live like the other rich and idle noblemen he meets in Paris. 'Il sentit la nécessité d'avoir des chevaux, de belles voitures, tous les accessoires du luxe moderne.'[23] ('He felt the necessity of having horses, fine carriages, all the accessories of modern luxury.') Three pages later his desires are satisfied: 'Il prit un petit appartement dans la rue du Bac, avec une écurie, une remise et tous les accompagnements de la vie élégante à laquelle il se trouva tout d'abord condamné.'[24] ('He took a small apartment in the rue du Bac; with a stable, a coach-house and all the accompaniments of the elegant life to which at first he found himself condemned.') But between the desire and its satisfaction have come a large number of other events, many of them of the repetitive and cumulative kind we have already noticed. The actual length of time that has passed is indefinite but we feel that it is more than the time taken to read three pages.

There is one other feature to note in Balzac's presentation of time. After a number of general scenes he presents one particular scene that is like the preceding ones in its main outlines, but which epitomizes their characteristics and is seen as part of a progression that leads up to that particular scene and which at the same time significantly advances the action. Such a scene is the first meeting of Victurnien and Mme de Maufrigneuse. They meet at one of the many brilliant receptions that Victurnien now attends, and here are gathered many of the new friends he has made. It is his love for Mme de Maufrigneuse, beautiful, etherial and angelic in appearance, which is the real cause of Victurnien's moral, and hence social and political, collapse.

James employs an analogous method of creating a composite picture in the second chapter of *The Wings of the Dove*. Here Kate Croy looks out over the park from a high window in a room that is above that of her aunt, Mrs Lowder. Although the latter sits far away downstairs she is a presence in her niece's room. And Kate discovers something new about her own position and her life every day from her window—these are the things she observes, not the park itself. This goes on all winter.

She knew so much that her knowledge was what fairly kept her there, making her at times circulate more endlessly between the small silk-covered sofa that stood for her in the firelight and the great grey map of Middlesex spread beneath her lookout.[25]

This room, with its sofa, window and fire, becomes the focal point for all the subsequent reflections so that a number of days are united by these elements. Kate passes in and out of the house but she returns to this post where she lingers above while her aunt remains below, and where she can hear the roar of London which seems the roar of a siege.

The great advances James had made in condensing time after the writing of *Roderick Hudson* can be seen if we look at Chapter 31 of *The Portrait of a Lady* (1881). Isabel returns to Florence after an interval of some months, an interval, James tells us, full of incident. How is he to give us the sense of these incidents, their force and value, their essential significance to Isabel, their sense without all their surface? He gives us a precisely indicated picture of Isabel in a room of Mrs Touchett's Florentine house, with the window open onto the garden, in an attitude that is suggestive in numerous ways. We are invited to observe Isabel as we might an actress playing a 'big' scene—we know something has happened from her position and her movements, her steady gaze followed by her rapid pacing of the room. We are watching the effects upon her *now* of what she has done in that interval that has yet to be given to us in its concretion of incident and detail. What is the meaning of her movements and her gaze? Is she trying, as we might suppose, to see her visitor before he arrives in the house? James assures us that this is not so, and implies that she had rather *not* see him. We are forced to try to work out what her movements and hesitations mean. Hence the narrative takes on a new density. For James purposely hides from us at this point the identity of her expected visitor, Caspar Goodwood. That these movements and expressions are related to the passage of time and its effects is shown in the sentence: 'Grave she found herself, and positively more weighted, as by the experience of the lapse of the year she had spent seeing the world.'

Another typical technique is that in which past events are made into miniature pictures or dramatic scenes, integrated into a more traditional narrative summary, as in the following passage:

She had never had a keener sense of freedom, of the absolute boldness and wantonness of liberty, than when she turned away from the platform at the Euston Station on one of the last days of November, after the departure of the train that was to convey poor Lily, her husband and her children to their ship at Liverpool.[26]

Here we *see* Isabel's movement—the turning away—and find ourselves in a station with the suggestion of the train moving away from her—suggestions that are developed more fully a few lines later. This particular little scene, briefly sketched as it is, is of great importance for at that moment Isabel is all alone in the world, without any family connections near to impede her or restrict her sense of freedom. And her sense of freedom, felt so intensely here, contrasts ironically, although only implicitly at the moment, with her caged feeling later in the novel after she has married Osmond. The continuation of this little scene conveys gesture, movement and even laughter.

Isabel watched the train move away; she kissed her hand to the elder of her small nephews, a demonstrative child who leaned dangerously far out of the window of the carriage and made separation an occasion of violent hilarity, and then she walked back into the foggy London street.[27]

This scene is then expanded and continued; it stands for a central event in her life, a turning-point in Isabel's career. She feels she has the whole world in front of her and she can do whatever she likes. For the moment she walks to her hotel. In the lines that follow we walk along the streets with Isabel, reliving her visual impressions, partaking of her thoughts and feelings, meeting a policeman, and in the manner in which his directions are conveyed, nearly hearing his words and his voice. Here a walk of some length is conveyed, not as it would happen serially in time, but in its accumulation of impressions.

The early dusk of a November afternoon had already closed in; the street-lamps, in the thick, brown air, looked weak and red; our heroine was unattended and Euston Square was a long way from Piccadilly. But Isabel performed the journey with a positive enjoyment of its dangers and lost her way almost on purpose, in order to get more sensations, so that she was disappointed when an obliging policeman easily set her right again. She was so fond of the spectacle of human life that she enjoyed even the aspect of gathering dusk in the London streets—the moving crowds, the hurrying cabs, the lighted shops, the flaring stalls, the dark, shining dampness of everything.[28]

This accumulation of visual impressions leads us naturally on to another method James uses to summarize: imagery. There are images of distilled experience such as this: 'Isabel . . . made use of her memory of Rome as she might have done, in a hot and crowded room, of a phial of something pungent hidden in her handkerchief.' Without in any way trying to tell us what those memories were or where and how they were experienced, James gives us the significance of them to Isabel, and the distillation of something precious is implied in the image of the phial of perfume as well as its strangely exhilarating effect.

There are other images that render the total impression made by a character, and hence summarize and condense, for the actual scenes or acts that might be the ground for these judgements are omitted: 'She [Isabel] liked her [Mme Merle] as much as ever, but there was a corner of the curtain that never was lifted; it was as if she had remained after all something of a public performer, condmened to emerge only in character and in costume.'[29] This last image is related to Isabel's impression of Mme Merle and to what we know and learn of her: that she is always playing a part, and often a very subtle and elusive one. Hence it is not an isolated image, functioning only for its immediate purpose, but finds itself in a context of images and ideas that run throughout the novel. Another such image, even more closely connected to others and to central themes in the novel, is the following: '[Isabel] only felt older—ever so much, and as if she were "worth more" for it, like some curious piece in an antiquary's collection.'[30] When we recall that Isabel falls in love with Osmond whose fine and careful selection of works of art is taken by her as a sign of his refined taste and sensibility, we can see that this image has tragically ironic overtones and that it fits in with all those images of Majolica and other precious bibelots that come in the chapters that tell of Rosier's passion for Pansy.

Running through this account of the intervening months are references to Gilbert Osmond. Isabel remains silent about him, but this silence 'was in direct proportion to the frequency with which he occupied her thoughts'. When she does not stop at Florence Mrs Touchett takes it as a sign that Osmond is less of a question with her than formerly and we are told that she, Mrs Touchett, is relieved when she learns that he has not left for Rome to join Isabel. The chapter ends with Isabel back in Florence, and the next opens with Isabel in the same position as at the start of the preceding chapter—in front of the open window. One way James has of giving us the sense of elapsed time is in his repeated hints that something has happened to bring Goodwood back to Rome. The reader knows on what conditions Isabel had agreed to see Goodwood again yet the details are withheld from him, but obviously not from either Isabel or Goodwood. Here the actors know more than the audience and we are therefore forced in reading to pass through a time-sequence that is different from that of the events yet paralleling it as we take up one suggestion after another and try to imagine the past. It is remarkable too what is thus summarized for us: the three weeks that Osmond passed in Rome with Isabel and Mme Merle after their return from the East—mentioned in a few words only—and what passed through Isabel's mind to make her finally accept him. We have no love scenes, no words of endearment, no engagement between the lovers at all. We see only what effect the engagement has on Goodwood, Mrs Touchett, Ralph and Isabel.

Thus by the time he was to write *The Portrait of a Lady* James had learned many of the lessons of Balzac in the presentation of the sense of the lapse of time. He uses, as did Balzac, summarizing images and telescoped actions. His own concentration on centres of consciousness provided him with new means of achieving foreshortening, and allowed him to absorb these Balzacian techniques into a new context and give them new meaning. The methods he had learned are hence so assimilated and transmuted that they are thoroughly integrated into James's own manner and entirely serve his own purpose.

<h2 style="text-align:center">III</h2>

Description in a novel is often 'pseudo-referential': 'pseudo' because the references after all are not to anything outside the novel (unless of course the novelist wishes to describe a well-known building or street, etc.; even then we do not feel the need to 'verify' his report). A simple example would be the descriptions in such a novel as *Life at the Top*: here we have details as to the furniture, colour of the curtains, type and colour of the car, brands of drinks, make of radiogram, etc. because from these we are to infer the social status or pretensions of the owners, their standard and mode of living. Now it has long been thought that to a large extent Balzac's descriptions function in much the same way: that they are meant to be documentary and informative. This view derives, it would seem, in large measure from Taine's famous essay on Balzac. Here he presents Balzac as working in much the same way as a *savant*: carefully gathering information about the streets and houses that his characters live in, the disposition of their rooms, their furniture and their clothes, their cutlery and their glassware. He is a prodigious taker of 'notes' and only after he has settled his characters in a specific setting does he proceed to elaborate his story. The rationale of this Taine explains thus:

Car telle est la nature; les détails y sont infinis et infiniment déliés; l'homme intérieur laisse son empreinte dans sa vie extérieure, dans sa maison, dans ses meubles, dans ses affaires, dans ses gestes, dans son langage; il faut expliquer cette multitude d'effets pour l'exprimer tout entier. Et, d'autre part, il faut assembler cette multitude de causes pour le composer tout entier. Les mets qui vous nourrissent, l'air que vous respirez, les maisons qui vous entourent, les livres que vous lisez, les plus minces habitudes où vous vous laissez glisser, les plus insensibles circonstances dont vous vous laissez presser, tout contribue à faire l'homme que vous êtes; une infinité d'efforts se sont concentrés pour former votre caractère, et votre caractère va se déployer par une infinité d'efforts; votre âme est une lentille de cristal, qui rassemble à son foyer tous les rayons lumineux élancés de l'univers sans bornes, et les renvoie dans l'espace sans bornes, étalés comme un éventail.[31]

(For such is Nature, the details of which are infinite and infinitely subtle. The inner man leaves his mark upon his outward life, in his house, his furniture, his transactions, his gestures and his language. One must explain this multitude of effects in order to express him in his entirety. And on the other hand, we must assemble this multitude of causes in order to compose him in his entirety. The food which nourishes you, the air you breathe, the houses which encompass you, the books you read, the slightest habits to which you have given way, the most imperceptible circumstances which you allow to beset you, all contribute to make you the man you are. An infinity of efforts have been concentrated to form your character and your character will display itself in an infinity of efforts. Your soul is a lens which brings together at its focus all the luminous rays launched from the unbounded universe and sends them forth into unbounded space, spread out like a fan.)

Taine's argument comes then to this: Balzac's method is right because it is scientifically correct. The language of the passage emphasizes the cause and effect relationship that Taine says exists between our circumstances and ourselves as individual personalities; we make our environment and then our environment makes us. We use externals as signs of the nature of people and to explain what they are to us. Therefore the details that Balzac piles up are to be seen as the same kind of facts that a sociologist or behavioural psychologist would look for and as having the same validity. But I believe Taine has got it wrong, and that Balzac's details are not documentary evidence as to the causal formation of his characters, but instead are a rhetorical device to convince us of the 'reality' of his characters, and that these details fulfil an important *artistic* purpose that is not concerned with an empirically verifiable depiction of person and place; that Balzac's imagination worked upon and transformed what it took from the external world, rather than confined itself to what it was presented with; and that no desire to be 'accurate' and 'scientific' checked Balzac's creative powers. As Angus Wilson has noted: 'A novelist, it seems to me, makes as much or as little use of the real world as he needs to project his vision of life.'[32] And Pierre Laubriet comments in the introduction to his edition of *César Birotteau* (1964): 'Ce n'est pas pour sa valeur documentaire, mais pour sa valeur symbolique que la description a sa place dans le roman balzacien; poète d'abord, Balzac n'est réaliste que par surcroît.'[33] ('Description has its place in the Balzacian novel not for its documentary but for its symbolic value. A poet first, Balzac is only a Realist into the bargain.')

From our point of view, however, the most important testimony is that of James himself. Writing of Balzac he noted 'his unequalled power of putting people on their feet, planting them before us in their habit as they lived—a faculty nourished by observation as much as one will, but with the inner vision all the while wide-awake, the vision for which ideas are as living as facts and assume an equal intensity.'[34] And James further remarked that the things Balzac invented were as real as the things that he knew, that his actual experience was overlaid with layers of imaginary experience. This explained for him how Balzac could have such a prodigious experience of life, and yet spend so much time in writing and inventing— he paid out of himself, he nourished his visions from within and not from his occasional sorties into the world.

The d'Esgrignon mansion, 'Le Cabinet des Antiques' of the title, plays a central role in this novel which we may call Balzac's *Golden Bowl*. The passage in which it is described is too long to quote in full, but the most important elements are seen in what is here quoted.[35] Certain keynote expressions are given early: the drawing-room is like 'une cage de verre' where the occupants, curious animals, can be observed by anyone passing by in the streets. And the visionary and hallucinatory quality of the description is indicated by this revealing phrase: the room appears to be one of those curiosities that border 'sur les limites du réel et du fantastique'.[36] These keynotes are blended in the following description.

Sous ces vieux lambris, oripeaux d'un temps qui n'était plus, s'agitaient en première ligne huit ou dix douairières, les unes au chef branlant, les autres desséchées et noires comme des momies; celles-ci raides, celles-là inclinées, toutes encaparaçonnées d'habits plus ou moins fantasques en opposition avec la mode; des têtes poudrées à cheveux bouclés, des bonnets à coques, des dentelles rousses. Les peintures les plus bouffonnes ou les plus sérieuses n'ont jamais atteint à la poésie divagante de ces femmes, qui reviennent dans mes rêves et grimacent dans mes souvenirs aussitôt que je rencontre une vieille femme dont la figure me rappelle quelques-uns de leur traits . . . je n'ai jamais plus retrouvé nulle part, ni chez les mourants, ni chez les vivants, la pâleur de certains yeux gris, l'effrayante vivacité de quelques yeux noirs. Enfin ni Maturin ni Hoffmann, les deux plus sinistres imaginations de ce temps, ne m'ont causé l'épouvante que me causèrent les mouvements automatiques de ces corps busqués . . . Il s'agitait là des figures aplaties, mais creusées par des rides qui ressemblaient aux têtes de casse-noisettes sculptées en Allemagne. Je voyais à travers les carreaux des corps bossués, des membres mal attachés dont je n'ai jamais tenté d'expliquer l'économie ni la contexture; des mâchoires carrées et très apparentes, des os exorbitants, des hanches luxuriantes. Quand ces femmes allaient et venaient, elles ne me semblaient pas moins extraordinaires que quand elles gardaient leur immobilité mortuaire, alors qu'elles jouaient aux cartes. Les hommes de ce salon offraient les couleurs grises et fanées des vieilles tapisseries, leur vie était frappée d'indécision; mais leur costume se rapprochait beaucoup des costumes alors en usage, seulement leurs cheveux blancs, leurs visages flétris, leur teint de cire, leurs fronts ruinés, la pâleur des yeux leur donnaient à tous une ressemblance avec les femmes qui détruisait la réalité de leur costume. La certitude de trouver ces personnages invariablement attablés ou assis aux mêmes heures achevait de leur prêter à mes yeux je ne sais quoi de théâtral, de pompeux, de surnaturel. Jamais je ne suis entré dans ces garde-meubles célèbres, à Paris, à Londres, à Vienne, à Munich, où de vieux gardiens vous montrent les splendeurs des temps passés, sans que je les peuplasse des figures du Cabinet des Antiques . . .puis j'admirais avec un sentiment de jalousie ce délicieux enfant, Victurnien, chex lequel nous pressentions tous une nature supérieure à la nôtre. Cette jeune et fraîche créature, au milieu de ce cimetière réveillé avant le temps, nous frappait par je ne sais quoi d'étrange.[37]

(Beneath these ancient ceilings, tawdry finery of an age gone-by, eight or ten dowagers moved about in the foremost row, some with doddering heads, some as dried up and black as mummies, these rigid, those bowed, but all caparisoned in more or less fantastic gowns in opposition to the fashion of the times; powdered heads with curled hair, caps with bows of ribbons, tarnished lace. The most farcical or the most serious paintings have never attained to the incoherent poetry of these women who return in my dreams and grimace in my memory as soon as I meet an old woman whose face recalls to me some of their features . . . I have never again found anywhere, neither in the dying nor in the living, the same pallor of certain grey eyes or the terrifying vivacity of certain black ones. In fact, neither Maturin nor Hoffmann, the two most sinister imaginations of our times, has terrified me as much as have the automatic movements of these corseted bodies . . . Stirring about there were faces flattened but furrowed by wrinkles, and resembling the heads carved on nut-crackers made in Germany. Through the window panes I saw hunch-backed bodies with their badly attached limbs, neither the function nor the structure of which have I ever tried to explain; jaws very square and very apparent, enormous bones, and luxuriant hips. When these women got to their feet they seemed no less extraordinary to me than when they kept their deathly immobility, playing at cards. The men of this salon showed the grey and faded colours of old tapestries, their life was smitten by indecision, but their dress was fairly close to the fashion; only their white hairs, their withered faces, their wax-like complexions, their ruined brows, the paleness of their eyes gave all of them a resemblance to the women which destroyed the reality of their costume. The certainty of finding these personages invariably at table or seated at the same hours had the effect of giving them, to my eyes, their indescribably theatrical, pompous and unearthly air. Never since have I entered those celebrated store-rooms at Paris, London, Vienna, or Munich, where the old watchmen show you the splendours of former times, without peopling them with the figures from the Collection of Antiquities . . . and then I admired with a jealous feeling this delicious child, Victurnien, in whom we all had a presentiment of a nature superior to our own. This young and fresh creature, in the midst of this cemetery awakened ahead of time, produced an indescribably strange effect on us all.)

The details are selected for their suggestiveness, for their power of psychological or moral evocation. This is a salon where everything is old, decaying, superannuated, out-of-date, outmoded, obsolete, dépassé. The people are survivals of another age, with ideas and manners no longer in touch with the present or with reality. There is something strange and supernatural about them. Everything is worn, weary and decrepit. There are elements in the description which dwell on the moribund aspect of the inhabitants of the salon: women 'au chef branlant' ('with doddering heads'), others 'desséchées et noires comme des momies' ('dried up and black as mummies'), men with 'leurs visages flétris . . . leurs fronts ruinés' ('their withered faces . . . their ruined brows'). These images lead naturally into those metaphors or adjectives and adverbs that summarize the whole significance of their lives: 'ces vieux lambris, oripeaux d'un temps qui n'était plus' ('these ancient ceilings, tawdry finery of an age gone-by'), women 'encaparaçonnées d'habits plus ou moins fantastiques en opposition avec la mode' ('caparisoned in more or less fantastic gowns in opposition to the fashion of the times'). With particular justice Balzac has here selected metaphors that suggest the age of knights and feudalism. This is a place which has ceased to live and yet is not buried. The appearance of the inmates when playing cards is of an 'immobilité mortuaire', they are museum pieces like those of London or Paris: 'splendeurs des temps passés'. All this leads to a brilliantly succinct metaphor that summarizes the whole nature, physical and moral, of the salon and its habitués: 'ce cimetière réveillé' ('this awakened cemetery'). The one small element of hope of rejuvenation and life lies in Victurnien, 'cette jeune et fraîche créature' whose appearance contrasts so startlingly with that of all the other occupants.

But this description does more: it acts as the ground and reference point for many other images and metaphors in the novel so that its presence and significance is central to the whole structure and meaning of the novel. In a passage shortly before this one we have had a description of Mlle Armande d'Esgrignon, the Marquis's sister and aunt to Victurnien. 'Quand mon maître de dessin me fit copier des têtes d'après l'antique, je remarquai que ces têtes étaient coiffées comme l'était Mademoiselle d'Esgrignon.' ('When my drawing-master made me copy heads after the antique, I noticed that these heads had their hair arranged like that of Mademoiselle d'Esgrignon.') And the connection of this personage with the fundamental values and preoccupations of the novel is underlined a few lines later: 'Aujourd'hui jamais ma folle imagination ne grimpe l'escalier en colimaçon d'un antique manoir sans s'y peindre Mademoiselle Armande comme le génie de la Féodalité.'[38] ('Today my unbridled imagination never clambers up the spiral staircase of an ancient manor without depicting there Mlle Armande as the presiding spirit of Feudality.')

The ancient monarchy is ruined, the former social structure has received blows from which it can never recover. But the Marquis d'Esgrignon, his sister, the Chevalier and their circle go on believing in former values and former social and political

54

relationships. An indissoluble union is formed through the imagery between the Marquis and what he represents socially and politically: 'Cette admirable ruine avait toute la majesté des grandes choses détruites.'[39] ('This admirable ruin had all the majesty of great things destroyed.') This ruin is the Marquis himself, but certainly much more has been destroyed than a man. Both his antiquity and his determination which ignores the true course of events are elicited in a later metaphor in which he is pictured 'se redressant contre le torrent des faits, comme un *antique* morceau de granit *moussu* [emphasis—P.G.] droit dans un abîme alpestre.'[40] ('. . . maintaining himself against the torrent of facts, like an ancient piece of mossy granite upright in an alpine abyss.') His devoted notary and former servant, Chesnel, who comes to the aid of the family in all its crises and finally saves the family from dishonour, is referred to as one of 'ces nobles champions des ruines'. The sacredness of his trust and the extent of his devotion is summed up in a metaphor that compares him to an old monk who 'aurait donné sa vie pour défendre une châsse vermoulue'[41] ('would have given his life to defend a wormy reliquary'). These images are of great poetic power, suggesting as they do the whole nature of the cause for which the notary is ready to sacrifice himself and his fortune. Furthermore both his attitude towards this cause and its viability are sharply juxtaposed in the succinct phrase: 'châsse vermoulue.' The idea that the Marquis is an ancient ruin surviving into the altered world of the Restoration and that he fails to see or understand the changes is central to the whole action of the story, as is Chesnel's devotion which itself is a survival of an older social order and ideas of obligation and service. But the power of the images which convey these ideas to us is dependent upon the original depiction and interpretation of the Cabinet des Antiques. One might find the building or buildings that served for the model of this salon, but one would not find the interpretation of their significance in the history of the France of the Restoration. That Balzac supplies to us.

So, clearly, the Cabinet becomes a grand symbol for the whole d'Esgrignon family, their friends and allies, and the relevance of their political and social opinions to the realities which surround them. It stands for the main themes of the novel. The Marquis and his friends try to live in an irrecoverable past—in a 'cimetière réveillé'. The Chevalier unconsciously corrupts the young Victurnien when he tells him of the exploits and adventures of the young men about town of the time of Louis XV 'sans apprécier la différence des temps'[42] ('without correctly evaluating the difference in the times'). The house and its inhabitants become a symbol for all the aristocracy who have failed to move with the times and to understand the new conditions that prevail. What they have failed to grasp is the importance now of money: 'ce grand relief de l'aristocratie moderne'[43] ('that great enhancement of modern aristocracy'). We remember that Victurnien is the hope of rejuvenation in the novel, so far as the aristocrats are concerned. And it is he who fails, partly through his own weaknesses, but as much through the bad education he has received. The connection between money and the life of the aristocracy is placed before us vividly: Victurnien runs up debts which Chesnel always arranges to pay, usually out of his own funds. The new power—and source of life—is money, and it is the rival of the d'Esgrignons, the parvenu du Croisier, who has this power and who represents Industry as they represent Honour.

The Cabinet des Antiques, a grand and unifying symbol whose presence is felt throughout the novel, stands then for a whole complex of attitudes and practices and serves as a central point of reference for other images and metaphors for its endangered position is that of one part of the aristocracy: the provincial legitimists who do not understand the condition of France and the laws and the changed sources of power—money rather than heredity—as well as the family of d'Esgrignon and their friends.

The hôtel des Esgrignons in *Le Cabinet des Antiques* is so solid in its specification that some French critics have spent much time in trying to identify the original. With some success, it is true, but—strange fact!—they have found that the 'original' doesn't correspond in all respects with Balzac's description of it. The same fate has attended the hôtel Grandet. No one is quite sure where it is in Saumur. This underlines the significant feature of Balzac's description: that it is there for much more than its quasi-referential qualities. It is creative in other ways: it brings together and focuses some of the major themes of the novel; it is both representative and emblematic of the d'Esgrignon view of life and it provides a clue for the interpretation of the ensuing action. The significance of the characters and their actions is partly explained by their surroundings and partly extended into a wider significance because of the representative value, symbolically expressed, of those surroundings. Unlike the practice—or at least the theories—of some of the later Realists, these surroundings do not determine the actions of the characters so much as explain them or provide clues to their appropriate interpretation. Furthermore, Balzac's description is woven into the structure of *Le Cabinet des Antiques* through the imagery it suggests or which recalls it. In much the same way the golden bowl in James's novel, although absent much of the time, serves as a central symbol and is recalled by many other images—cups, drinks, vessels, Maggie's desire to have her marriage intact. And it is used as a central fact in Maggie's final discovery of the actual relations that have existed between the Prince and Charlotte.

James does not go into the overwhelming detail that makes Balzac's houses seem incontrovertible presences. Instead he tends to *suggest* their physical characteristics: he paints more than builds them. Nevertheless James pursues intensity of presentation, and that intensity comes mainly from the way in which a house or object affects one of his principal characters, and from the degree to which that character's interpretation and reaction are important in the development of the novel. Furthermore, James, like Balzac, can use his houses or buildings to draw together some of the major themes of a novel. And he can use them to indicate important traits, attitudes and values of his characters. His descriptions as much as Balzac's play an important role in the total structure and development of his novels.

The Portrait of a Lady opens with a particularly serene and harmonious description of a late summer afternoon where tea is being taken on the wide lawn of the Touchetts' house. Its central importance is indicated when James says that it 'was the most characteristic object in the peculiarly English picture I have attempted to sketch'.[44] This house is not their ancestral home, as is that of the d'Esgrignon family in Balzac's novel. It does not, in its accumulated features, directly represent their particular abiding passions or dominant traits. But it is an important indication of the nature of Mr Touchett and of his son Ralph who inhabit it. The house, without being a summation of their history and an outward and visible sign of their dominant characteristics, is still expressive by suggestion. For it expresses an accumulation of pictorial values and the delicate working of time. And it is the first indication which Isabel receives of England and Europe. Part of its function therefore lies in the contrast which is implied later when we see her in her Albany home before her aunt discovers her, and part in how much it affects Isabel and how much she feels moved by it.

The Touchetts' house is presented as an object of contemplation which has much to offer an observer who is conscious of both aesthetic values and historical associations, and for whom these are important parts of his life. Such an observer is Isabel, and such are already to some extent Mr Touchett and to a greater degree his son Ralph. This is indicated in the manner of James's description, first of the house and then of Mr Touchett's own evaluation of it:

A long gabled front of red brick, with the complexion of which time and the weather had played all sorts of pictorial tricks . . . presented to the lawn its patches of ivy, its clustered chimneys, its windows smothered in creepers.[45]

[Mr. Touchett] now, at the end of twenty years, had become conscious of a real aesthetic passion for it, so that he knew all its points and would tell you just where to stand to see them in combination and just the hour when the shadows of its various protuberances—which fell so softly upon the warm, weary brickwork—were of the right measure.[46]

The house expresses through its details the mind and life of the inhabitants: peaceful, generous, warm and full of delicacy. Furthermore the house is open to the world, not imposing and domineering but gentle. There is a flow between the house and the lawn which expresses the experience that the house can be to Isabel.

Its full significance only comes out later in contrast with some of the other houses which are described. To emphasize Isabel's previous exclusion from experience and isolation from the greater world as well as the narrowness of her previous aesthetic experiences James places her first meeting with Mrs Touchett in the old family house in Albany. This house is commodious and rambling, but without the dignity, nobility or grace of the Touchett house. Its decay is without the grandeur which the passage of time has given the English house. The walls, admittedly interior, are a yellowish-white, not the red of the soft warm, weary brickwork of the other. Isabel is sitting in the 'office' which is off the library. Her very knowledge and its acquisition has something irregular and undirected about it. But above all she sits in a room whose door is bolted: 'She had never opened the bolted door nor removed the green paper (renewed by other hands) from its side-lights; she had never assured herself that the vulgar street lay beyond.'[47] We have here a clear image of how limited her life has been, how confined and circumscribed her intellectual and aesthetic opportunities. We see therefore more fully how important an impression the Touchett house is in her intellectual and aesthetic progress, and what Europe, at its best, has to offer her. The difference between her imagination and her circumstances is made clear later by expanding an image which, as we have just seen, is used in the description of the house itself. 'Her imagination was by habit ridiculously active; when the door was not open it jumped out of the window. She was not accustomed indeed to keep it behind bolts.'[48]

The significance of the Touchett house is further heightened by its implied contrast with Osmond's villa outside Florence. Osmond's villa again is not the summation of his social standing and material circumstances as it might be in Balzac. It is nevertheless indicative of his character and suggestive of the moral nature of the man who lives within. The details play a definite symbolic role. Indeed James achieves just the right blend of the pleasant, agreeable and slightly ominous as well as the consciously imposing. The effect created of the house is partly anthropomorphic. If the house were completely sinister, Isabel would never enter it. James, having highly conscious characters who analyse their responses, cannot indulge in heavy and obvious symbolism. The description does, however, carefully communicate the nature of Osmond, largely in the personification of the villa and the hints and suggestions lent to it.

The villa was a long, rather blank-looking structure . . . this antique, solid, weather-worn, yet imposing front had a somewhat incommunicative character. It was the mask, not the face of the house. It had heavy lids, but no eyes; the house in reality looked another way— looked off behind, into splendid openness and the range of the afternoon light . . . The windows of the ground-floor, as you saw them from the piazza, were, in their noble proportions, extremely architectural; but their function seemed less to offer communication with the world than to defy the world to look in . . . It [the interior room] was moreover a seat of ease, indeed of luxury, telling of arrangements subtly studied and refinements frankly proclaimed.[49]

A hint as to what is to come is given when Isabel pays her visit. An impression which the place gives, not directly attributed to Isabel but which it seems to be reasonable from the context to assume belongs to her, is that 'There was something grave and strong in the place; it looked somehow as if, once you were in, you would need an act of energy to get out.' This impression which suggests more than it indicates foreshadows the fate of the principal character, for her later marriage to Osmond will come to seem to her more of an imprisonment than an enhancement of life. James adds to the irony when he comments that at this stage however Isabel is more interested in advancing.

The description of the Palazzo Roccanera as seen by Edward Rosier (Chapter 36) plays a double function. It gives us an important new vision and interpretation of Osmond as he is represented in his Roman house. This is

a dark and massive structure overlooking a sunny *piazzetta* in the neighbourhood of the Farnese Palace. In a palace, too, little Pansy lived—a palace by Roman measure, but a dungeon to poor Rosier's apprehensive mind. It seemed to him of evil omen that the young lady he wished to marry, and whose fastidious father he doubted of his ability to conciliate, should be immured in a kind of domestic fortress, a pile which bore a stern old Roman name, which smelt of historic deeds, of crime and craft and violence . . . Rosier was haunted by the conviction that at picturesque periods young girls had been shut up there to keep them from their true loves, and then, under threat of being thrown into convents, had been forced into unholy marriages.[50]

This is a far more foreboding place than the Florentine villa in which Isabel first met Osmond. There are many sinister overtones: 'dungeon', 'evil omen', 'immured', 'fortress', 'crime and craft and violence'; and later, in part of the same passage not quoted above, 'disappointed and depressed', 'mutilated', 'dusty', 'damp'. Although at this stage we are not quite sure of the accuracy of the impression, as the palace is presented through the lightweight Rosier's mind, nevertheless the seeds of suggestion have been planted and an unfavourable impression made on the reader. But the description has a further relevance to the whole structure of the novel. We have not seen Isabel since her marriage. This is the first time one of the characters approaches her after that event. A great deal that has happened to her, as we see Rosier's impression confirmed, is therefore summed up for us in this palace and Rosier's reactions to it. The way the house stifles Isabel is already here forcibly suggested.

This description of the Palazzo Roccanera takes us back also to the opening scene on the lawn at the Touchett house alongside the Thames. Here Isabel feels a great expansion of her possibilities; life is richer and more promising of new impressions than ever before. Isabel is free to wander from room to room and from the inside of the house to the outside. This openness and communication with the world, symbolizing preparedness for experience—which is what Isabel has come for—is suggested in some of the first impressions we are given of the house.

Privacy here reigned supreme, and the wide carpet of turf that covered the level hill-top seemed but the extension of a luxurious interior. The great still oaks and beeches flung down a shade as dense as that of velvet curtains; and the place was furnished, like a room . . .[51]

Thus Rosier's impression marks an important transition in the novel. In the earlier sections much of the action took place out of doors or in houses which had an easy communication with the outside world. There are rambles in London squares, in Florence, in Rome, and Mrs Touchett's villa has its windows thrown open. But in the later stages, from the point of Rosier's visit onward, there is a greater air of confinement. Isabel is immured as much as Pansy in her husband's beautifully arranged house. More and more of the action takes place within doors or at night. She must flee from her house to see Ralph. This is an open act of defiance. So both symbolically and by relating the descriptions to the themes of the novel James has integrated them into its total structure.

In *The Princess Casamassima* (1885) the description of Medley, the beautiful country house which the Princess has rented, is even more important thematically.

After a hysterical scene at the Sun and Moon, an obscure, noisy, smoky pub full of ranters and half-baked revolutionaries

—where Hyacinth's commitment to terrorism reaches its highest pitch—the Third Book opens at Medley, and the contrast between Medley and all it stands for and the Sun and Moon is strikingly vivid. The Third Book also acts as a transition, in part, to the important visits to Paris and Venice which mark the reversal of values in Hyacinth's life. The visit to Medley might be expected to inflame a revolutionary the more; here is a house with all its antique grandeur, with its rooms which could house many more people than it does, representing a wealth that could only be gained at the expense of others, representing hereditary transmission—all the iniquities of private possessions and inherited wealth. The effect upon Hyacinth is not to reinforce his hatred of either the established order or the creatures of wealth and luxury. Nor does he come to hate the beauty that has been created out of the accumulated wealth. The effect is quite different—and structurally related in the most intimate fashion to the central themes of the novel. The description of Medley shows what Medley represents and it shows how Hyacinth reacts to what he sees, this reaction revealing the change in his values from the preceding book. The visit to Medley forms part of the hero's progress which continues with the Continental trip, and this progress in appreciation leads to his final suicide as he finds the claims of the Sun and Moon and the values inherent in Medley irreconcilable.

Here then is how Medley strikes the percipient observer Hyacinth as he takes it in from his window:

... the main body of the house ... was richly grey wherever clear of the ivy and the other dense creepers, and everywhere infinitely a picture: with a high-piled ancient russet roof broken by huge chimneys and queer peep-holes and all manner of odd gables and windows on different lines, with all manner of antique patches and protrusions and with a particularly fascinating architectural excrescence where a wonderful clock-face was lodged, a clock-face covered with gilding and blazonry but showing many traces of the years and the weather ... and there entered through his open casement the breath of a world enchantingly new and after his recent feverish hours unspeakably refreshing; a sense of sweet sunny air and mingled odours, all strangely pure and agreeable, and of a musical silence that consisted for the greater part of the voices of many birds. There were tall quiet trees near by and afar off and everywhere; and the group of objects that greeted his eyes evidently formed only a corner of larger spaces and of a more complicated scene. There was a world to be revealed to him; it lay waiting with the dew on it under his windows, and he must go down and take of it such possession as he might.[52]

The house is an initiation to a richer, more abundant life. Hyacinth is regaled as never before, with delicate food and a 'liquor that reminded him of some lines of Keats in the "Ode to a Nightingale" '. All his senses are awake, and not only his physical ones, but also his perceptions as to social forms, manners, customs, and ways of existing. He begins by wishing to avoid services that he is not accustomed to, but soon finds that 'his impulse to deprecate services departed, he was already aware there were none he should care to miss or was not quite prepared for.'[53] The sense of the past, which becomes so rich a part of his experience and so important in his altered commitment—not to revolution but to appreciation —present in the description of the house, is made more explicit with a reference to the first night he spends in the mansion. In the room in which he sleeps the 'long dressing-glasses emitted ghostly glances even after the light was extinguished.'[54] The whole nature of the place is to induce Hyacinth to experience things he has never had a chance to experience before: in the middle of the night he gets up to light his candle to look at the many engravings, prints and mezzotints which adorn the walls of his room. Out of the house in the park 'he rambled an hour in breathless ecstasy, brushing the dew from the deep fern and bracken and the rich borders of the garden, tasting the fragrant air and stopping everywhere, in murmuring rapture, at the touch of some exquisite impression.'[55] The house is there and its value is real and independent of Hyacinth; but its force in the novel, its becoming an integral part of the action depends upon Hyacinth's appreciation. This comes out in such passages as the following:

His whole walk was peopled with recognitions; he had been dreaming all his life of just such a place and such objects, such a morning and such a chance . . . Round the admirable house he revolved repeatedly, catching every aspect and feeling every value, feasting on the whole expression . . . There was something in the way the grey walls rose from the green lawn that brought tears to his eyes; the spectacle of long duration unassociated with some sordid infirmity or poverty was new to him; he had lived with people among whom old age meant for the most part a grudged and degraded survival. In the favoured resistance of Medley was a serenity of success, an accumulation of dignity and honour.[56]

In this way the precise details of the house are not described; we are given a solidity of specification, not so much in the physical features of the house—who would 'recognize' Medley? —but more in the response and evaluation of the characters to the house. Furthermore since the house does express 'values'— aesthetic and social—it is through their responses to these that the characters are illuminated. Balzac's characters tend to 'fit' their environment more closely, and to be expressed in their surroundings. James can specify less, in a physical sense, because it is the reactions to their environment that are important in the presentation of his characters, and because some, at least, can choose it. The Princess's occupation of Medley is in some ways an anomaly given her revolutionary commitments. She feels this and resolves it by her choice later of Madeira Crescent. Hence James can use the description of Madeira Crescent, and, in connection with Hyacinth, of Lomax Place, to present other modes of living and perception. These modes of perception are central to the novel's meaning.

It is Medley then which provides the ground for comparison and evaluation when Hyacinth returns to Lomax Place, the house where he has grown up in the care of his 'aunt' Pinnie.

The picture was the same, and all its horrid elements, wearing a kind of greasy gloss in the impure air of Lomax Place, made, through the mean window-panes, a dismal *chiaroscuro*—showed, in their polished misery, the friction of his own little life; yet the eyes with which he looked at it had new terms of comparison. He had known the scene for hideous and sordid, but its aspect to-day was pitiful to the verge of the sickening.[57]

Lomax Place has become the symbol for Pinnie's limited and stinted life, and the range of the experiences hitherto available to Hyacinth. It is the perfect expression of experiences possible and achieved.

But more important in the development of the themes of the novel, and hence more structurally related, is the description of the Princess's house in Madeira Crescent which Hyacinth visits only after his long pilgrimage to France and Italy. This is 'a low stucco-fronted edifice in a shabby, shallow semi-circle'. Grandeur, dignity, honour, transmission, historic associations and an opening to new experiences have previously been represented to Hyacinth in Medley. In the Princess's present habitation there is dinginess, ugliness, restriction of experience and pleasures to the common mean, and an expression of the Princess's new-found hatred for all that, for Hyacinth, redeems man's life from barbarity and makes it 'less of a bloody sell'. In the place of her treasures, her pictures and statues, of her fine books (or those of Medley) and the exquisite gardens, she has now surrounded herself with the cheap and tawdry, the blatantly ugly, and the vulgarly tasteless. The street is mean, meagre and fourth-rate and above all possesses 'that absence of style and elevation . . . which Hyacinth had already more than once mentally compared with the high-piled important look of the Parisian perspective.' Madeira Crescent does not exist apart from the fuller context of the themes of the novel—for James has specifically recalled for us the importantly metamorphic experience of Paris. The Princess therefore not only mortifies the flesh by her choice, even more importantly, she has chosen the means of 'mortifying the spirit as well'.[58] Hyacinth's perceptions of the differences between Madeira Crescent and Medley and Paris are important to the basic action of the novel. As we shall see more fully in a later chapter, the Princess's choice of the house in Madeira Crescent exemplifies the destructive spirit of the revolutionary passion.

Part Two

Flaubert, Realism
and the Search for Style

3
James's Evaluation of Flaubert's Achievement

James's preface to the 1902 translation of *Madame Bovary* published in the 'Century of French Romance' series represents the final summing up of his views on the novelist whose influence, after that of Balzac, was the most important and pervasive on his work.[1] There are a number of changes apparent between this article and that in *French Poets and Novelists* of 1878. In the first place the whole notion of Flaubert as a Realist has undergone a profound transformation brought about partly through the revelations and analyses of Emile Faguet's book *Gustave Flaubert* which James cites, refers to and praises. He makes use of Faguet's distinction between the two elements in Flaubert's character: the sense of the real and the sense of the romantic.

It is in the background and the accessories that the real, the real of this theme, abides; and the romantic, the romantic of this theme, accordingly occupies the front. Emma Bovary's poor adventures are a tragedy for the very reason that in a world unsuspecting, unassisting, unconsoling, she has herself to distil the rich and the rare. Ignorant, unguided, undirected, ridden by the very nature and mixture of her consciousness, she makes of the business an inordinate failure, a failure which in its turn makes for Flaubert the most pointed, the most *told* of anecdotes.[2]

To see Flaubert's realism as only *secondary* is a very real shift of emphasis, and in keeping with this change of perspective are other important changes. Gone are the reproaches of materialism and sensationalism, of approaching the subject from the outside, of being interested in the pictorial for its own sake. Gone too are the moral strictures on the *acts* committed by Emma Bovary. These had played an important part in his earlier judgement:

Women who get into trouble with the extreme facility of Emma Bovary, and by the same method, are unfortunately not rare, and

69

the better opinion seems to be that they deserve but a limited degree of sympathy. The history of M. Flaubert's heroine is nevertheless full of substance and meaning.[3]

In the later essay it is her consciousness that he judges, not her acts as such.

For James the power of the artist lies in his ability to represent, to conjure, to 'render' the person, place and scene. It is their ability to do this that makes the Realists so formidable. It is their inability to do this that so often makes the 'Idealists', the believers in the operation of the soul, the optimists, so ineffectual. 'To be even a little weak in representation is of course, practically and for artistic purposes, to be what schoolboys call a duffer.'[4] The power to evoke the material universe, the sensuous and sensual elements of experience, the physical presence of the earth, sky and sea, the tactile impressions of the moment, the appetites and desires and pains and pleasures of man's life—this power is that of the Realists because they are above all artists. And representation, for James, is something we value for itself. The general weakness of the Realists, however, in his opinion, is that they do not present character, the movement of the soul, the satisfactions of the affections or the moral sense. This applies in particular to Flaubert: 'Perhaps the best illustration of all would be the difference between the superiority of Gustave Flaubert as a painter of aspects and sensations and his lapses and limitations, his general insignificance, as a painter of ideas and moral states.'[5] His imagination is however so fine, and he is so accomplished at what he does attempt that it is some time before we notice that the moral and human is left out. Flaubert, to James, lacks experience and is indifferent to character and the higher kind of sensibility.[6] It is this absence of a certain type of representation that renders Flaubert's characters *vulgar* in James's opinion. Of Loti he writes:

What makes the facts vulgar, what justifies us in applying to Loti's picture of himself an ironic epithet or two, is his almost inveterate habit of representing the closest and most intimate personal relations as unaccompanied with any moral feeling, any impulse of reflection or reaction . . . The closer, the more intimate is a personal relation the more we look in it for the human drama, the variations and complications, the note of responsibility for which we appeal in vain to the loves of the quadrupeds. Failing to satisfy us in this way such a relation is not, as Mr. Matthew Arnold says of American civilisation, *interesting*. M. Pierre Loti is too often guilty of the simplicity of assuming that when exhibited on his own part it *is* interesting.[7]

But if Loti and Maupassant and the other members of the Realist school have nothing to tell us in the way of character, the possibilities of conduct or the part played by the *idea* in the world, and if they see man as the sport of fate, suffering or enjoying one recurring pleasure—the sexual—'their affirmation of all this is still, on the whole, the most complete affirmation that the novel at present offers us.'[8] We see here very clearly James's dilemma: the Realists render their vision of reality with greater force than anyone else but that vision is incomplete. Nevertheless, however inferior their grasp of essential elements in human nature, James always saw them as repaying study, the best of them, for the power of their evocation, their superb accomplishment, and the mastery of their style.

If the Realists—Flaubert, Maupassant, Loti, Zola—seemed to neglect the moral sentiments James would seem to neglect the physical and sensual side of mankind. To ennoble and to elevate meant, for James, passing beyond the physical, and hence the common and the vulgar. For James man's sensual and erotic life was always something gross. He could not accept the crudely materialistic way of viewing man's sexual relations which the Realists exploited, and could find the noble and refined only in the avoidance of such relations in any of their physical aspects. An illuminating example is to be found in his notebook entries that deal with the plan for *The Wings of The Dove*.

It has bothered me in thinking of the little picture—this idea of the physical possession, the brief physical, passional rapture which at first appeared essential to it; bothered me on account of the ugliness, the incongruity, the nastiness, *en somme*, of the man's 'having' a sick girl: also on account of something rather pitifully obvious and vulgar in the presentation of such a remedy for her despair—and such a remedy only. 'Oh, she's dying without having had it? Give it to her and let her die'—that strikes me as sufficiently second-rate[9].

Certainly as James presents it here such love would be both second-rate and vulgarly carnal. How does he transform the idea—the relationship that is to develop between them—into something noble and *humanly* valuable?

71

I seem to get hold of the tail of a pretty idea in making that happiness, that life, that snatched experience the girl longs for, BE, *in fact*, some rapturous act of that sort—some act of generosity, of passionate beneficence, of pure sacrifice, to the man she loves. This would obviate all 'marriage' between *them*, and everything so vulgar as an 'engagement', and, removing the poor creature's yearning from the class of egotistic pleasures, the dream of being possessed and possessing, etc., make it something fine and strange.[10]

The evolution of a noble and beautiful idea of conduct—part of the beauty that should be in a work of art for James—is here inseparable from an idealism that finds physical love, in its essential nature, vulgar, common and egotistical.

Now we may see more clearly the inadequacies, as James conceived them, of Emma Bovary. By 1902 James had accepted *Madame Bovary* as a classic. The central question was *why*? Was it the inherent dignity of the subject, of the central character herself? To this James gave an emphatic 'No'. 'The dignity of its substance is the dignity of Mme Bovary herself *as a vessel of experience*—a question as to which, unmistakably, I judge, we can only depart from the consensus of French critical opinion.' [Emphasis—P.G.][11] That a subject is low and mean, inherently uninteresting means for James that there is a *mind* in which certain experiences do not take place, or cannot take place, that certain perceptions and feelings are unattainable in such a character's consciousness. The main subject of interest in a novel is always, for James, character; and character is consciousness. People in a novel are of interest to James only in so far as their minds are of interest, and these minds, in turn, to be interesting, must be conscious of themselves, capable of reason, intention, will, reflection and discrimination as well as of passion and instinct. Our interest is concentrated on certain individuals and their experience, and a necessary quality of experience for it to be human, for James, is that it should be conscious experience. To be driven by fate or instinct or circumstance is to be without inherent interest or *dignity*. The best minds are the best furnished and the most refined, and these minds are not vulgar, common or those of people living in and crushed by sordid circumstances. We can see here how James combines a number of moral and social criteria into the definition of a noble or dignified subject. So it is because of what Emma lacks in her points of contact with the world, her lack of a fine mind, that James finds *Madame Bovary* insufficient as a novel. 'Our complaint is that Emma Bovary, in spite of the nature of her consciousness and in spite of her reflecting so much that of her creator, is really too small an affair.'[12]

James goes on to ask: 'Why did Flaubert choose, as special conduits of the life he proposed to depict, such inferior and in the case of Frédéric such abject human specimens?'[13] James commits here a certain fallacy. He draws deductions as to the nature of Flaubert's own mind from the type of mind that Flaubert did or did not portray. 'He wished in each case to make a picture of experience—middling experience, it is true—and of the world close to him; but if he imagined nothing better for his purpose than such a heroine and such a hero, both such limited reflectors and registers, we are forced to believe it to have been by a *defect of his mind*.'[14] (Emphasis—P.G.) The reason, he says later, that Flaubert never addressed himself to the really furnished, the complicated character of man and woman, the finely civilized was because he could not. Now it is certainly true that a man can only put into his books what he has in his mind, the qualities of perception, intelligence, reflection and understanding of the motives of men and women, but it does not follow from the absence of certain *portrayed* characteristics or types of behaviour or thought that the author himself was incapable of them. We may speak of the imaginative world created by a writer, and of the qualities of that writer's imagination as they are revealed in what he has written. We can observe what subjects seemed to be his main interests, what aspects of life appeared to him worthy of the effort of recording, explaining and examining. James was always conscious, in fact, of the multiplicity of possible windows in the House of Fiction. For him each was valid as long as the pictures to be seen from it could be rendered. Yet at times, as in this essay on Flaubert, James saw some windows as better than others. Flaubert's 'defect' really lay in his not presenting the same type of consciousness as James did. For James the demand for beautiful subjects was as much an aesthetic principle as the demand for proportion, arrangement and disposition.

James therefore finds the answer to what makes *Madame Bovary* a classic, in spite of the limited nature of the central character, to lie in its formal qualities.

The form is in *itself* as interesting, as active, as much of the essence of the subject as the idea and yet so close is its fit and so inseparable its life that we catch it at no moment on any errand of its own . . . The work is a classic because the thing, such as it is, is ideally *done*, and because it shows that in such doing eternal beauty may dwell.[15]

That was the final lesson of Flaubert, a lesson, however, that could be fully learnt only when James had altered his opinions about the 'L'Art pour l'Art' movement and had more intimately absorbed its basic convictions. Before this, James found hints in Flaubert's search for style that could be of use to him, and worked out his own techniques to achieve aims similar to those which Flaubert had proposed.

4
Flaubert's Influence on James's Technique

I

Of first importance in a comparison of Flaubert's and James's techniques is the way Flaubert intermingles his description with the states of mind of his characters. Chapter 8 (Part I) of *Madame Bovary* will serve as an example. The description here is not only indicative—informing us of what is there to be seen—but more importantly what is described is strictly subordinated to a revelation of Emma's mind and feelings: these things act upon her sensibility and imagination in this particular way. For example, Emma notices that 'Charles's trousers pinch his belly'. This is indicative of Emma as much as it is of Charles, for she notices the detail *now* when it clashes with the elegance and luxury of the mansion where they are dining. The detail reveals Charles's penury and indifference to appearance. It is also, at this point in the novel, the sort of detail that irritates Emma who above all wants to make a good impression and be part of this rich and elegant world. It places him for her in relation to the other men she sees that evening, and places him to his serious disadvantage.

The whole of this chapter of *Madame Bovary* is of central importance. For already Emma has suffered disillusionment in her marriage—it has not brought her the happiness she had expected, but so far there has been nothing else to which she could attach her dreams and romantic longings. Here Emma comes into contact for the first time with that world of wealth, luxury and aristocratic prestige which has formed an essential part of her day-dreams. Here she can measure the distance that separates her prosaic life from the life of ease and voluptuous enjoyment for which she yearns. And because her encounter with this world is brief she can go on investing it with romantic associations. Flaubert here unites three functions in his descriptions: he tells the reader what there is there to be seen and experienced; he tells him what Emma herself sees and how it affects her; and he provides us with material which allows us to judge Emma's interpretation of events without ever going beyond what Emma herself can observe. (In Jamesian terms, he keeps a restricted point of view.) And much of the description acts in more than one capacity at a time.

Even the most impersonal and detached description, while informing the reader of the setting, works by suggestion. The opening paragraph of this chapter describes briefly, without Balzacian accumulation or interpretation, the château. The château is presented for its effect upon Emma; its reality is assured not by its incontrovertible physical presence but by Emma's own. The colourless and matter-of-fact language in which the location of the château and its appearance are described conveys not only its grandeur but also Emma's passive acceptance of it as she approaches it. As she penetrates into the château the notes of suggestion, and the sensations appealed to, grow more numerous and more precise; their footsteps and voices echo in the marble paved vestibule as in a church. As they pass through the billiard room Emma notices the men around the table: 'des hommes à figure grave, le menton posé sur de hautes cravates, décorés tous, et qui souriaient silencieusement en poussant leur queue,' ('. . . men with serious faces, chins resting on high cravats, all wearing decorations, who smiled silently as they pushed their cues.') Flaubert here takes up a middle ground between direct authorial presentation and analysis on the one hand and a presentation entirely in terms of a character's feelings, interpretations and judgements on the other. (This middle ground is very much the manner of James in his novels from *The Portrait of a Lady* to *The Tragic Muse*.) We have the material upon which Emma's imagination can work; and we have just *this* material because it is upon such things that it *will* work. This emphasizes how much description here is an integral part of the novel, for our recognition of these details as significant is dependent upon our knowledge of Flaubert's previous presentation of Emma. The point of view—Emma's—carefully controls the selection of details. And this is part of Flaubert's 'impersonality': for he does not tell us about the place or people in themselves, or give us his own feelings and reactions to them. They don't exist except in their relevance to his central character. And this same reticence, and the means of controlling it, is developed by James first by centring everything in relation to one character

—as Isabel in *The Portrait of a Lady*—or later by developing his centres of consciousness which exclude the author's direct participation. This controlling 'point of view' in Flaubert's novel is shown too in the selection of the portraits and their inscriptions.

Sur la boiserie sombre du lambris, de grands cadres dorés portaient, au bas de leur bordure, des noms écrits en lettres noires. Elle lut: 'Jean-Antoine d'Andervilliers d'Yverbonville, comte de la Laubyessard et baron de la Fresnaye, tué à la bataille de Coutras le 20 octobre 1587.' Et sur un autre: 'Jean-Antoine-Henry-Guy d'Andervilliers de la Vaubyessard, amiral de France et chevalier de l'ordre de Saint-Michel, blessé au combat de la Hougue-Saint-Vasst le 29 mai 1692, mort à la Vaubyessard le 23 Janvier 1693.'

(On the dark wooden panelling hung great gilt picture frames bearing on their lower edges names written in black letters. She read: 'Jean-Antione d'Andervilliers d'Yverbonville, Count of la Vaubyessard and Baron of la Fresnaye, killed at the battle of Coutras, 20 October, 1587.' An on another: 'Jean-Antoine-Henry-Guy d'Andervilliers de la Vaubyessard, Admiral of France and Knight of the Order of St Michael, wounded at the battle of Hougue-Saint-Vasst 29 May 1692, died at la Vaubyessard 23 January 1693.')

Yet Flaubert passes beyond Emma's sensibility if not beyond the things that would impress her. This is essential to his ironic method. We must not, for Flaubert's purposes, be enclosed in Emma's mind. The description therefore must also establish the necessary distance between the reader and Emma. Thus for example we have finely rendered visual impressions, as the light breaks over the paintings and is reflected from the varnish, and patches of clear colour stand out from the gloom. Here Flaubert renders an effect that tells, we are sure, on Emma, but analysed and presented in a way beyond her.

Brunissant les toiles horizontales, elle se brisait contre elles en arêtes fines, selon les craquelures du vernis; et de tous ces grands carrés noirs bordés d'or sortaient, çà et là, quelque portion plus claire de la peinture, un front pâle, deux yeux qui vous regardaient, des perruques se déroulant sur l'épaule poudrée des habits rouges, ou bien la boucle d'une jarretière en haut d'un mollet rebondié.

(As it burnished the horizontal canvases it [the light] broke into delicate streaks, following the cracks in the varnish, and from all these dark gold-framed rectangles emerged, here and there, some brighter patches of paint—a pale forehead, a pair of eyes that looked straight at you, perukes which tumbled down upon the powdered shoulders of red coats, or else the buckle of a garter above a plump calf.)

This dual use of description—both to reveal Emma's state of mind through what she experiences and, by passing beyond her, to show her limitations or suggest an ironic evaluation of her—is shown too in the depiction of the dinner (paragraphs 6-8 of Chapter 8). At first the focus is entirely on Emma: 'Emma se sentit, en entrant, enveloppée par un air chaud, mélange du parfum des fleurs et du beau linge, du fumet des viandes et de l'odeur des truffes.' ('Emma felt herself, on entering, enveloped in warm air, a mixture of the scent of flowers and clean linen, of the smell of meat cooking and the scent of truffles.') However Flaubert soon modulates into another key: we pass to the objects that she experiences and here the description is no longer dependent upon her sensibility or the analytical powers of her intelligence. All is controlled by what is relevant to her experience, but not limited to the manner in which she would experience it. It is not Emma who would be able to speak to herself in this way:

Les bougies des candélabres allongeaient des flammes sur les cloches d'argent; les cristaux à facettes, couverts d'une buée matte, se renvoyaient des rayons pâles; des bouquets étaient en ligne sur toute la longueur de la table, et dans les assiettes à large bordure, les serviettes, arrangées en manière de bonnet d'évêque, tenaient entre le bâillement de leurs plis chacune un petit pain de forme ovale.

(The silver dish-covers elongated the flames reflected from the candles in the chandeliers; the crystal glasses were clouded over and sent a palish light from one to the other; the bouquets stood in a line the whole length of the table and in the wide-rimmed plates the table-napkins, folded into bishops' mitres, each held a small oval roll tucked into its opening.)

Such careful selection of detail, such precise notice of the effects of light are marks of Flaubert's sensibility. They reveal, by implication, the limits of Emma's own responses.

The distance between Emma and what is described is further-more essential for the effect of the depiction of the Duc de

Laverdière. He is physically repulsive and in his dotage, a decaying old rake and debauchee. But Emma sees him in a romantic light and the irony is gained by the juxtaposition of a repellent old man and Emma's imaginative transformation:

Un domestique, derrière sa chaise, lui nommait tout haut, dans l'oreille, les plats qu'il désignait du doigt en bégayant; et sans cesse les yeux d'Emma revenaient d'eux-mêmes sur ce vieil homme à lèvres pendantes, comme sur quelque chose d'extraordinaire et d'auguste. Il avait vécu à la Cour et couché dans le lit des reines!

(Behind his chair a footman called out in his ear the names of the dishes to which he pointed, mumbling, with his finger, and Emma's eyes, in spite of themselves, constantly reverted to this old man with the pendulous lips as to something extraordinary and majestic. He had lived at Court and slept in the bed of queens!)

The 'discovery' of a place only as one of the characters becomes aware of the scene, the slow unfolding and development of characters, the minute analysis of motive and feeling and the importance of the most apparently insignificant detail in the analysis and interpretation of character belong also to Henry James's method. And in his introduction to the English translation of *Madame Bovary* of 1902 James shows his awareness of these different aspects of Flaubert's technique even though he does not give details or cite specific examples. 'The work is a classic because the thing, such as it is, is ideally *done*, and because it shows that in such doing eternal beauty may dwell ... Emma interests us by the nature of her consciousness and the play of her mind, thanks to the reality and beauty with which those sources are invested ... Then her setting, the medium in which she struggles, becomes in its way as important, becomes eminent with the eminence of art; the tiny world in which she revolves, the contracted cage in which she flutters, is hung out in space for her.'[1]

We can see James's emulation of Flaubertian features in a number of different novels. In *The Tragic Muse* Nick Dormer and his sisters and their mother are first seen in the garden at the Palais de l'Industrie in Paris where the annual Salon of painting and sculpture is held. That they are here when we first see them is of crucial importance for the themes of the novel. The Salon could have provided the occasion for a set piece of description of the works exhibited. The Goncourts in *Manette Salomon*, for example, describe certain paintings in great detail, analysing the composition, the arrangement of shapes and forms, specifying the exact shades of colour, the nuances of tone, and the play of light on the different canvases. But for James the place and its objects exist in their solicitations of different responses from his characters: bored indifference on the part of Grace, contemptuous and virtuous indignation on the part of their mother at the 'horrors' her younger daughter Biddy will see, generous enthusiasm and artistic stimulation on the part of Nick. As Nick turns to go away with Biddy, leaving Grace and their mother on a bench, to look at more paintings and sculptures, including a marble group showing a man with the skin of a beast about his loins tussling with a naked woman, his mother exclaims:

'Do you really think it's necessary to the child's development? . . . What we've been through this morning in this place, and what you've paraded before our eyes—the murders, the tortures, all kinds of diseases and indecency!'

Nick's full response to this challenge does not come until a few paragraphs later:

'This place is an immense stimulus to me; it refreshes me, excites me, it's such an exhibiton of artistic life. It's full of ideas, full of refinements; it gives one such an impression of artistic experience. They try everything, they feel everything. While you were looking at the murders, apparently, I observed an immense deal of curious and interesting work . . .'[2]

In each case it is the nature of the reponse that is significant and the objects that elicit it are indicated but briefly or in but the most general terms.

A similar technique is observable in an early chapter of *The Portrait of a Lady* in a scene which is even more analogous with the one just discussed from *Madame Bovary*. Isabel, who has only just arrived at Gardencourt, in her first encounter with Europe and a beautiful country house, is eager for Ralph to show her the pictures in the gallery even though it is late and Ralph has indicated that the light is insufficient so that it might be best for them to put off the visit until the next day.

The lamps were on brackets, at intervals, and if the light was imperfect it was genial. It fell upon the vague squares of rich colour and on the faded gilding of heavy frames; it made a sheen on the polished floor of the gallery. Ralph took a candlestick and moved about, pointing out the things he liked; Isabel, inclining to one picture after another, indulged in little exclamations and murmurs. She was evidently a judge; she had a natural taste; he was struck with that. She took a candlestick herself and held it slowly here and there; she lifted it high, and as she did so he found himself pausing in the middle of the place and bending his eyes much less upon the pictures than on her presence. (Chapter 5)

We have here even less designation of the pictures, their subjects or their dates than in Flaubert's passage. But the dates and subjects were relevant in *Madame Bovary* because of the way they would act upon Emma's romantic sensibility, excite her interest in the nobility and encourage her to dream of luxury and ease. We have, nevertheless, a similar awareness of the play of light in the descriptions in both novels. Flaubert indulges this perhaps more for is own sake than for its immediate relevance to Emma; at least the sensitiveness to light and its suggestions are not necessary to our understanding of Emma's mind for she is not much affected by such plastic and aesthetic values. But Isabel Archer *is* and they are part of her experience and her appreciation of the moment, in the same way as the meaning of Medley in *The Princess Casamassima* depends on Hyacinth's powers of appreciation.

Isabel's character is gradually revealed and built up through a series of small incidents. When she arrives at Gardencourt the reader knows very little about her except that she is Mrs Touchett's independent American niece. What she is—her wit, her intelligence, her play of mind, her sensitivity and her love of freedom—comes out in her conversation. Her past, or some of it, is given to us in recapitulatory and analytic chapters following upon her first appearance. But this past gives us only some of her characteristics, and above all does not hem her in; she is left '*disponible*'. It is her openness to new impressions, her youth and inexperience, and her desire for knowledge and life which are emphasized. The succeeding events do not follow from the initial circumstances. Eugénie Grandet's past and her house are essential elements in the history that she is to live; Isabel's are indicative of her mind and her limitations, but she escapes from her house and these circumstances do not constantly weigh upon the present and interact with it. Much more of Isabel's character is discovered in her response to Ralph's pictures, her visit to Lord Warburton's house, her rejection of both Warburton and Goodwood, her meetings in Florence with Osmond and her slow ramblings in Rome amongst the ancient ruins and Renaissance glories, than in the summarizing chapters. Often the incidents in themselves are minor. Madame Merle at the piano with Osmond reveals immensities to the observant Isabel. A very large part of James's novel is spent preparing us for Isabel's decision to marry Osmond. There is a multiplicity of incident and analysis in his preparation for this act. In both Flaubert's and James's novel then we find the same long, minute preparation before the heroine commits herself, one to a lover, the other to a husband.

James carried the intermingling of character and place to much greater lengths than did Flaubert, particularly in the novels he wrote after 1895. Take the opening scene from *The Wings of the Dove*:

It was at this point, however, that she remained; changing her place, moving from the shabby sofa to the armchair upholstered in a glazed cloth that gave at once—she had tried it—the sense of the slippery and of the sticky . . . The vulgar little street, in this view, offered scant relief from the vulgar little room; its main office was to suggest to her that the narrow black housefronts, adjusted to a standard that would have been low even for backs, constituted quite the publicity implied by such privacies. One felt them in the room exactly as one felt the room—the hundred like it or worse—in the street. Each time she turned in again, each time, in her impatience, she gave him up, it was to sound to a deeper depth, while she tasted the faint flat emanation of things, the failure of fortune and of honour.[3]

Everything is seen and interpreted through Kate's consciousness. The shabby sofa and the sticky glazed cloth are real enough, but we are aware of them only because she is conscious of them. Their real significance lies in their meaning for her. Her sense of the vulgarity and poverty of her father's surroundings is important for the impetus they give to her desire to escape from them. They help to explain her intense revulsion from her surroundings and her preparedness to plot to gain Milly's fortune. If we read the passage attentively we are clearly aware, nevertheless, that James is doing more than subordinating the milieu to the perceiving mind. This leads us to a matter of some importance in our comparative study: the attempt by both James and Flaubert to create a unified but flexible language enabling different modes of perception and consciousness and different types of speech to be presented in the same prose medium without any loss in the aesthetic pleasure of a finely fashioned, harmonious and carefully cadenced prose.

II

Flaubert wished to forge a language that would be beautiful in itself but capable at the same time of presenting conversation and thoughts themselves banal, trivial and commonplace. For Flaubert there was one and only one perfect way to express a particular idea or feeling—style was absolute and not relative to a particular author. Each thing to be represented and each passion, feeling or idea had its own proper expression and the search of style was to find the expression. 'La correction (je l'entends dans le plus haut sens du mot) fait à la pensée ce que l'eau de Styx faisait au corps d'Achille: elle la rend invulnérable et indestructible.'[4] ('Correctness [I take the word in its highest sense] does to thought what the waters of the Styx did to the body of Achilles: makes it invulnerable and indestructible.') This last phrase reminds us of James's famous letter to Walpole: 'Form alone *takes*, and holds and preserves, substance.' It is not a long step from this belief in the unique expression and the eternity of style to another proposition: that rhetoric or style is the justification of what is said. 'On reconnaît la clarté et la justesse de la conception à la clarté, à la lumière, à la solidité et à la beauté des mots qui l'énoncent.'[5] ('One recognizes the clarity and the justice of the conception by the clarity, radiance solidity and beauty of the words which utter it.')

Something must now be said about Flaubert's style, about what he sought to achieve and how he achieved it, before seeing how James, particularly in the later novels, adapts the aims and methods of Flaubert to his own quite different type of novel and range of characters. One of Flaubert's principal techniques is the use of 'le style indirect libre'.[6] One of its principal uses is to permit Flaubert to move from his own narrating voice to the reported speech and thoughts of his characters without too great a break in the phrasing and movement of the prose. It allows him to give the substance of the language of his characters, as they speak it or think it, without taking full responsibility for it, so that it can be reported ironically. At the same time these words, which often are more common and vulgar, more banal or more emphatic than the language of the narrator, can be fitted into one consistent pattern. The usual verb tense in Flaubert is the imperfect—'l'éternel imparfait' in Proust's phrase. This imperfect is intimately related to the realism of *Madame Bovary* and Flaubert's composition by scenes: for it expresses the stuff and continuity of life and links the different succeeding tableaux. As a result we feel the passage of life, its intensities and its langours. More importantly the use of the imperfect allows Flaubert to pass from narration to 'style indirect libre' without any break. Thibaudet quotes the following passage from *Madame Bovary*:

Un homme au contraire ne devait-il pas tout connaître, exceller en des activités multiples . . . Mais il n'enseignait rien celui-là, ne savait rien, ne souhaitait rien. Il la croyait heureuse; et elle lui en voulait de ce calme si bien assis.

(But ought not a man, on the contrary, to know everything and excel in many different spheres . . . But he neither taught anything, knew anything, nor hoped for anything, that one. He thought she was happy, and it was because of this entrenched composure of his that she felt so much resentment towards him.)

And he comments:

Le dernier imparfait n'appartient plus au même ordre, et pourtant on ne s'en aperçoit pas, on passe à lui insensiblement. La force de ces imparfaits de discours indirect consiste à exprimer la liaison entre le dehors et le dedans à mettre sur le même plan, en usant du même temps, l'extérieur et l'intérieur, la réalité telle qu'elle apparaît dans l'idée et la réalité telle qu'elle se déroule dans les choses.[7]

(The last imperfect no longer belongs to the same class and yet we are unaware of this coming to it, as we do, imperceptibly. The strength of these imperfects in indirect speech consists in their expressing the link between the outer and the inner, in putting on the same footing, by using the same tense, the external and the internal, reality as it appears to the imagination and reality as it discloses itself in objects.)

Flaubert has thus fashioned a style that allows him to combine the reflections and feelings of his characters with the descriptions and narration of external events in one linguistic medium. However we must not forget that the direct speech of Flaubert's characters is highly individual and characteristic: Homais is not to be mistaken for Charles or Bournisien. The use of the imperfect, however, helps Flaubert to pass from the most diverse spoken idioms to the musical and carefully composed narrative phrases.

I believe that James, particularly as he passes into the later phase and becomes more consciously occupied with style, a preoccupation that his essays about Flaubert make evident, is seeking to create an even more unified style than Flaubert's. He is pursuing, in his own way, one of the major quests that Flaubert undertook. The means will be somewhat different both because the languages are different and because the modes of consciousnesness and speech patterns that James wished to absorb into his unified structure are different. One of the reasons, perhaps the principal one, why the characters in James's later novels speak as no one in any society has ever spoken, and why they talk as the narrator writes, is that James is consciously seeking a linguistic medium that can pass from one purpose to another—dialogue, description, narration and analysis—with the least possible discontinuity. In some novels, such as *The Ambassadors* (1903), this uniformity of discourse of the central characters may act as a means of assessing the attitudes of people in the novel: the nearer they are to the manner of narration the nearer they are to the moral centre of the novel.[8] Hence Waymarsh and the Pococks who speak in their unreformed American are far from the language of Mme de Vionnet, Strether and Maria Gostrey and are far from the central values of the novel. This may be true of *The Ambassadors* but it is not applicable, I believe, to some of the other later novels where all the characters are merged into the language that permeates the whole of the book. The narrator in *The Aspern Papers* is also the rogue, and it is difficult to differentiate the speech of Kate Croy and Merton Densher, let alone either of these from that of Milly Theale. Indeed this is true too of *The Golden Bowl* (1904) to such an extent that Mr Verver hardly seems an American robber baron at all. This merging of styles, for the purpose of giving a unified surface, has the drawback, then, of leading to that notorious ambiguity of the later novels: we are given too few linguistic signs to tell one person from another and to assess their attitudes properly. All of James's characters are so intelligent and self-conscious that this is a virtue, and it seems even more a virtue than perhaps it is always meant to be because the language is indistinguishable from that of the narrator himself. However an advantage is gained too: by merging the language of narration and dialogue, James is able at times to make that dialogue particularly pointed and suggestive. The weight of the whole book seems to be behind it. In *The Wings of the Dove* we can see how James forms this unified language in more detail.

In *The Wings of the Dove* the dialogue immediately follows on and develops out of the narrative. It is a way for the characters to assess 'where they are', which itself is a result of the preceding narrative. We can see this interpenetration of dialogue and narrative in the following example taken from the opening of Book Sixth:

'I say, you know, Kate—you *did* stay!' had been Merton Densher's punctual remark on their adventure after they had, as it were, got out of it; an observation which she had not less promptly, on her side, let him see that she forgave in him only because he was a man.

Densher's speech is followed by narration that informs us of Kate's response. Whether she replies in words or possibly by some action, we are not sure. In this novel above all it is perfectly possible for people to understand each other's meanings without a word passing. James has in fact purposely blurred the distinction between narrative and dialogue by making a very extensive use of indirect speech. This mode was not invented by Flaubert but he certainly developed it to a degree and employed it with a suppleness that was unprecedented, and his 'followers'—Daudet, the Goncourts, Maupassant and Zola—continued to exploit it. In English it is found notably in

Jane Austen, and it appears that it is a more 'normal' and less of a 'stylistic' device in English than in French. But certainly James uses it to a degree that is uncommon and finds he needs more and more words that will take the place of 'say' or 'tell'. A very incomplete selection from a few pages gives: 'denouncing', 'welcomed him back', 'appealed to', 'propounded the theory', 'urged', 'announced', 'enunciated', 'to mention to', 'professed', 'slipped in the observation that', 'he made it out . . . with', 'formulated . . . as', 'arranged it'. The last seven come on three pages: we can feel an almost Flaubertian horror of repetition, and although some of the phrases are certainly recognized synonyms for 'speaking' or 'saying' there are those that are peculiarly James's own and understandable as part of his effort to avoid the common 'he said' or 'he cried'. Their basic function is to help the transition from narrative to dialogue by words that would not normally introduce speech: 'he made it out . . . with', etc.

The sentence that immediately follows the passage from Book Sixth quoted above is: 'She had to recognize, with whatever disappointment, that it was doubtless the most helpful he could make in this character.' Is this sentence a report of Kate's speech or is it a reflection that she makes to herself? It is, surely, intentionally ambiguous. A little later we have: 'But the amount of light men *did* need!—Kate could have been eloquent at this moment about that.' Is the first sentence a report of what she did say, as it appears to be? And if so what is its relation to the second: 'Kate could have been eloquent' etc.? Does Kate say this to Densher as well or does she only think it? If she thinks this second sentence does this then imply that the first sentence after all is not reported speech but interior monologue? James hardly gives us enough clues to decide these questions. This equivocation continues with 'What, however, on his seeing more, struck him as most distinct in her was her sense that, reunited after his absence and having been now half the morning together, it behoved them to face without delay the question of handling their immediate future.' This observation could be the result of what Kate said or what Densher had observed in her actions and in those mysterious understandings that take place between characters in this novel.

James has then forged a narrative language that incorporates into itself those things that a character says to himself, those that he says to another (given in the equivalent of 'style indirect libre') and the interpretation of events made by a character. This interpretation itself is based on a combination of spoken words, looks, gestures and acts. The result is the elimination of the narrator as much as possible—or the blurring of the distinction between the language of the narrator and the language of the characters. This blurring is not quite complete: there are events for whose authenticity we have to rely on the narrator. But the distinction between narration and the interpretation of events by a character is not sharp—terms that indicate a character's reaction are intermingled with an account of events: 'This need [the personal need of Kate and Merton for each other] had had twenty minutes, the afternoon before, to find out where it stood, and the time was fully accounted for by the charm of the demonstration.' The 'charm' is clearly what Densher feels. But it is not only in this word that the fusion between the various elements—dialogue, reflection, narration —takes place. 'To find out where it stood' and 'fully accounted for' are phrases that are conversational, rather than the prose of narration, although they can be, as demonstrated here, adapted to exposition. James indeed, because of the exigencies of his type of 'impersonality'—the presentation of the story as much as possible through the minds of the characters who act as 'reflectors'—has created a mode of narration, as had Flaubert before him, that is half-way between dialogue and normal impersonal narration. His characters and their consciences become narrators but not story-tellers. And James, like Flaubert, modulates from directly reported dialogue to reported speech (given in his own 'style indirect libre') to narrative. The lack of explicit transitions serves to unite the prose into one whole.

When he had praised her for it on alighting from his train she had answered frankly enough that such things should be taken at a jump. She didn't care to-day who saw her, and she profited by it for her joy. To-morrow, inevitably, she should have time to think and then, as inevitably, would become a baser creature, a creature of alarms and precautions. It was none the less for tomorrow at an early hour that she had appointed their next meeting.[9]

As in the passage from *Madame Bovary* which was quoted earlier there is an intermingling of the inner and outer worlds, for we pass from Kate's reported speech to the statement that she made an appointment for the following day. Kate's speeches are not part of an inner world merely because they translate her thoughts and feelings, but because the whole passage is in a sort of 'style indirect libre': Kate's remarks are presented as *remembered* by Densher. They are part of *his* thoughts and feelings. Hence the use of so much reported speech in the passage actually heightens the consciousness of Densher, for it is *he* that rehearses all of this as 'he makes out' what has happened. The range of a character's knowledge and perception is greatly increased through the distinctive style which involves so much use of narrated dialogue. The decision to centre the narration in the consciousnesses of the characters leads to the forging of a distinctive style to accomplish this narrative transformation, and in turn this style creates new possibilities, in fiction, at least, for the range and subtlety of the minds being exhibited. Style truly is a way of viewing the world—as Flaubert had proclaimed. And in James's hands it creates a fictional humanity far more conscious, inquiring and percipient than we normally are.

Flaubert's use of the imperfect tense as a means of unifying the structure of his narrative allowed him to move from narration to dialogue and back again as well as to suggest continuity and the passage of time.[10] James too has a predilection for a particular verb mood in *The Wings of the Dove*—the conditional —which he used extensively.

James used the conditional tense in those passages which indicate the steps in analysis that a character is performing in an attempt to understand more fully the exact nature of his relationship with another character—when he is trying to work out, as James puts it, 'where they are'. This the character does by projecting a possible act and foreseeing its consequences. And since the character fills in the imagined details this gives another dimension to the action, for we have imagined acts that yet do not happen, but for our understanding of the character are as valuable as those acts that do. And equally we have speeches that are not made, but are imagined and reported directly or indirectly, which are also as much a part of the characterization as those that are made. Here is an example:

If Kate had consented to drive away with him and alight at his house there would probably enough have occurred for them, at the foot of his steps, one of those strange instants between man and woman that blow upon the red spark, the spark of conflict, ever latent in the depths of passion. She would have shaken her head—oh sadly, divinely—on the question of coming in; and he, though doing all justice to her refusal, would have yet felt his eyes reach further into her own than a possible word at such a time could reach. This would have meant the suspicion, the dread of the shadow, of an adverse will.[11]

What would have happened between them if they had done something that they did not do is narrated through Densher's own consciousness: hence the *apparent* third-person narrative manner, for much of what is being given would only seem credible if it were a third-person narrator and not a character who guaranteed its accuracy.

In the following example we have an instance of narrative that must be given by a third-person narrator but which is presented in terms that remind us of the character whose consciousness (again Densher's) is the centre, and hence once more transforms that narration into something that lies between impersonal third-person narration and interior monologue: 'He walked northward without a plan, without suspicion, quite in the direction *his little New York friend*, in her restless ramble, had taken a day or two before.'[12] (Emphasis—P.G.) That Milly had taken such a walk cannot—at this stage of the story—be known to Densher at all; it is only the omniscient narrator who can tell us this. But by infusing the narrative with the perceptions and manner of thinking of Densher ('his little New York friend') we are made to feel his presence even here. Flaubert achieves somewhat similar effects by his use of 'style indirect libre' and the imperfect tense. Charles Bovary meditates on his life before his marriage to Emma and finds that only now for the first time is he happy (Chapter 5, Part I). In the sentence below beginning 'L'univers, pour lui', etc. we have moved from Charles's immediate reflections to authorial comments which nevertheless still inform us of Charles's state of mind. The narration then reverts to 'style indirect libre' to give us Charles's thoughts as he formulates them to himself and then passes, finally, into a recital of his actions.

Ensuite il avait vécu pendant quatorze mois avec la veuve, dont les pieds, dans le lit, étaient froids comme des glaçons. Mais, à present, il possédait pour la vie cette jolie femme qu'il adorait. L'univers, pour lui, n'excédait pas le tour soyeux de son jupon; et il se reprochait de ne pas l'aimer, il avait envie de la revoir; il s'en revenait vite, montait l'escalier, le coeur battant.

(And then for fourteen months he had lived with the widow whose feet, in bed, were as cold as blocks of ice. But as of now he possessed for life this pretty woman whom he adored. For him the universe did not extend beyond the silken compass of her petticoat. He reproached himself for not loving her adequately and longed to see her again. He hurried back and climbed the stairs with a beating heart.)

James's narrative language employs phrases that are colloquial and slangy—the slang of the fashionable and chic—and rhythms that are those of speech. And the dialogue is highly stylized and reflects the language of the narrative. The 'style indirect libre' is used not only for what people say but also for internal discourse. The fact that James uses the same style for all of these purposes creates a surface that seems both to resonate and to hang together like a finely-wrought coat of golden mail.

James then is carrying on stylistic 'researches' begun by Flaubert in *Madame Bovary* in novels that are very different in temper and tone, in moral outlook and in the extent of his characters' consciousness. The lesson, the example has been thoroughly absorbed, perhaps even forgotten, but is none the less powerful and pervasive for its transubstantiation.

5
Two Modes of Possessing:
Conquest and Appreciation

Stendhal, Balzac, Flaubert, Maupassant and Henry James—each, through certain of his characters, made a distinctive analysis of his society and the times in which he lived. But though these characters are children of their ages they are even more children of their authors' personal temperaments, imaginations and moral visions. Julien Sorel, in Stendhal's *Le Rouge et le Noir*, for example, is the young man of the 1830s, haunted by the Napoleonic legend with its career open to all talents, living in the society of the Restoration which has closed its doors to the talented but impoverished youth of the provinces, reserving its awards for the well-born and the well-placed, while he is determined to make his way through the Army or the Church to success: wealth, fame, power and pleasure. Rastignac, in *Le Père Goriot*, determines to make an assault upon society and carve out a place for himself within it. He rises from impoverished obscurity, the son of a respectable, long-established family of the lesser country nobility, to a position of power and influence. And to do so he must lose his moral innocence, sacrifice his better feelings, exploit his family, particularly his devoted sisters, and be tempted by and succumb to some of the counsels of the diabolical Vautrin. Above all he must possess—not love—women, for it is his position as the *amant en pied* of Madame de Nucingen, the wife of an immensely rich financier, which gives him his chance and makes possible his famous apostrophe to Paris: 'À nous deux maintenant!' And this same woman is one of the insensible and insatiable daughters of Père Goriot who has sacrificed his wealth and his life to their pleasures and fantasies. Maupassant's Bel-Ami is obviously a spiritual relative of Rastignac and Julien Sorel. He is an ex-army officer who feels the disgrace of poverty and pushes his way to the top. His means are journalism of a none too savoury sort, his good looks and his unscrupulous exploitation of the attachments he can create. By compromising the daughter of his wealthy and influential employer, whose wife is the latest of his many mistresses, he achieves a splendid marriage which will lead him to the Palais Bourbon. And not satisfied with this coup, before he has even left the church in which the marriage has taken place, he is assured by the looks of another woman, Mme de Marelle, who has loved him the most but whom he has treated abominably, that she will once more submit to his desires and become his mistress!

Besides the importance that the personal possession of women plays in the hero's progress, we can observe that all the novels so far mentioned have a common feature: their authors' comprehension of the intense interconnection between power, wealth and pleasure. They are not ashamed or apologetic about these realities, however ambiguous or ambivalent their appreciation of the way the attainment of these successes may affect the sentimental or moral life of their heroes. And since these realities have not fundamentally changed nor the relation of men to their conquest and control, these novels have still their sense of a permanent relevance for us. James stands, consciously, in this line of the great social novelists of the nineteenth century; his contributions being *The Bostonians, The Princess Casamassima* and the great short stories of the 1880s.[1]

I

In considering how James handles the theme of personal possession in *The Princess Casamassima*, how he closely relates the social and the personal, and comparing James's handling with Flaubert's use of similar material in *L'Éducation sentimentale*, we can best see James's relations with French Realism and his distinctive differences. For James was quite conscious that he was in part being a 'Realist'. He visited a prison to take notes in the approved Realist or Naturalist fashion. The prison itself is an appropriate realistic setting. But the prison is only one element. The whole subject is one that would be approved by the Realist school. For the hero, the young Hyacinth Robinson, is the illegitimate son of a French dressmaker and an unknown Englishman, presumed by some to be a lord. He is brought up by a friend of his mother, Miss Pynsent, and sees his mother only once, on her death-bed in the prison where she is serving her sentence for the murder of his putative father. Not only is his heredity mixed, part French and English, and his birth illegitimate, but his parents' characters imply profligacy, unbridled passions and criminal violence. He enters life then with a past charged with lust, licentiousness and murder. To this is added his environment and upbringing. His circumstances are straitened and he lives in respectable poverty in an obscure and dingy quarter of London, never actually starving but never more than able to make ends meet, with the woman he calls his 'aunt', Miss Pynsent. At the appropriate age he is apprenticed to a bookbinder, through the assistance of Miss Pynsent's lifelong friend, Anastasius Vetch, a violinist in a theatre orchestra. He shows capabilities above the average, both in intelligence and sensibility, and he excels at the art of bookbinding, giving evidence thus of artistic abilities.

It is through Hyacinth's vocation as a bookbinder that a third Realistic element is introduced: the movement of social revolution through anarchistic terrorism. Hyacinth comes to know Monsieur Poupin, a master bookbinder and a French exile from the fall of the Commune in 1871. And through him he comes to know Paul Muniment, a more serious and earnest leader. He attends the meetings of working men's clubs with Muniment and on one fatal night is taken to meet the great German head of the movement, Hoffendahl, and pledges himself to commit, unquestioningly, whatever act of terrorism he may be commanded to enact within the next five years.

Now all of these ingredients: the tainted heredity, the meagre and poverty-stricken upbringing, and the social revolutionary movement with its idealistic hopes of a better social order coming out of terror and violence, are recognizable elements in the novels of the French Realists, particularly Flaubert's *L'Éducation sentimentale* and Zola's *Germinal*. And yet for all their similarities, how differently they are handled by James.

James visited his prison, but on the whole his attitude towards documentation was quite different from that of someone like Zola.

To have adopted the scheme was to have had to meet the question of one's 'notes', over the whole ground, the question of what, in such directions, one had 'gone into' and how far one had gone;

and to have answered that question—to one's own satisfaction at least—was truly to see one's way.

My notes then, on the much-mixed world of my hero's both overt and covert consciousness, were exactly my gathered impressions and stirred perceptions, the deposit in my working imagination of all my visual and all my constructive sense of London . . . If one was to undertake to tell tales and to report with truth on the human scene, it could be but because 'notes' had been from the cradle the ineluctable consequence of one's greatest inward energy: to take them was as natural as to look, to think, to feel, to recognize, to remember, as to perform any act of understanding . . . To haunt the great city and by this habit to penetrate it, imaginatively, in as many places as possible—*that* was to be informed, *that* was to pull wires, *that* was to open doors, *that* positively was to groan at times under the weight of one's accumulations . . . What it all came back to was, no doubt, something like *this* wisdom—that if you haven't for fiction, the root of the matter in you, haven't the sense of life and the penetrating imagination, you are a fool in the very presence of the revealed and assured; but that if you *are* so armed you are not really helpless, not without your resources, even before mysteries abysmal.[2]

We might be tempted to think that this settles the matter; to some degree of course it does, for James is surely right to insist that without the penetrating imagination all the facts and authoritative sources in the world will not produce good fiction. On the other hand we know that Flaubert, in writing *L'Éducation sentimentale* (1870), read a great deal about the Revolution of 1848, wrote to friends to enquire about specific points and to collect their eye-witness recollections of the scenes that they had been involved in, and consulted the newspapers of the period in order to avoid any inconsistency in his chronology. Of course a novel that relies, in part at least, on reconstructing specific recent events must get its basic facts right. Nevertheless, the problem of selection, emphasis, interpretation and penetrating imagination remains, for Flaubert and Zola as much as for James. For if the years 1840-8 are livingly presented to us in *L'Éducation sentimentale* it is because Flaubert has breathed life into his characters and selected those attitudes, beliefs, habits, passions and motives that we can believe moved the men and women of his time. But equally one can see Flaubert consciously aware of what radical Republicans actually thought and said: the words and the slogans that were the furniture of their minds, the fixed categories of their commentary and protest. Of this kind of Realism James gives us much less. There is for example no Sénécal—the rigid, doctrinaire Republican of Flaubert's novel —in *The Princess Casamassima*.

From James's point of view, expressed frequently in his reviews and articles on Flaubert, the latter, as was true of many of the Realist school, was an adept in rendering appearances and surfaces, but failed to render the moral and immaterial nature of his characters. One might say that Sénécal is the sum of his *bêtises*: of his specific criticisms and the formulas that express his desire for, and his idea of the nature of, the brave new world he wishes to see created and participate in creating. The centre is revealed by the externals: he reveals himself by the way he pontificates at certain moments. Neither Sénécal nor Deslauriers nor Dussardier, nor any of the other Republicans, ever reach that degree of universality and essential characterization that we find in Paul Muniment, although neither Paul nor anyone else in James's novel gives us as much outward evidence of revolutionary socialist commitment as Sénécal or some of the others in Flaubert's work. This may explain why James's novel, for many, does not seem the 'social document' that it is.[3] James, having penetrated to the core of the movement, to the passions that animate the desire for revolution, and having captured the essence of the kind of men and women who would be the leaders, followers or aspiring hangers-on, expressed these insights in the same language as that he employed in other novels and stories of this period. Hence the characters in *The Princess Casamassima* lack that touch of particular expression that strikes one as right and accurate, that reflects the mould of thought taken by people of a particular persuasion at a particular historical moment. Thus Sénécal speaks in the idiom of the radical Republican reformer more fully than do Paul or the Princess in that of socialist anarchists. But Paul is a more prophetic figure in his persisting traits and in his essential 'greatness'. Paul could be a Lenin—or a Stalin— but Sénécal is only a police agent.

Paul Muniment is surely one of James's most successful secondary characters and repays comparison with Deslauriers as well as Sénécal in *L'Éducation sentimentale*. Deslauriers and

Frédéric Moreau—the hero of the novel—become friends when they are adolescents and this friendship continues into their maturity. Fraternity, in each novel, has its practical test in the relationship between these pairs of young men. Frédéric at first has somewhat the same admiration and respect for his older friend as Hyacinth has for Paul.

Both Paul and Deslauriers exploit their younger friends yet in quite dissimilar ways. Deslauriers comes to Paris to live with Frédéric, and to a large extent at his expense. Frédéric's feelings are more expansive and generous than those of his friend: the affection is more on his side than on Deslauriers'. Flaubert presents Deslauriers' exploitation of this friendship in very concrete terms: Deslauriers wants to establish a journal and expects Frédéric to supply the money. He uses Frédéric's confidence to make the acquaintance of Mme Arnoux so that he can attempt to make her his mistress, presuming all the while that Frédéric has already succeeded himself and that it is always easier to seduce a woman who has succumbed once than one who has not. Through Frédéric again he comes to know the wealthy and influential M. Dambreuse. And when Frédéric's momentary attempt to enter politics fails through his inability to find support from a political club, Deslauriers abandons him too. The exploitation and betrayals are definite, precise, but limited, mean, base and ignoble. Deslauriers' ideas of power are equally circumscribed. He wants to be rich, to cut a figure in the world, to become a deputy or minister, and to have some wealthy woman as his mistress. And he dreams, in establishing a newspaper, to be able to wield the power of a petty tyrant.

Deslauriers touchait à son vieux rêve: une rédaction en chef, c'est-à-dire au bonheur inexprimable de diriger les autres, de tailler en plein dans leurs articles, d'en commander, d'en refuser.[4]

(Deslauriers' old dream was nearly within his grasp: an editorship, which meant the inexpressible happiness of managing others, of hacking about their articles, of commissioning and refusing their contributions.)

Paul's control over Hyacinth and his exploitation of the latter's affection for him is at once far more profound, less petty and more sinister. His power goes far deeper because it is a moral and an affective power. His ultimate ambitions are vague—it is jokingly suggested by some during the course of the book that he could become Prime Minister. This is almost too modest an assessment of his potentialities, we are made to feel. For his influence over others is extensive—and cold-blooded. He induces adoration in Lady Aurora who visits his sister out of charity, devoted friendship in Hyacinth, and passionate submissiveness in the Princess. As James clearly sees this is a more dangerous power than that envisaged by Deslauriers. For if it is exploited, as it is by Paul Muniment, it is a far more effective instrument and morally more damaging and evil than the petty betrayals and machinations of Flaubert's figure. Paul inspires love, friendship and devotion but remains aloof from them. This is what makes him, in the Princess's phrase, 'a great man'. Being a Jamesian figure Paul has little overt coarseness or vulgarity in his indifference: which only makes it more difficult to cope with or even to appreciate. Overt vulgarity, indeed, would prevent him from being effective with people of the calibre of Hyacinth and the Princess.

Deslauriers' attempt on Mme Arnoux is entirely carnal; Paul Muniment on the other hand succeeds in ousting Hyacinth from the Princess's affections. He succeeds, that is, in depriving him of something humanly far more significant: the love, esteem and affection of the Princess, of the special place he occupied in her life. Whether Paul Muniment has become her lover is left vague. But fundamentally it doesn't matter. The important loss is the affective one and the physical act of possession would be but one more, unnecessary sign of Hyacinth's loss and his replacement by Paul in an even more intimate relationship with the Princess than he ever enjoyed. For the Princess talks to Paul, seeks his regard and respect, in a way that she had never done with Hyacinth. As he recognizes, his loss is even more poignant in that he loses something that he cannot claim ever to have possessed. His loss is therefore total.

Paul looks upon all people around him as instruments. Hyacinth's friendship and enthusiasm are seen as worthwhile only in so far as they are useful to the revolution: Lady Aurora's love is desirable as long as it impels her to visit his invalid sister; the Princess's love and admiration and willingness to sacrifice herself are useful because they mean a supply of funds for the cause. For Paul is no vulgar adventurer seeking only his own personal gratifications: he can sacrifice all to the greater cause. This is precisely what makes him both prophetic and frightening. Paul exercises, in the decision he takes about Hyancinth, in the use he makes of his friendship for himself and his temporary enthusiasm at an evening meeting, a power of life and death. For it is he who takes Hyacinth to see Hoffendahl, the anarchist leader, and it is as a result of this meeting that Hyacinth makes his pledge to carry out any act of terrorism they may ask of him. His good conscience about this—his disclaimer of any responsibilities, his assertion that Hyacinth is 'free' and need not carry out the command to commit a political assassination at a country house party if he does not want to, his unmoved state at Hyacinth's affectionate attachment to him and his willingness to use this dependence, his viewing of the matter as merely that of a person who presented himself with the right qualities for the job at the right time—makes him out as a real leader.

In Flaubert's novel all the early idealism and enthusiasm of friendship is frittered away. Deslauriers and Frédéric meet again at the end of the novel, both unsuccessful, disillusioned and weary. The ideal of friendship has been undermined by a series of pettinesses and misunderstandings. One is left with the taste of ashes. In James's novel Hyacinth's friendship has been exploited and he has been destroyed. But he remains a man capable of acting from principle and with his integrity undiminished; he commits suicide rather than commit the assassination he has been ordered to carry out. His idealism and affection, however tragically exploited, have not collapsed in the general ruin. More tragic yet reassuring is his fate.

A revealing comparison may be made of the different ways in which the nature of the revolutionary movement itself is treated in *The Princess Casamassima* and *L'Éducation sentimentale*. Flaubert's treatment is mordantly ironic: the actors he presents are of a crushing mediocrity and basic ignobility which leave the reader feeling depressed and soiled, as if he had witnessed the delousing of a group of street vagabonds. Undoubtedly Flaubert is trying to give us, through them, an explanation, and a human not an economic, political, or sociological one, for the failure of the Revolution of 1848 and for its petering out in the *coup d'état* of the 2nd of December. His characters are narrow, petty in their conceptions, envious, full of spleen, and denigrating, even of their friends. In one centrally important scene Flaubert brings them all together at Frédéric's house, and after Frédéric has treated them generously they all, on making their way home from his flat, find something to deride in the way he has entertained them. The most vocal of the critics is Sénécal whose last act in the novel is the killing, in his function as a police officer, of his former Republican friend Dussardier. This latter indeed has remained a Republican, but he has only his simplicity and generosity with which to defend himself. He believes straightforwardly in the idea of the Republic and that it will usher in the golden age, but he is incapable of either argument or analysis. And in the end he is 'liquidated'.

Sénécal is an important and significant type: authoritarian, dogmatic, severe, a rigid moralist. As a foreman at Arnoux's factory he is a harsh and hated taskmaster. His humanitarianism is one of equalitarian order:

'La démocratie n'est pas le dévergondage de l'individualisme. C'est le niveau commun sous la loi, la répartition du travail, l'ordre!'[5]

('Democracy is not a shameless abandonment to individualism. It means an equal standing under the law, the division of labour, order!')

Flaubert and James both see in their revolutionaries an intrinsic and necessary hatred of elegance, luxury and art. In the struggle for social justice these are considered by the revolutionaries as examples of injustice, or obstacles to its accomplishments, or mere frivolities. Sénécal expressly reproves any delight in art which cannot be useful to the cause of the people:

L'Art devait exclusivement viser à la moralisation des masses! Il ne fallait réproduire que des sujets poussant aux actions vertueuses; les autres étaient nuisibles.
'Mais ça dépend de l'exécution?' cria Pellerin. 'Je peux faire des chefs-d'oeuvre!'
'Tant pis pour vous, alors! on n'a pas le droit . . .'
'Comment?'
'Non! monsieur, vous n'avez pas le droit de m'intéresser à des choses que je réprouve! Qu'avons-nous besoin de laborieuses

bagatelles, dont il est impossible de tirer aucun profit, de ces Vénus, par exemple, avec tous vos paysages? Je ne vois pas là d'enseignement pour le peuple! Montrez-nous ses misères, plutôt! enthousiasmez-nous pour ses sacrifices! Eh! bon Dieu, les sujets ne manquent pas: la ferme, l'atelier . . .'[6]

(Art should aim exclusively at the moral improvement of the masses! Only those subjects which encouraged virtuous actions should be represented, the rest were harmful.

'But that depends upon the performance', cried Pellerin. 'I can produce masterpieces!'

'So much the worse for you! No one has the right . . .'

'What?'

'No, sir, you haven't the right to make me interested in things of which I disapprove! What need have we of laboured trifles which profit us not in the least—these Venuses, or your landscapes, for example? I don't see any instruction for the people in them. Show us their miseries! Arouse our enthusiasm for their sacrifices! Good God, there is no lack of subjects—the farm, the workshop . . .')

And when he is invited to Frédéric's exquisitely arranged flat for the house-warming party he strikes his matches against the beautiful yellow damask wall-hangings. His views on the function of plays are rigidly doctrinaire and socially moralistic. On the subject of the spectacles being presented at the Gymnase:

Sénécal s'en affligea. De tels spectacles corrompaient les filles du prolétaire; puis on les voyait étaler un luxe insolent.[7]

(Sénécal deplored them. Such shows corrupted the daughters of the proletariat; furthermore they flaunted an insolent luxury.)

The high point of this scene comes when Deslauriers, after drinking to the Republic to come, smashes a beautiful Venetian glass.

James's analysis is similar but goes deeper. The Princess finds that she must, to be consistent in her new-found commitment to the cause of the 'people', abandon all her former possessions: paintings, statues, beautiful furniture, exquisitely bound books. Her reasons are not unlike those of Sénécal, although expressed with less hatred and bitterness, for she gives up what she has had, and he attacks those who have from the point of view of one of the deprived. The Princess explains to Lady Aurora:

'When thousands and tens of thousands haven't bread to put in their mouths I can dispense with tapestry and old china . . . The world will be beautiful enough when it becomes good enough,' the Princess resumed. 'Is there anything so ugly as unjust distinction, as the privileges of the few contrasted with the degradation of the many? When we want to beautify we must begin at the right end.'[8]

When Hyacinth visits her new home in Madeira Crescent he sees how far her self-denying asceticism has gone, for she lives in an ugly mediocre house with vulgar furniture and atrocious decorations. She does this because these surroundings are appropriate to the lower-middle classes, the 'people', and will help her feel nearer to them. Her reception in her altered circumstances of the beautifully bound volumes that Hyacinth presents to her—representative of his affection and attachment to her as much as his ability and desire to create beautiful things—is cold and indifferent. Her values now are such that an interest in fine bindings would be thought frivolous and irresponsible. It is a question, she says, of serving either God or Mammon. The importance of this rejection of the offered fine bindings is evident if we remember that Hyacinth is more than just an ordinary bookbinder: he is an artist. The general significance of the Princess's actions is provided by one of Hyacinth's reflections.

The Princess gave up these things in proportion as she advanced in the direction she had so audaciously chosen; and if the Princess could give them up it would take very transcendent natures to stick to them.[9]

The Princess is more indicative of the real nature of the revolutionary passion than Sénécal, Deslauriers or Dussardier in *L'Éducation sentimentale*. For the Princess has known the beauties she can do without; she is, after all, we have been told, not only the most beautiful, but the cleverest woman in Europe. If then the passion for social justice and social democracy is inimical to 'all the traditions of the past', if the rising democracy won't care for perfect bindings or the finer sorts of conversation, if 'all that had been, as it were, rescued and redeemed from it [the misery of the people]; the treasures, the felicities, the splendours, the successes of the world' are to be seen as iniquities and obstacles to the new spirit, then the

Princess, intelligent and cultivated as she is, is a more prophetic and representative type than the deprived and miserably envious, narrowly ambitious and carpingly critical personages created by Flaubert.

II

In Flaubert's novel, as we have observed, there is a great enmity shown towards 'the monuments and treasures of art, the great palaces and properties, the conquests of learning and taste' but nowhere within the novel is there a centre of opposition or an affirmation of the value of art as a supreme expression of civilization, as that which makes life less of a 'bloody sell'. Flaubert's novel itself might be thought of as such an affirmation—it is only the effort of his imagination to recreate and interpret the life he has seen that redeems that life. Flaubert transcends Frédéric and his weaknesses, as well as those of all the more petty creatures he depicts, wriggling worm-like in their envy, greed, lust and ambition, because he can create *L'Éducation sentimentale* whereas all his characters are sterile failures. James on the other hand places art, and the value it expresses and symbolizes, in the centre of the novel and in Hyacinth, with his 'generosity of imagination', presents someone who is able to acknowledge its central importance in a world the counterpart of Flaubert's of envy, greed and spoliation.

Here we touch upon something that is of prime importance for James and which allies him to a strong French tradition, and by the way in which he embodies that tradition he makes his own distinctive contribution. The fabric of civilization that has been built, its grandeurs, splendours, treasures and felicities, are a possession of the human race—they are not merely the luxurious toys of a privileged and pampered few. They are not, for James, inessential ornaments of the rich, which we can easily do away with in some new order of social justice. Indeed what James presents, through Hyacinth, is precisely this fear that they would be done away with—as the Princess does without them. Their evaluation and the just recognition of their importance relies on some other principles than social justice and democratic egalitarianism. They must be valued for reasons different from those that demand the material improvement of the masses. And they are not to be identified, for James, as merely class-acquisitions which can and should disappear with the classes which may, in the past, have encouraged and promoted their existence. They represent human possibilities and human achievements—and ones of the profoundest human value. James shows over and over again, in fact, that their appreciation and proper evaluation is not a matter of class, for time and again those born with all the material and hereditary possibilities for their appreciation ignore their intrinsic value. It is the free intelligence (and a free intelligence is a cultivated intelligence)—often American, frequently feminine (such as Isabel Archer's), that sees their true value and saves them or recaptures, through their appreciation, their fertilizing force for human sensibility. Such a role is played by Hyacinth. And because he is, materially and socially, an outsider, one whose intelligence and sensibility measure their true worth for *all* humanity, his testimony is that much more important. And Hyacinth, it is important to emphasize, is neither snob nor social climber. Hence his responses show how, for James, civilization is a human achievement, of value to all who aspire to full humanity, no matter under what political or social conditions that civilization might have been created. There are many other virtues possessed by less fully sensitive and intelligent people than Hyacinth: Miss Pynsent's devotion and unselfish love and care for the unfortunate abandoned child of her friend, Hyacinth's mother; Mr Vetch's disinterested friendship and benevolence towards Hyacinth; Lady Aurora's charity—all these are cases in point. These qualities are important, but James does not equate what is valuable in existence with what is virtuous. A virtuous life may be spent without intellectual or aesthetic appreciation, but this is not the fullest life. It does not represent the highest good of which man is capable. And James does not feel called upon, any more than Aristotle did, to suggest that the good or best life must be one which is shared by all, and for which the common feelings and virtues of the majority are alone sufficient qualifications. Yet it is a life that any man *may* enjoy and hence is of permanent human significance.

This emphasis on art and the treasures in which it is embodied places James, in one sense, within a French tradition—

his reiterated praise of the French for their sense of form is evidence of this. And Hyacinth's first perception of what is to be enjoyed and valued even in a world as imperfect as it now is, comes to him most forcibly in Paris. Neither in George Eliot nor in Dickens would James have found such a positive affirmation of these values as he did in both the works and the opinions of his French peers.

But in the mode of possessing Paris there is a vital difference between James and those French novelists we have examined. A central act of many of James's heroes and heroines is the 'taking possession' of a place. A late example comes from 'The Velvet Glove' (1909)—in which another Princess figures, and who, because she is a princess, embodies romance and the potentiality of life for the central figure, the American novelist, John Berridge. It is Paris that once more acts upon the imagination:

His companion had said something, by the time they started, about their taking a turn, their looking out for a few of the night-views of Paris that were so wonderful; and after that, in spite of his constantly-prized sense of knowing his enchanted city and his way about, he ceased to follow or measure their course, content as he was with the particular exquisite assurance it gave him. *That* was knowing Paris, of a wondrous bland April night; that was hanging over it from vague consecrated lamp-studded heights and taking in, spread below and afar, the great scroll of all its irresistible story, pricked out, across river and bridge and radiant *place*, and along quays and boulevards and avenues, and around monumental circles and squares, in syllables of fire, and sketched and summarized, further and further, in the dim fire-dust of endless avenues; that was all of the essence of fond and thrilled and throbbing recognition, with a thousand things understood and a flood of response conveyed, a whole familiar possessive feeling appealed to and attested.[10]

The basic response and the mode of taking possession of Paris is the same as in Hyacinth's case. The place, the external world is subordinated to the human world as well as to the individual will, intelligence and sensibility of the observer through his responsiveness and extended sympathetic understanding. He does not use the world, or possess some power over it or acquire some social, political or economic position within it. It is his because he *feels* it and assimilates it into the

105

structure of his lived responses. It is humanized and possessed by his receptivity. Hence the act of 'possession' in James is frequently associated with strolling and lounging about the streets. This is exemplified in Chapter 29, Book IV of *The Princess Casamassima*:

> Hyacinth had been walking about all day—he had walked from rising till bedtime every day of the week spent since his arrival . . . He had seen so much, felt so much, learnt so much, thrilled and throbbed and laughed and sighed so much during the past several days that he was conscious at last of the danger of becoming incoherent to himself and of the need of balancing his accounts . . . He had his perplexities and even now and then a revulsion for which he had made no allowance . . . but the great sense that he understood and sympathized was preponderant, and his comprehension gave him wings—appeared to transport him to still wider fields of knowledge, still higher sensations.[11]

His characters possess the city through the windows of a carriage or whilst sitting at a café table or breaking the thick crusty Parisian bread (as Lambert Strether in *The Ambassadors*). People of Jamesian sensibility are contemplative, passive and absorptive rather than pragmatic, active and assertive. In Balzac the hero would take possession or begin to take possession of Paris by taking physical possession of the Princess, as Rastignac begins his conquest through becoming the lover of one of Goriot's wealthy and well-placed daughters. When at the end of *Le Père Goriot* Rastignac looks down at the Paris spread at his feet and throws out his challenge the conquest that he is about to undertake is understood in terms of acquiring definite political, social and economic power within the organized structures of the capital. Balzac might 'possess' Paris by his imagination but his heroes yearn to possess it by their wills and to effect their purposes within and through the institutions where recognized power exists. And Balzac of course was not free from the same yearnings for wealth, power and position. Nor is the position different for Maupassant's Bel-Ami as he exclaims 'À nous deux!' on the steps of the Madeleine, consciously echoing Rastignac. Deslauriers dreams of political power and wealth, and Frédéric's idea of amorous success is to become the lover of Mme Arnoux.

Both James and these French authors express, but in their characteristically different ways, the agglutinative imagination of man as he tries to subsume the world to himself. But James's mode of possession is by receptive assimilation rather than by exertion of the will and the acquisition of the power to command or to own. James's recurring expression for himself and those heroes who possess some part of himself, perhaps the most important part, is that he was 'a person on whom nothing is lost'. A finely organized sensibility is a way of appropriating the world—and leaving it all to be equally appropriated by someone else—and of abolishing those terrifying distinctions between the self and the non-self.

On which way the world is 'possessed'—by acquisition or by sensitive receptivity—depend the nature and quality of a civilization and the possibility of the existence of civilized natures within it. Hyacinth's choice is that of generous admiration rather than that of envious acquisition. His death is an affirmation of that civilization which he no longer wants to destroy but to enjoy. And James, through this death and the circumstances that bring it about, may therefore be said to have made an even more radical critique of acquisitiveness than Balzac, Flaubert or Maupassant.

Part Three

Art for Art and Aesthetic Realism

6
Henry James and 'L'Art pour l'Art'

The beginnings of the 'L'Art pour l'Art' movement go back to Gautier's preface to *Mademoiselle de Maupin* (1835-6). His primary aim was to declare the freedom of art from any moral, political or social-economic theory that would claim that art has a special function to serve in instructing others in the truth of its precepts, in purifying their morals, or in advancing the well-being of the people. He had several groups in mind in his defence of art. One was that of the moralizing journalists who took upon themselves the defence of the public's virtue. His attack upon them is witty and provocative, exposing their hypocrisy and praising the flesh and honest erotic pleasure. More significantly he rejects the idea of art being 'moral' at all. Morality is bourgeois prudence and respectability and as such he is prepared to by-pass it altogether, asserting that the greatest good is pleasure and that Art is a source of pleasure in the Beautiful. This rejection of 'morality' has caused some confusion, and it has been forgotten that Gautier identifies morality with a specific and limited code of conduct, that embraced by the Catholic and '*bien-pensant*' bourgeoisie of the Restoration. He is claiming for art higher and independent ends rather than arguing that morality itself needs reinterpreting. But this view can be seen as giving art a very important place in the life of man and one that has ends worthy of man's pursuit. His argument is ethical rather than moral although his tactic is to dismiss morality as irrelevant to art altogether.

But the main part of the preface deals with the views of the social utilitarians represented by *Le Globe*, which had been taken over by the followers of Saint-Simon in 1830. His attack is directed against those who want art to be useful in the promotion of social progress and committed to particular social and political choices. If 'useful' is taken to mean that which ameliorates the material conditions of life or contributes to social and economic progress (however understood) then art, Gautier declares defiantly and proudly, *is* useless. And the converse is true, too: 'Il n'y a de vraiment beau que ce qui ne peut servir à rien; tout ce qui est utile est laid.' ('There is nothing truly beautiful but that which serves no useful purpose; everything that is useful is ugly.') Art does not make anything at all necessary to life, does not promote the manufacture of one useful item.

Gautier both represents and reinforces a very important current of thought in France, an appreciation of which is vital for an understanding of the difference between French and English literature in the nineteenth century. In a broad sense this difference lies in the freedom of the French novel from the moral domination of young unmarried ladies. As Henry James himself puts it, George Eliot and Dickens had an 'eye to the innocent classes'. The French novelist earlier and more consciously rejected such a limitation. When Flaubert claims an impersonality for the artist similar to that of God, the artist's right to stand back from his creations, he is asserting the right of the artist to ignore any didactic or moralizing purpose, and not to make use of his creations to point a moral or adorn a tale, to distribute praise or blame.

Art, for Gautier, has an existence and supreme value apart from the events that may involve the destinies of men and nations. He developed the concept of the artist in his ivory tower devoted to transcendent aims to the full:

> Comme Goethe sur son divan
> À Weimar s'isolait des choses
> Et d'Hafiz effeuillait les roses,
>
> Sans prendre garde à l'ouragan
> Qui fouettait mes vitres fermées
> Moi j'ai fait *Émaux et Camées*
>
> (As Goethe on his divan
> At Weimar held himself aloof from things
> And plucked the roses from Hafiz
>
> So I, paying no attention to the hurricane
> Which beat against my closed windows
> Have made *Émaux et Camées*)

The artist is dedicated to producing exquisite works and this dedication should proceed even in time of war, that most 'serious' event. 'Art for Art must be understood in these revolutionary terms—as a rejection of the standards of 'L'Industrie et le Progrès, ces ennemis de l'art' as Baudelaire put it. Gautier's paradoxical answer to the question: What is the use of poetry?—that it is useless, has the merit of showing the falseness of the questioner's criteria in judging art. The Beautiful, that is, demands another standard of judgement than that used in deciding either on political action or the truth of scientific propositions. The standard is not, for Gautier, the amount of personal emotion or confidences that is poured forth by the artist and that the reader is asked to overhear. For Gautier there is a realm of the Beautiful which the artist discovers and makes known to others: there are beautiful objects, colours, forms, rhythms and sequences of words and these the poet or artist presents.

Art has its own province and its own rigorous demands. To create a beautiful work of art is in itself a difficult enough task, and sufficiently valuable. No other justification is needed. Art then became an ideal, a way of life, and a religion. To achieve the beautiful became a goal that few were felt capable of understanding and even fewer of achieving. And no matter how differently they interpreted the demands of 'Art for Art' nor how divergent their practices, all the group were united in their belief in the supreme importance of art, seen as a self-justifying activity of the human mind. In the following pages we shall see how much of James's own thinking about art and the novelist's craft came to resemble that of Gautier and his descendants.

I

James had some adverse things to say about the 'L'Art pour l'Art' movement. Furthermore, James and the 'L'Art pour l'Art' movement appear, on the face of it, to a high degree opposed. Part of the reluctance to accept that James had anything in common with the 'L'Art pour l'Art' movement is due to confusion between Gautier's views and what came to be known in England as 'Aestheticism'—the doctrine that life should be lived merely for moments of aesthetic appreciation.

We must recognize, however, that the phrase 'l'art pour l'art' is ambiguous. In the whole movement we need to distinguish three quite distinct strands. Firstly, Gautier, Flaubert, the Goncourts and the others insisted that the artist has the right to select his subject-matter wherever he will and that the value of a work of art is not to be measured by its conformity to political or social codes of usefulness. The artist's greatest value, according to them, is in the freedom of his imagination and without this freedom his creativity is hampered. The significance of a work of art, as commentary on human experience, is not to be assessed by its providing text-book examples of virtue rewarded and vice punished. Secondly, for this group art has its own inherent morality. For the work of art is itself an object of delight. The mind engaged in the contemplation and appreciation of a work of art is performing activities which are themselves moral goods. Furthermore, and more importantly, in a work of art we see our condition more clearly in proportion to the intelligence and achievement of the artist. A greater awareness of what life is like is an increase in our moral awareness. Thirdly, there is the view that the value of art lies in its formal properties. In an extreme form it may be asserted that it is the sensuous delight provided by the materials and their organization which gives a work its sole value. And 'Aestheticism' then goes on to pronounce these values as the only ones that matter in life. Those who adhered to 'Aestheticism' in this narrower sense often took Gautier as a forerunner, but as we have seen this is not all he had to say. James in his novels makes clear the distinction between the validity of the first two sets of propositions and the sterility to his mind of the third in the extreme form of 'Aestheticism. If much of what the first two sets assert seems now critical commonplace, this is a measure of the permanent value of 'L'Art pour l'Art'.

Among other important elements in the movement as it develops and is refracted in the works of the great French novelists and poets of the middle and latter part of the nineteenth century are: the emphasis placed on a work of art as the expression of the individual temperament of the artist; the importance of representation and the writer's 'impersonality'; the religion of art and the creation of an alternative world of art; the primacy of the created world of art over landscape and nature as the sources of artistic and human inspiration; and the emphasis on style as a mode of seeing and interpreting the world and as that which gives permanence and value to a work of literature. The extent to which these concerns, as well as those already mentioned, find their way into James's novels and stories reveals his deep affinity with much of what the movement stood for.[1]

Out of the consideration of the relation of a work of art to moral and social questions developed another important aspect of the 'L'Art pour l'Art' movement: the impersonality of the artist as championed for example by Gautier, Flaubert, Maupassant and the Goncourts. There often seems to have been confusion as to what was being claimed by an artist's 'impartiality' or 'impersonality' (the terms seem to have been used more or less synonymously).[2] Some of this confusion came about from the way this desire for impartiality was expressed, for some authors made the analogy with science. This was a tactical move: it was a way of stressing their point and emphasizing their difference, particularly from those writers they thought too sentimental or too personal. But like many analogies and metaphors this is deceptive when taken too literally or pressed too far. By proclaiming the importance of impersonality these authors wished to assert that a work of art, particularly the novel, should present characters with their own personalities, distinct from that of the author, and that these should be allowed to act out their fates according to their own natures and circumstances, without any *overt* comment or criticism on the part of the author or without his 'rigging' the story to tell a particular edifying moral. They found themselves opposed to the confessional literature of excessive sensibility (as exemplified in Rousseau, for example), or the personal lyricism of a Lamartine or a Hugo, or the writers who used the novel as a platform for promoting social reforms, as George Sand, say, in her period of social romanticism. Impersonality is a revolt against lyricism, self-confession, autobiography and the *roman à thèse*. The impersonal artist abandons his own immediate and superficial personality to absorb himself in that of his creations. Flaubert makes this point quite clear. In a letter to George Sand (1866) he wrote:

Il faut, par un effort d'esprit, se transporter dans les personnages, et non les attirer à soi.[3]

(We must make the mental effort to project ourselves into our characters rather than assimilating them to ourselves.)

On the relation between art and science, he had this to say in a letter to Louise Colet (1853):

C'est là ce qu'ont de beau les sciences naturelles: elles ne veulent rien prouver. Aussi quelle largeur de faits et quelle immensité pour le pensée! Il faut traiter les hommes comme des mastodontes et des crocodiles. Est-ce qu'on s'emporte à propos de la corne des uns et de la mâchoire des autres?[4]

(That is what is fine about the natural sciences; they do not seek to prove anything. Consequently what a breadth of facts and what an immense area for thought. One must treat men as one does mastodons and crocodiles. Does one lose one's temper in respect of the horn of the one or the jaw of the other?)

To Flaubert the writer's task is to represent, to render life and to avoid drawing conclusions. James over and over again returns to the importance of 'doing', of creating the illusion of life, or 'rendering'. He is here in perfect harmony with Flaubert, for the essence of Flaubert's artistic creed is succinctly summed up in this phrase: 'L'art est une représentation; nous ne devons penser qu'à représenter.'[5] (Art is a representation; we should think of nothing but representing.')

The analogy with science is misleading because of course the objectivity of science has a different aim from the objectivity of the impersonal artist. Science seeks to establish laws which are capable of being substantiated by experimental evidence. Or if Karl Popper's analysis is preferred, science establishes laws which, capable of being refuted according to well-understood procedures, have not been refuted. But a novel cannot be 'refuted'. It can falsify experience, but that is hardly the same thing. And of course the personality of the artist is stamped on every word, phrase, cadence, paragraph, incident, image and structural pattern—and on the choice of subject and the types of characters chosen. This was not denied by those—at least the more clear-sighted of them—who demanded 'impersonality'. They simply demanded indeed that the artist's personality be so stamped, that it be everywhere but nowhere visible; that he be himself *through* his work of art rather than *in* it by depicting his private experiences or voicing his own opinions. The less quotable personality he had the more he would have an artistic one. Hence style became the supreme sign of the individual artist, and the manner of his being one.

116

Therefore equally with the demand for impersonality went the claim that a work of art is a particular way of seeing the world and that each artist has his own way of doing so. Zola claims that a novel is the world seen 'à travers un tempérament'; James remarks that 'Art is really but a point of view, and genius but a way of looking at things.'[6]

II

James wrote his famous 'Art of Fiction' as a reply to Walter Besant's lecture at the Royal Institution, 'Fiction as one of the Fine Arts' (April, 1884). In the earlier part of that year he had spent some time in Paris, and discussed the art of the novel with Daudet, Edmond de Goncourt, Zola and Maupassant. His letters from Paris tell us how important and stimulating he had found these discussions. There are in fact remarkable similarities between James's position in his essay and Maupassant's later preface to *Pierre et Jean*. It is unlikely that Maupassant read James's essay; James always found that the French were too inbred and too indifferent to English fiction, including his own. This is not a case of 'influence' in any narrow causal sense, but rather of a common viewpoint and shared discussions. Much of what James had to say was common currency in the French circles into which he was admitted, and much of this derived from the 'L'Art pour l'Art' movement considered in its broader aspects.

James urges the right of the novelist to represent whatever he wants in whatever manner he sees fit, the novel's function being to represent life. And in this argument for the novelist's freedom he draws on the analogy with painting which was a staple of 'Art for Art' theory about literature from Gautier onwards.

The only reason for the existence of a novel is that it does attempt to represent life. When it relinquishes this attempt, the same attempt that we see on the canvas of the painter, it will have arrived at a very strange pass. It is not expected of the picture that it will make itself humble in order to be forgiven; and the analogy between the art of the painter and the art of the novelist is, so far as I am able to see, complete. Their inspiration is the same, their process (allowing for the different quality of the vehicle), is the same,

117

their success is the same. They may learn from each other, they may explain and sustain each other. Their cause is the same, and the honour of one is the honour of another.[7]

The obverse of this is that the novel 'ought to be artistic', that its purposes are best fulfilled when it is so, and that the search for form is essential to its being worth anything at all.

In his article on Maupassant (1888) James reviewed Maupassant's work and began his discussion with a consideration of the preface to *Pierre et Jean*. There Maupassant had concluded that only a few people ask the right thing from a writer: 'Make me something fine in the form that shall suit you best, according to your temperament.' James commended this statement of the case. 'This seems to me', he wrote, 'to put into a nutshell the whole question of the different classes of fiction, concerning which there has recently been so much discourse. There are simply as many different kinds as there are persons practising the art, for if a picture, a tale or a novel be a direct impression of life (and that surely constitutes its interest and value), the impression will vary according to the plate that takes it, the particular structure and mixture of the recipient.'[8] This is common ground to both Maupassant and James, and was a central point in Zola's theory as well. And the preface to *Mlle de Maupin* lies behind them all as their common ancestor.

Since there is a multiplicity of temperaments there can be no *a priori* rules about the artist's subjects or manner of treatment. James and Maupassant are at one on this point. The only responsibility a novel has, says James, is to be interesting. The ways to be interesting 'are as various as the temperament of man, and they are successful in proportion as they reveal a particular mind, different from others. A novel is in its broadest definition a personal, a direct impression of life: that, to begin with, constitutes its value, which is greater or less according to the intensity of the impression.'[9] Maupassant contends that there are many different kinds of novels and it is a form which expresses 'les tendances les plus opposées, les tempéraments les plus contraires, et admette les recherches d'art les plus diverses.'[10] ('. . . the most opposed tendencies, the most contrary temperaments and admits the most diverse researches of art.') And like James he claims that 'le talent provient de l'originalité, qui est une manière spéciale de penser, de voir, de comprendre et de juger.'[11] ('. . . talent arises from originality, which is a special manner of thinking, seeing, comprehending and judging.')

So for each of these critics, who are also novelists, it is only the execution that we can properly judge. James states: 'We must grant the artist his subject, his idea, his *donnée*: our criticism is applied only to what he makes of it.'[12] 'The execution belongs to the author alone; it is what is most personal to him, and we measure him by that.'[13] Maupassant, after stating that what the reader should demand is something beautiful in whatever form suits the artist and according to his temperament, comments:

L'artiste essaie, réussit ou échoue. Le critique ne doit apprécier le résultat que suivant la nature de l'effort . . .[14]

(The artist tries, succeeds, or fails. The critic should only appraise the result according to the nature of the endeavour.)

For both the novel is the form that allows the greatest range of personal visions to be expressed, and this is precisely its value. Since this is so, and since from this very openness comes the interest and value of the novel, both James and Maupassant insist that the independence of the artist from arbitrary restrictions on his subject-matter dictated by 'moral' concerns is a matter of vital necessity for the health of the novel as an art form.

James argues against there being a sensible distinction between the story of a novel and its treatment except in so far as the story can be thought of as the initial subject:

This sense of the story being the idea, the starting-point, of the novel, is the only one that I see in which it can be spoken of as something different from its organic whole; and since in proportion as the work is successful the idea permeates and penetrates it, informs and animates it, so that every word and every punctuation-point contribute directly to the expression . . . the story and the novel, the idea and the form, are the needle and thread.[15]

This insistence on the inseparability of form and meaning, of subject and treatment—that the subject resides in the treatment, the meaning in the expression—was one of Flaubert's central and constantly reiterated positions. Cassagne in his great study of the writers of the 'L'Art pour l'Art' movement noted that, for them:

Une première proposition est que la forme et l'idée sont indissociables, ou mieux sont identiques, ne font qu'un, ne sont séparables que par une exercise d'abstraction illusoire.[16]

(A first principle is that the form and the conception are indissociable, or better that they are identical and make but a unity, and are only separable by an illusory act of abstraction.)

And he quotes various dicta of Flaubert: that style is not only a way of expression but also 'une manière de penser', and 'une manière absolue de voir les choses.'[17] James's sense of the indissoluble link between style and subject grew stronger as he grew older and the last manner is in part explicable as an expression both of this belief and the greater technical agility he acquired not only in individual sentences but in the overall patterns he created and the different styles of narration he adopted for different stories or novels. He made powerful play with the necessary link between language and subject in a letter to Auguste Monod, who translated some of James's works into French. He is here speaking of the first autobiographical volume, *A Small Boy and Others* (1913).

You understand the value I attach to your attention to what I do—yet I confess that it is a relief to me this time to have so utterly defied translation. The new volume will complete that defiance and express for me how much I feel that in a literary work of the least complexity the very form and texture are the substance itself and that the flesh is indetachable from the bones! . . . But without having in the least sought the effect, it does interest me, it does even partly exhilarate me to recognize that the small Boy, while yet so tame and intrinsically safe a little animal, is locked fast in the golden cage of the *intraduisible*![18]

James had achieved in prose what Gautier had taken to be of the essence of verse; the use of words in all of their possibilities so that it would not be possible to use other words and retain the same meaning. His prose reverberates with a polish that Flaubert could take as a tribute of emulation: 'le style est à lui seul une manière absolue de voir les choses.' ('. . . style is in itself an absolute manner of seeing things.')

At the conclusion of 'The Art of Fiction' James begins to deal with the question of the morality of the novel. And here he draws again upon the pictorial analogy:

Will you not define your terms and explain how (a novel being a picture) a picture can be either moral or immoral? You wish to paint a moral picture or carve a moral statue: will you not tell us how you would set about it? We are discussing the Art of Fiction; questions of art are questions (in the widest sense) of execution; questions of morality are quite another affair, and will you not let us see how it is that you find it so easy to mix them up?[19]

James goes on to attack, not the moral earnestness and seriousness of the English novel, but its moral timidity: being moral isn't simply a question of avoiding certain subjects. The mark, he says, in opposition to Mr Besant, of the English novel is not its moral purpose but its moral diffidence. And if a novelist is to have a purpose the least dangerous one 'is the purpose of making a perfect work'.[20] James is certainly not flouting morality, but he is indicating that morality does not lie in always having the young person in mind when writing, and more positively he suggests that the artist's morality consists in being an artist—not in pursuing some supposed moral purpose. His last words of advice are: 'Remember that your first duty is to be as complete as possible—to make as perfect a work.'[21] These conclusions could not be more in harmony with what Gautier, Flaubert, the Goncourts, Daudet and numerous others had urged and were urging in their own ways. The morality comes through the work, and there is a morality in the very pursuit of perfection.

III

It is not only in the theory of the art of the novel that we can trace James's affiliation with the 'L'Art pour l'Art' movement and its spiritual associates and descendants. The close association of the plastic and literary arts is one of the characteristics of the movement as much as the adaptation of the terminology of painting to literary works. James evidences this not only in his use of the example of painting and sculpture in his defence of the liberty of the writer to choose his subject and in his insistence that a work of art has no moral significance unless it has artistic significance first, but also in his characteristic vocabulary applied to works of literature: portrait, tone, values, etc.

But the connection is even more profound; it finds expression in the way nature itself is seen and in the importance of the arts in the education of heroes and heroines, as well as in the novels that treat the lives of artists as their central subject. As Cassagne remarked:

Souvent ils n'ont été à la nature qu'à travers l'art. Souvent ce sont les tableaux qu'ils connaissaient, ou ceux qu'ils concevaient, qui leur ont appris à connaître la nature.[22]

(Often they reach nature only through the medium of art. Often it is the paintings they have known or those that they have conceived which have taught them to know nature.)

Closely related to this general point of view is the belief that physical nature is less interesting and humanly valuable than nature represented in works of art or transformed by man's imagination: museums, churches, statues, great buildings, palaces—the accumulation of man's efforts to create are more interesting than raw nature. Flaubert writing to George Sand from Switzerland (July 1874), expresses himself thus:

Je ne suis pas *l'homme de la nature* et je ne comprends rien aux pays qui n'ont pas d'histoire. Je donnerais tous les glaciers pour la Musée du Vatican. C'est là qu'on rêve.[23]

(I am not a man of nature and countries which have no history mean nothing to me. I'd give every glacier for the Vatican Museum; it's there that one dreams.)

James expresses himself in very nearly the same terms. His most powerful descriptions are not of mountains, lakes or streams but of palaces, piazzas, the Grand Canal, old churches and worn stones. Writing of Switzerland in 1872 he had this to say:

Switzerland represents, generally, nature in the rough, and the American traveller in search of novelty entertains a rational preference for nature in the refined state . . . I relish a human flavour in my pleasures, and I fancy that it is a more equal inter-course between man and man than between man and mountain.[24]

One has only to contrast this tepid reaction to the Swiss mountain scenery with the pages on the Rows of Chester, the Milan Cathedral, the sense of the past at Haddon Hall, the paintings of Tintoretto and the Last Supper of Da Vinci in the same volume to feel how much local colour and the historic sense are important elements in James's whole reponse to

Europe and how much of it is filtered through literature or art before it comes out in his prose.[25]

The same cast of mind may be seen in the novels of the Goncourts. In the opening chapter of *Renée Mauperin* (1864) the eponymous heroine calls attention to what she considers to be a beautiful scene: her companion is not impressed and she insists:

'Si, c'est beau! je vous assure que c'est beau . . . Il y a eu à l'Exposition, il y a deux ans, un effet dans ce genre-là . . .'[26]

('But it *is* beautiful! I assure you that it is beautiful . . . At the Exhibition, two years ago, there was that kind of effect . . .')

And in their description of the ensuing scene the Goncourts consciously imitate a painting. For one of the results of the interest in painting and of the theoretical strength that the movement took from the example of the plastic arts was an intensification of the rendering of sensation and the physical appearance of things. For writers who were also 'naturalists' this training was of the utmost importance. Here the opening paragraphs of *Renée Mauperin* describe what Renée, bathing in the Seine, sees:

Et d'un regard elle indiqua la Seine, les deux rives, le ciel.

De petits nuages jouaient et roulaient à l'horizon, violets, gris, argentés, avec des éclairs de blanc à leur cime qui semblaient mettre au bas du ciel l'écume du bord des mers. De là se levait le ciel, infini et bleu, profond et clair, splendide et déjà pâlissant, comme à l'heure où les étoiles commencent à s'allumer derrière le jour. Tout en haut, deux ou trois nuages planaient, solides, immobiles, suspendus. Une immense lumière coulait sur l'eau, dormait ici, étincelait là, faisait trembler des moires d'argent dans l'ombre des bateaux, touchait un mât, la tête d'un gouvernail, accrochait au passage le madras orange ou la casque rose d'une laveuse.[27]

(And with a glance she indicated the Seine, its two banks, the sky.

Little clouds were playing and rolling on the horizon, violet, grey, and silver, with flashes of white at their crests, which seemed to place, low in the sky, the surf of the sea shore. Thence the sky arose, infinite and blue, profound and limpid, resplendent and already growing pale, as at the hour when the stars begin to shine behind the day. High above two or three clouds were floating—solid, motionless, suspended. A vast light spread over the water, now sleeping here, now sparkling there, making silvery moires tremble in the shadows of boats, touching a mast, the head of a rudder, catching on its way a washer woman's orange kerchief or pink mob-cap.)

More extreme examples of the domination of the pictorial arts in description are to be found in *Manette Salomon* (1867). Here the Goncourts indulge themselves in a description of Paris, drawing extensively on the technical vocabulary of paintings: the tiles of the houses are the colour of 'marc de raisin'; the large mass represented by the roofs, tinted in the colour just described, spread out and darken to a 'noir-roux' as they approach the quays; the cloud produced by all the exhalations of Paris hangs over the hill at the edge of the horizon and this cloud finishes in 'déchirures aiguës sur une clarté où s'éteignait, dans du rose, un peu de vert pâle' ('sharp-torn edges on a clear background where amidst pink a little pale green was spreading.'): nearer may be observed 'un grand plan d'ombre ressemblant à un lavis, d'encre de Chine sur un dessous de sanguine.'[28] ('. . . a large area of shadow resembling a wash of Indian ink on a base of red-chalk.')

One of the most striking examples in James's writings of nature experienced as art, and only fully experienced because it is like art, lies in Strether's intensely rendered excursion outside Paris when he walks through the countryside and finally comes upon the river where he discovers Mme de Vionnet and Chad in their boat. During the whole of this episode he imagines himself in a Lambinet painting. The experience is intense, special, emotionally heightened, humanly significant because, to a large extent, of the overtones of the remembered painting, because Strether is searching to recapture the ideal and transformed world of art in life. And James, more subtly and delicately than the Goncourts in their description of Paris (the hints of painting in *Renée Mauperin* are more emphatic) mixes the present impression and the recalled work by the terms of his description.

The oblong gilt frame disposed its enclosing lines; the poplars and willows, the reeds and river—a river of which he didn't know, and didn't want to know, the name—fell into a composition, full of felicity, within them; the sky was silver and turquoise and varnish; the village on the left was white and the church on the right was grey; it was all there, in short—it was what he wanted: it was Tremont Street, it was France, it was Lambinet.[29]

The whole of the day passes within this picture, and other images are part of the definition of the experience; what happens to Strether is his drama, the landscape is the stage, his experiences are enhanced by their being like events in a story by Maupassant. These are all elements in Strether's view of what he is doing and of its significance; it is through such analogies that the experience is most fully lived, realized and made humanly valuable. The experience is oblique and filtered, interpreted through art, pictorial and literary, which penetrates every part and every moment of it. And at the end of this chapter in which Strether has been living in a picture James gives a fuller description of what Strether sees as he sits at the bottom of the garden of the inn, waiting for his dinner to be prepared. This description makes full use of pictorial terms and analogies:

The valley on the farther side was all copper-green level and glazed pearly sky, a sky hatched across with screens of trimmed trees, which looked flat, like espaliers; and though the rest of the village straggled away in the near quarter the view had an emptiness that made one of the boats suggestive.[30]

The appearance of the boat carrying Chad and Mme de Vionnet is the right note—to complete the picture. The agitation caused by the intrusion of the real carnal relationship between Chad and Mme de Vionnet which now stares Strether in the face is the greater because it is not the right note, morally, to complete his aesthetic enjoyment. But having established a tone in the description of the day, Strether's behaviour, and Chad's and that of Mme de Vionnet, all of whom avert violence and attempt to gloss over the awkwardness of the encounter, is more understandable: the artistic setting makes possible a certain kind of harmonious and restrained human behaviour or at least makes the participants seek to make their behaviour accord with the tone of the preceding setting.

'A New England Winter' (1884) provides an earlier case. An important difference between James and the Goncourts comes out here. James to a large extent interiorizes his descriptions. When he presents Boston pictorially it is as one of his observers, Florimond Daintry, sees or might see it. In this he follows Flaubert more than the authors of *Renée Mauperin*. As we have seen, when they, in *Manette Salomon*, present Paris it is in terms that are of the studio, in the terminology of the craft of painting. When Florimond Daintry sees Boston pictorially the description does not stand independent of the observing consciousness; not only is Boston as a visual presence made vivid to us but we are aware of the particular way Florimond has of seeing it and James is as interested in giving us an impression of, and making an oblique comment on, Florimond's particular cast of mind as he is in giving us Boston.

. . . he raised his eyes to the arching blueness, and thought he had never seen a dome so magnificently painted . . . he was an impressionist . . . He was of course very conscious of his eye; and his effort to cultivate it was both intuitive and deliberate . . . It was not important for him that things should be beautiful; what he sought to discover was their identity—the signs by which he should know them.[31]

As an impressionist Florimond is here gently satirized by James. Nevertheless through Florimond James can give us many visual impressions that he does not give either through his aunt or his mother. Furthermore since Florimond sees pictorially James can describe pictorially even when the object presented is not filtered directly through Florimond's eyes and reflections but given to us because that is the way Florimond would notice it. Thus:

The long straight avenue lay airing its newness in the frosty day, and all its individual façades, with their neat, sharp ornaments, seemed to have been scoured, with a kind of friction, by the hard, salutary light. Their brilliant browns and drabs, their rosy surfaces of brick, made a variety of fresh, violent tones, such as Florimond liked to memorize, and the large clear windows of their curved fronts faced each other, across the street, like candid, inevitable eyes.[32]

The validity of this and other parts of the description is not dependent on Florimond's thought or response; we are not as immersed in Florimond's consciousness as we are in Strether's. The narrator is the traditional third-person omniscient author. But the presence of Florimond provides James with an opportunity of seeing Boston with a different eye from that of the native inhabitants: Florimond is a returning ex-patriate. His eye is therefore partly alien and James can use this fact to present an analysis of the American scene; the visual impressions have their social significance. Florimond Daintry is not the sole object of James's irony. Through him and the impression Boston makes on him, James can tell us this about the city and its manners:

This continuity of glass constituted a kind of exposure, within and without, and gave the street the appearance of an enormous corridor, in which the public and private were familiar and intermingled.[33]

James has developed a strong visual sense in himself and has a taste and interest in the scene for its own properties. In Florimond he has a reasonable excuse for this delight.

The upper part of Beacon Street seemed to Florimond charming— the long, wide, sunny slope, the uneven line of the older houses, the contrasted, differing, bulging fronts, the painted bricks, the tidy facings, the immaculate doors, the burnished silver plates, the denuded twigs of the far extent of the Common, on the other side; and to crown the eminence and complete the picture, high in the air, poised in the right place, over everything that clustered below, the most felicitous object in Boston—the gilded dome of the State House.[34]

James in this story shows the ability to make a general portrait of a place in easy, light references to the appearances of things—appearances which tell of the more than physical nature of the place. Certainly the work of Gautier which helped him develop his descriptive prose in his travel sketches is important in this development as much as his own few years of training in the visual arts. And the example of the Goncourts and Daudet as well as Flaubert is there too. But James is more careful than the Goncourts to link his description to an observer who, it is reasonable to expect, will be interested in what there is to be seen. The Goncourts' description is often autonomous and does not affect the course of the story or the feelings of the characters in any direct way. Nature, even seen through art, seems to be more independent than in James. This is even true in *Manette Salomon* when the painter Coriolis wanders through the forest of Fontainebleau day after day; the descriptions are noticed, at the most, by Coriolis, but they are not really made a part of his consciousness. So in the end nature leads a life that is apart from the characters and often opposed to them; they sink and it remains fresh. The effect is otherwise in James's descriptions of the Boston scene and Florimond Daintry, who is actively connected with what is being presented even if that is not given to us as exactly what he sees and thinks. The observers are more conscious of what there is to observe in James, whereas the Goncourts present themselves as more conscious than their characters. But undoubtedly the French experiments in visual description were a great stimulus to James's rendering of appearances. James is aware of the visual properties of the objects before him, is consciously building up a picture, and making an interpretation of the scene before him.

IV

For Gautier, Flaubert, the Goncourts and others of the 'L'Art pour l'Art' movement as for James, art is not a distortion of reality, a filter which prevents the consciousness from perceiving things as they are, a presupposition which mars the native intelligence and blurs the uneducated eye so that it fails to come into immediate relationship with the world in spontaneous perception, unprejudiced and receptive of the freshness and wonder of the world. On the contrary the experience of art for these writers is a heightening of consciousness, a preparation for the full value and meaning of the relationship between things. Their vision is cultivated, civilized and sophisticated. And because it is, it is, in their view, more meaningful. They are not apologetic about the accumulated layers of perceptual interpretation which art has given them and through which they see the world. They do not wish to strip themselves of their educated responses so that they can see things in their pristine quality. Quality, on the contrary, comes through the cultivation and education of the eye into taste and a richer consciousness of what is to be seen. James is always seeing the present as rich with the past and much of the most important part of this past is what art has achieved and passed on to us. Hence the importance for James, as for the Goncourts, of an aesthetic education for his heroes and heroines.

An early instance of the appreciation and understanding of art as a guide to the interpretation and evaluation of character is to be found in the Goncourts' *Renée Mauperin* (1864). Renée, as we have already seen, points out the beauty of the river-side scene to her companion, who fails to respond to it and does not see it as a painted and exhibited landscape as she does. Her companion, a young man called Reverchon, a suitor selected as respectable and even desirable by her parents, is a thoroughly mediocre personage and is subsequently rejected by Renée. Part of his mediocrity is demonstrated by this failure of his aesthetic sensibility. More importantly, throughout the novel, an appreciation of what is beautiful, and not merely what is beautiful in nature but what is beautiful in art, is a guide to the moral nature of the characters. This comes out clearly in a discussion about Italy. Henri, Renée's brother, a young, ambitious lawyer, pragmatic and ruthless, morally callous—he has been, unbeknown to his family, the lover of Mme Bourjot whom he gets to accept and even promote his marriage to her daughter because of her dowry and the excellent connections this will provide for him—has found nothing to admire in economically backward, technically retarded Italy. On the other hand the most understanding of all Renée's friends, Denoisel, the man who educates her feelings and tastes, opens her mind and develops her intelligence, stimulates her to think independently, and who represents an aristocratic indifference to place-hunting and self-seeking promotion, whose sentiments are noble and disinterested, is also the man of exquisite artistic taste and perceptions. It is he who teaches Renée to draw as well as to think.

Isabel Archer's education begins with an appreciation of Gardencourt. A great deal of her experience of Europe is aesthetic, and her judgement, knowledge and taste all flower. When she, in her eagerness, asks Ralph to show her the paintings at Gardencourt on her first night there we are told that 'She was evidently a judge; she had natural taste.' And when she finishes looking at them she remarks, 'Well, now I know more than I did when I began.' Her responsiveness to paintings is not an isolated feature of her character but an integral part of her whole generous response to life. But it is important in itself because it makes directly for fullness of life and experience. Her aesthetic education continues in Florence and Rome, and James devotes some pages to it and her responsiveness. The following passage denotes a continuous and developing experience of Florence:

In the clear May mornings before the formal breakfast . . . she wandered with her cousin through the narrow and sombre Florentine streets, resting a while in the thicker dusk of some historic church or the vaulted chambers of some dispeopled convent. She went to the galleries and palaces; she looked at the pictures and statues that had hitherto been great names to her, and exchanged for a knowledge which was sometimes a limitation a presentiment which proved usually to have been a blank. She performed all those acts of mental prostration in which, on a first visit to Italy, youth and enthusiasm so freely indulge; she felt her heart beat in the presence of immortal genius and knew the sweetness of rising tears in eyes to which faded fresco and darkened marble grew dim.[35]

And the educative role of perception continues in Mrs Touchett's great old Florentine villa with its monumental court and its high cool rooms with carven rafters and pompous frescoes from the sixteenth century. For in such a place Isabel is aware of the murmur and echo of the past. Such an awareness acts constantly on her imagination—and extends her sense of the nature and complexity, the richness and accumulation of human life in its creations and its great acts.

James's use of aesthetic response as a means of indicating character is complex. It is interesting to note that Henrietta Stackpole's reponse to Rome is quite different from Isabel's. James is here mainly having some good-natured fun, satirizing certain chauvinistic American reactions to the Old World, as exemplified for example in Twain's *Innocents Abroad*. Like Twain, Henrietta finds, in the original edition of the novel, that the Capitol in Washington is more impressive than St. Peter's. (In the New York Edition this is changed; she is now struck, on her visit to the Forum, that ancient Rome was paved like modern New York.) Henrietta, for all her good qualities, cannot see that it would be offensive to the Touchetts to be written up in her newspaper and only desists because Isabel asks her to. And Henrietta, not accidentally surely, advises Isabel, more or less openly, to leave her husband at the end of the novel and go off with Casper Goodwood. Divorce is easy in the United States, particularly in the Western States, and she cannot understand Isabel's persistence in a course that seems to mean nothing but unhappiness to her. Isabel's finer moral sense seems to be related to her more acute responsiveness to all that the past and human artistic effort has achieved for us.

Henrietta is blind to the finer distinctions in both art and morals.

But to be interested in art is not in itself a guarantee of moral awareness; it depends very much on the manner of the interest in and the awareness of aesthetic values. Osmond is an obvious case in point; and part of Isabel's tragedy is that she is deceived by Osmond's apparent good taste. He is, as Ralph declares, a sterile dilettante, but because he seems so aware of what is beautiful Isabel is taken in. She can be taken in because he seems to have achieved an awareness that she values. But his attitude is a pose and is not a generous response to the human significance of art as is hers. Here Ralph plays an essential role; for his is a cultivated consciousness in which the aesthetic and the moral are both refined. He understands Osmond's sinister limitations, the sterility of his collector's passion. But Ralph is Isabel's guide to the beautiful in Florence and Rome; he has achieved that finer aesthetic consciousness that Isabel seeks. And he is the most disinterested and morally finest man in the novel. The aesthetic education of his heroine is an important part of her development as a human being, but James uses the way in which people respond to art and not, of course, just their interest in collecting beautiful objects, as his way of distinguishing one character from another. The frivolous and superficial Edward Rosier who has a fine collection of faïence is another case in point.

We can see very much the same distinctions at work in *The Spoils of Poynton* (1897). Mrs Gereth and Fleda Vetch meet on the common ground of the appalling bad taste and ugliness of the Brigstocks' country house, Waterbath, and their appreciation of its vulgarity. No one else seems conscious of it. Mrs Gereth has spent a lifetime in achieving a masterpiece of taste and arrangement at Poynton. Her son's marriage to the blooming, flushed, bouncing and vulgar Mona Brigstock will drive her out and deliver the possessions that have been her life to Mona. Mona has no appreciation for the things for their beauty; she only wants them as possessions and because they go with the house. Her passion is pure acquisitiveness and her sensibility non-existent. When Fleda visits Poynton she too takes 'possession' of the place and its achievement, but her 'possession' is entirely an act of appreciation, of understanding, of feeling the value and the great beauty that has been created by Mrs Gereth. But James also draws an important distinction between Mrs Gereth's attitude and Fleda's, the place that appreciation, sensibility and discrimination have in each of their lives.

> . . . Fleda at least could see the absurdity . . . which gave the measure of the poor lady's strange, almost maniacal disposition to thrust in everywhere the question of 'things', to read all behaviour in the light of some fancied relation to them . . .
>
> Almost as much as Mrs Gereth's her taste was her life, though her life was somehow the larger for it.[36]

Mrs Gereth's passion for her 'things' and her attachment to her house on the other hand are not, we are told, 'vulgar avidity'.

> It was not the crude love of possession; it was the need to be faithful to a trust and loyal to an idea. The idea was surely noble; it was that of the beauty Mrs Gereth had so patiently and consummately wrought.[37]

It is because Fleda is so much herself an aesthetic being and can understand both the supreme beauty that Mrs Gereth has wrought and the pain of having to give all this up that she becomes, at least in the beginning, Mrs Gereth's ally. But there is a finer discrimination seen only by Fleda: if Mrs Gereth's passion is not 'crude possession' it is one that limits her.

V

In his treatment of the theme of the artist and the artistic life James further shows his affinities with the 'L'Art pour l'Art' movement. In *The Tragic Muse* an adverse view of Gabriel Nash is explicitly included in the novel; Nick Dormer, the scion of a political family but who wants to be a painter, refers to the way his mother thinks of him: as the exponent of some dangerous French doctrines which are undermining Nick's virtues, his sense of responsibility and his public spirit. He is viewed, by her, as the exponent of a dangerous aestheticism. This view is implicitly satirized through the manner in which Nick tells of it. To Julia Dallow, the rich and powerful widow all expect Nick to marry, Nash is anathema; but Julia has no time for the aesthetic, her ambitions are all political and her hopes for Nick are parliamentary and ministerial. Gabriel obviously represents a very different set of values and the basic conflict between the life of the artist and its demands and a political career and its rewards which are incompatible with a devotion to art as more than an amateurish pastime and a frivolous enjoyment is dramatized, comically, in this opposition between Gabriel and Julia. It is given a more profound expression in the conflicts between Nick and Julia and Miriam Roche, 'The Tragic Muse' and Peter Sherringham, the young diplomat who falls in love with her, or those within Nick and Peter themselves. It is important to remember that Gabriel is first seen in the Salon in Paris where Nick immediately seizes upon him as someone who can help him. Nick recognizes in him a support and an ally, essential to him in his struggle to be an artist and not to become entirely absorbed in a political career. Gabriel expresses his opposition to the active life of 'doing' in paradoxes and exaggerations, but it is only when Gabriel has ceased to be necessary to Nick, when his function as a catalyst has been fulfilled, that he fades away. And at many places in the novel what he has to say is given direct approval; Nick finds himself not only agreeing with Gabriel but feeling that he has taken the words right out of his mouth; it is Gabriel too who recognizes the value of Nick's work and tells him to carry on. The terms in which he does so are worth close attention:

'Nicholas Dormer . . . for grossness of immorality I think I have never seen your equal.'[38]

In these words one of the central themes of the novel is brought into a clear and sharp focus: the conflict between moral duty as normally understood and the morality of an achieved work of art with the consequent duty of an artist to create as well as he can. Nick is 'immoral' because having a great talent he neglects it. As Nash explains:

'I called you just now grossly immoral, on account of the spectacle you present—a spectacle to be hidden from the eye of ingenuous youth: that of a man neglecting his own fiddle to blunder away on that of one of his fellows. We can't afford such mistakes, we can't tolerate such license.'[39]

And after he has assured Nick that he has a great instrument to play on he continues:

'I like it, your talent; I measure it, I appreciate it, I insist upon it . . . I have to be accomplished to do so, but fortunately I am. In such a case that's my duty. I shall make you my business for a while. Therefore,' Nash added, piously, 'don't say I'm unconscious of the moral law.'[40]

That these arguments bear a strong kinship with those of the 'L'Art pour l'Art' movement should by now need no further demonstration. Their importance, however, is reinforced by their effect upon Nick, the latter's acceptance of much of what Gabriel has to say, and the satirical portrayal of the usual English view of the immorality of art. As Nick remarks to his sister, Bibby, about their mother:

'She has inherited the queer old superstition that art is pardonable only so long as it's bad—so long as it's done at odd hours, for a little distraction, like a game of tennis or of whist. The only thing that can justify it, the effort to carry it as far as one can (which you can't do without time and singleness of purpose), she regards as just the dangerous, the criminal element. It's the oddest hind-part-before view, the drollest immorality.'[41]

Painting is only one of the arts which, in the novel, have to fight against the prejudice of their immorality and establish their own moral significance. The discussions about the theatre centre on the morality of doing something well. The artistic and dramatic point of view is represented by Mme Carré, the actress of the Comédie Française; the moralistic by Mrs Rooth.

'We are very, *very* respectable,' Mrs Rooth went on, smiling and achieving lightness, too. 'What I want to do is to place my daughter where the conduct—and the picture of conduct, in which she should take part—wouldn't be absolutely dreadful. Now, *chère madame*, how about all that? how about the conduct in the French theatre—the things she should see, the things she should hear?'

'I don't think I know what you are talking about. They are the things she may see and hear everywhere; only they are better done, they are better said. The only conduct that concerns an actress, it seems to me, is her own, and the only way for her to behave herself is not to be a stick. I know no other conduct.'

'But there are characters, there are situations, which I don't think I should like to see *her* undertake.'

'There are many, no doubt, which she would do well to leave alone!' laughed the Frenchwoman.

'I shouldn't like her to represent a very bad woman—a *really* bad one,' Mrs Rooth serenely pursued.

Mme Carré's eventual reply to this is explicit enough; she has played nothing but bad women and when she does so she tries to make them real. Miriam, whom her mother is so concerned to protect, offers to recite something from Augier's *L'Aventurière*, a play in which the heroine is a common adventuress—and actress—who has made her fortune by way of going from the arms of one lover to those of another. Before the recitation can begin Mme Carré breaks forth once again:

'You mix things up, *chère madame*, and I have it on my heart to tell you so. I believe it's rather the case with you other English, and I have never been able to learn that either your morality or your talent is the gainer by it. To be too respectable to go where things are done best is, in my opinion, to be very vicious indeed; and to do them badly in order to preserve your virtue is to fall into a grossness more shocking than any other. To do them well is virtue enough, and not to make a mess of it the only respectability. That's hard enough to merit Paradise. Everything else is base humbug! *Voilà, chère madame,* the answer I have for your scruples!'[42]

It is not by accident therefore that James places the opening scenes of *The Tragic Muse* in Paris. Here is the Salon to be visited by Nick Dormer—the annual consecration of the pictorial art, which has so much to tell him, and so many 'horrors' for his mother. And Miriam Rooth can learn the art of acting which she can then bring to redeem the vulgarity and triviality of the English stage only in Paris. Mme Carré represents the tradition and the training of the French stage and gives voice to the conviction that 'doing' is in itself a morality.

But it is not only in the conversations between Mme Carré and Mrs Rooth or the remarks of Nash and Nick that the essential difference between the moralistic and the artistic point of view—which includes a morality for the artist—is dramatized. Peter Sherringham suffers from his love for Miriam which has come about from his interest in and attachment to the theatre. But that attachment does not go so far as his marrying an actress and allowing her to remain one. The novel triumphantly affirms Miriam's decision to stay on the stage and be great there rather than as the wife of an ambassador.

Near the end of the book comes a great affirmation of the eternal value of art. This is given through the reflections of Nick Dormer after he has made his decision to give up his political career forever and to dedicate himself to the art of portrait painting. He is thinking about the masterpieces of the past:

These were the things that were the most inspiring, in the sense that they were the things that, while generations, while worlds had come and gone, seemed most to survive and testify. As he stood before them sometimes the perfection of their survival struck him as the supreme eloquence, the reason that included all others, thanks to the language of art, the richest and most universal. Empires and systems and conquests had rolled over the globe and every kind of greatness had risen and passed away; but the beauty of the great pictures had known nothing of death or change, and the ages had only sweetened their freshness. The same faces, the same figures looked out at different centuries, knowing a deal the century didn't, and when they joined hands they made the indestructible thread on which the pearls of history were strung.[43]

This recalls a whole line of French writers, Balzac included, but none more than Gautier whose poem 'L'Art' James had quoted in full in *French Poets and Novelists*.[44] The following are its concluding stanzas:

> Tout passe.—L'Art robuste
> Seul a l'éternité.
> Lebuste
> Survit à la cité.
>
> Et la médaille austère
> Que trouve un laboureur
> Sous terre
> Révèle un empereur.
>
> Les dieux eux-mêmes meurent.
> Mais les vers souverains
> Demeurent
> Plus forts que les airains.
>
> Sculpte, lime, cisèle;
> Que ton rêve flottant
> Se scelle
> Dans le bloc résistant!

> Everything passes away—Robust Art
> Alone possesses eternity.
> The bust
> Lives after the City.

And the austere medal
Which a ploughman finds
    Under the earth
Reveals an emperor.

The gods themselves die.
But sovereign verses
    Remain
Stronger than brass.

Sculpt, file, carve
That your wavering vision
    Fix itself
In the resisting block!

In 'The Author of *Beltraffio*' (1884) James treated explicitly the theme of Art for Art and its conflict with accepted morality. One part of James's notebook entry for this story is particularly interesting. After outlining the essential conflict in the story—the distaste Mark Ambient's wife feels for all of his works because to her they represent a great immorality, as do his dedication to art, Italy, aestheticism and beauty—he concludes: 'the general idea is full of interest and very typical of certain modern situations.'[45] The story then presents a dramatization between a morally utilitarian view of art represented in the wife and moral aestheticism represented in Mark Ambient.

Ambient's most important work, *Beltraffio*, was, says the narrator:

the most complete presentation that had yet been made of the gospel of art; it was a kind of aesthetic war-cry . . . there had not as yet been, among English novels, such an example of beauty of execution and value of subject. Nothing had been done in that line from the point of view of art for art.[46]

There are two aspects to his artistry: truth to life, and the creations of a perfect form and an infallible surface for conveying that truthfulness. Ambient is 'the artist to whom every manifestation of human energy was a thrilling spectacle, and who felt for ever the desire to resolve his experience of life into a literary form.'[47] And for him the creation of a form is not separate from presenting the truth, presenting life as fully and comprehensively as possible. This is made explicit when he declares to the sympathetic narrator: 'I want to be truer than I have ever been . . . I want to give an impression of life itself.'[48] (The reader can recall for himself how much this echoes the views of James in 'The Art of Fiction'.) This impression can only be obtained through a faultless form, an immaculate surface. James uses the metaphor made current by Gautier in comparing the effect of a perfect verbal surface and achieved formal structure to cups, vases, hammered metal and a polished plate. As Ambient is made to say: 'This new affair must be a golden vessel, filled with the purest distillation of the actual; and oh, how it bothers me, the shaping of the vase—the hammering of the metal!'[49] And after referring to the difficulty of catching life in the vessel of art he returns to the difficulties of rendering:

'Ah, polishing one's plate—that is the torment of execution!... The effort to arrive at a surface—if you think a surface necessary—some people don't, happily for them!'[50]

These are not only the sentiments of Mark Ambient: they echo what James had heard in the company of Flaubert, Daudet, the Goncourts and Zola. And they find their way not only into this but other stories and into his own letters and critical writings. Ambient carries his doctrine of perfection of form to an extreme. To write badly, to choose the second-best word is, he declares, 'the highest social offence I know; it ought—it absolutely ought—I'm quite serious—to be capital.'[51]

His intense dedication to art makes him feel life more intensely. The narrator declares, and we may assume that James basically agrees, that there is much to be said for any interest which can make a man feel so much. The moral issue between Ambient and his wife is made clear: he is dedicated to beauty and attempts at all times and with every effort to reproduce it. But equally he wishes to show life as it is, he cares to see all things as they are and to reproduce them in his fiction. No truncating and no evasions. His wife's view is indeed similar to the moral view of literature which James touches on more lightly in his article 'The Art of Fiction' of the same year. James in that piece denied that morality was to be found by not treating certain subjects. Ambient quotes his wife's opinion, which we know, from a previous conversation between the narrator and Ambient's sister, to be that the novel should have a purpose, in strongly disapproving terms:

'. . . . her conception of a novel . . . is a thing so false that it makes me blush. It is a thing so hollow, so dishonest, so lying, in which life is so blinked and blinded, so dodged and disfigured, that it makes my ears burn.'[52]

And he ends his exposition with a Flaubertian cry that James was to echo later in his own correspondence and in other stories dealing with writers: 'There is a hatred of art—there's a hatred of literature!'

The conflict between the two views of art and life is dramatized in the struggles of Ambient and his wife over their son and his education. Ambient makes a significant remark in this connection. He quite agrees that as a child or even as an adolescent his son should not read his works. Novels, that is, are not to be judged from the point of view of what is suitable to children— the perennial 'jeune fille': what is appropriate to young virgins to know or read is not the standard from which to view art. The damage is not to youth, but to art. This position echoes not only the Art for Art viewpoint but also James's in 'The Art of Fiction'. The story itself points its own conclusion unambiguously. Mrs Ambient allows her son to die rather than permit him to grow up and read his father's work. It is her morality, her narrow interpretation of the function of art, that is destructive. It denies not only the role of art, but in its specious defence of moral purity it also destroys life itself. The greatest morality —as James declared and Flaubert and the 'L'Art pour l'Art' movement declared with him—lies in the perfect rendering of the fullest possible human experience. Hence this story once more finds James closely allied with many aspects of the 'L'Art pour l'Art' movement.

VI

Towards the end of *The Tragic Muse* Gabriel Nash warns Nick Dormer against becoming a fashionable amateur and allowing himself to be absorbed by Julia Dallow and rendered impotent as an artist. Similarly Miriam Rooth is offered the passionate love of Peter Sherringham and all the luxuries and splendours the world can provide in return for her abandoning her art. Thus James presents the essential conflict between the desires of life, including sexual desire, and the demands of art. (And he does so in a way that in itself suggests both symmetry and completeness: themselves aesthetic values.) His observation of his own surroundings—and the social demands made on artists, the incompatibilities, as he saw them, between the demands of a normal human existence and the search for perfection in works of art—supplied him with the material. The stories of the artists and writers of the 1880s and 1890s show marked affinities nevertheless with the ideas and suppositions of the 'L'Art pour l'Art' movement. As Cassagne has remarked:

Or il n'est pas douteux que l'école de l'art pour l'art n'ait considéré l'amour, heureux ou malheureux, légitime ou non, comme nuisible au développement de l'artiste. [53]

(For there is no doubt that the Art for Art movement considered love, happy or unhappy, legitimate or otherwise, as harmful to the artist's development.)

And he goes on to quote Flaubert's remark to Maupassant: 'Un homme qui s'est institué artiste n'a plus le droit de vivre comme les autres.' [54] ('A man who has set himself up as an artist no longer has the right to live as others.')

It is interesting to note in this connection that part of the inspiration for 'The Lesson of the Master' itself came from a French example:

. . . as I was talking with Theodore Child about the effect of marriage on the artist, the man of letters, etc. He mentioned the cases he had seen in Paris in which this effect had been fatal to the quality of the work, etc.—through overproduction, need to meet expenses, make a figure, etc. And I mentioned certain cases here. Child spoke of Daudet—his *30 Ans de Paris*, as an example in point. 'He would never have written that if he hadn't married.' [55]

'The Lesson of the Master' (1888) is a tale which, in many ways, could have been written by one of the members of the 'L'Art pour l'Art' movement. Most likely, any of these would have made the tale more unrelieved in its sombreness, omitting any character that does win through to decent perfection— whose renunciation succeeds. It is unlikely that any member of the 'L'Art pour l'Art' group would have portrayed a man of the lucidity of Henry St George whose unselfish generosity 'saves' the young and admiring writer, Paul Overt. The special distinction of James's tale is the rendering of the apparent grace, charm and physical well-being which accompany the artistic failure of Henry St George. This bright surface is a very important part of the meaning of the story; this apparent delightfulness is precisely the snare.

At the centre of the story is the conflict and the choice between living life as an artist and living it as a man and human being. James makes it quite clear that the two *are* incompatible and quite distinct, although what art tries to do is to recreate a loveliness, a freshness and a vitality which are found in life and whose fullest expression is found in a beautiful young woman. But art is parasitical; there is a necessary choice between the perfection of the life and the perfection of the work. Within the story, beauty, and human loveliness, are concrete and physically manifested, not abstract ideas. James uses the female form as the fullest expression of beauty, although he has divested it of all the overtly sensuous and provocatively voluptuous connotations with which someone like Gautier would have surrounded it. Paul Overt, the young author and admirer of the Master, is sitting next to Miss Fancourt. The feeling she appealed to

was responsive admiration of the life she embodied, the young purity and richness of which appeared to imply that real success was to resemble *that*, to live, to bloom, to present the perfection of a fine type, not to have hammered out headachy fancies with a bent back at an ink-stained table.[56]

Life is the starting-point for the artist, and here its appeal and the sense of the paleness of art in comparison with the normal experience of life is rendered as powerfully as possible so that Paul Overt's choice and the Master's lesson will have their greatest illustrative value. The two writers—Paul Overt and the Master, Henry St George—are discussing the young woman a little later:

'One would like to represent such a girl as that,' Paul continued.
'Ah there it is—there's nothing like life!' said his companion. 'When you're finished, squeezed dry and used up and you think the sack's empty, you're still appealed to, you still get touches and thrills, the idea springs up—out of the lap of the actual—and shows you there's always something to be done. But I shan't do it—she's not for me!'[57]

There is an intentional ambiguity in this phrase 'she is not for me' which James exploits throughout the story. Paul, as they continue to discuss Miss Fancourt, sees her as material for literature; she becomes transformed for him into 'a sketch of a fine subject', and as he listens to the Master's words 'he lost himself in gazing at the vision—this hovered there before him— of a woman's figure which should be part of the glory of a novel.' The other possible sense of 'she's not for me' comes out later. For that she is not for the Master becomes somewhat obscure to Paul as he sees him paying a great deal of attention to her, taking her to picture galleries, calling on her in the late afternoons. The contrast, and its significance, is made clearer for us when it is the Master who marries her: she is therefore 'for him' as a man, but not as an artist, not as a 'fine subject . . . a woman's figure which should be part of the glory of a novel.' That function is left to Paul Overt for he is capable of going on as a writer of distinction, of dedication.

We know from the start of the story that the Master's powers have not kept up with his earlier performances. Paul Overt, that is, is conscious of the fact that Henry St George has had three great successes—artistic successes—but that since then the quality of his work has declined. It is important for the significance of the tale that only Overt and Henry St George himself are aware of what has happened. All the others are totally unaware of the change. This deterioration in the Master's performance is part of the contradiction and mystery that the young man feels he must try to understand. An indication is given by the description of the Master's wife whom he meets before he does Henry St George himself. She is a very pretty, young-looking woman, who is very smartly dressed in clothes that come from Paris. Her prosperity is too great to have come from literature alone, and although Paul knows that authors' wives are not all of a type, 'he had never before seen one look so much as if her prosperity had deeper foundations than an ink-spotted study-table littered with proof sheets.'[58] She looks more like the wife of a man who 'kept' books rather than wrote them. This is damning enough, but her most insidious effect is her power to interfere with his artistic integrity by censuring what he writes. 'I never made him do anything in my life but once—when I made him burn up a bad book. That's all!' she tells him.[59] Paul senses that the burned book 'would have been one of her husband's finest things'. Not only has she destroyed a work of art but she has turned literature into an industry like another. For her writing is a trade, with so many volumes to be turned out. Mrs St George utters the wish that Miss Fancourt could induce her husband to write a few more books.

Our young man stared—he was so struck with the lady's phraseology. Her 'Write a few' seemed to him almost as good as her 'That's all'. Didn't she, as the wife of a rare artist, know what it was to produce *one* perfect work of art? How in the world did she think they were turned off?[60]

The answer is given later when Paul Overt visits the Master's home and enters his study, whose four walls are covered with books and where the only window is a skylight so that he cannot look out and be distracted. Here he is locked up every morning by his wife. There is a tall desk where he 'could write only in the erect posture of a clerk in a counting-house'. This is the perfect image for the transformed and debased artist— the central subject of the story.

For the 'Lesson' is what the Master has become; his worldly success serves as a warning to the aspiring young writer that he must 'keep it up'—try to achieve a decent perfection in his work and not lose sight of his own aims. The Master worships, he says, false gods and his artistic life is the result of his betrayal of his own talent. He explains what he means:

'The idols of the market; money and luxury and "the world"; placing one's children and dressing one's wife; everything that drives one to the short and easy way. Ah, the vile things they make one do!'
'But surely one's right to want to place one's children.'
'One has no business to have any children,' St George placidly declared. 'I mean of course if one wants to do anything good.'
'But aren't they an inspiration—an incentive?'
'An incentive to damnation, artistically speaking.'[61]

The Goncourts treated this conflict between the demands of marriage and the demands of artistic perfection in both *Charles Demailly* and *Manette Salomon*. The first is a novel about writers and the literary life, including the journalistic fringes, and the second portrays the lives and struggles of different types of painters: Anatole who is more attracted to the Bohemianism of the life of the artist than to Art, Garnotelle who is the hard-working, essentially conventional and academic painter who wins the Prix de Rome and is commercially successful but artistically null, and Coriolis, who is a real original painter of talent and an essentially new vision. It is for Coriolis that marriage is a real danger and he senses this quite clearly himself. The Goncourts explain his—and their—viewpoint, one which is very reminiscent of the ideas expressed explicitly and implicitly in 'The Lesson of the Master'.

Selon lui, le célibat était le seul état qui laissât à l'artiste sa liberté, ses forces, son cerveau, sa conscience. Il avait encore sur la femme, l'épouse, l'idée que c'était par elle que se glissaient, chez tant d'artistes, les faiblesses, les complaisances pour la mode, les accommodements avec le gain et le commerce, les reniements d'aspirations, le triste courage de déserter le désintéressement de leur vocation pour descendre à la production industrielle hâtée et bâclée, à l'argent que tant de mères de famille font gagner à la honte et à la sueur d'un talent. Et au bout du mariage, il y avait encore la paternité qui, pour lui, nuisait à l'artiste, le détournait de la production spirituelle, l'attachait à une création d'ordre inférieur, l'abaissait à l'orgueil bourgeois d'une propriété charnelle.[62]

(According to him celibacy was the only condition that left the artist his liberty, his powers, his intellect, his conscience. He still held the view that it was because of the woman, the wife, that so many artists gradually gave way to their weaknesses and were complacent to the dictates of fashion, made compromises with profit-making, renounced their aspirations, found the melancholy courage to abandon the disinterestedness of their vocation and stoop to a hasty and botched industrial production and to money, which so many mothers of families cause to be earned by the shame and sweat of a talented man. And in the end marriage brought paternity which, for him, was harmful to the artist, diverting him from productions of the spirit and attaching him to an inferior order of creation, dragging him down to the bourgeois pride in a flesh and blood property.)

Sacrifices are not worth much unless the sacrifice entails real privation; temptation resisted has to be temptation strongly felt if there is to be any virtue in the resistance. So Paul Overt finds the home of the Master most attractive, and he is dazzled by the success and honour he has achieved. He would like to be able to compose in Henry St George's book-lined study. The morality of art however is strict, austere and ascetic. It takes great strength in a writer to keep to his ideal, and to seek perfection. And the audience that he writes for is an élite. As the Master tells Paul Overt:

> . . . not more than two or three people will notice you don't go straight. The others—*all* the rest, every blest soul in England, will think you do—will think you *are* keeping it up: upon my honour they will! I shall be one of the two or three who know better. Now the question is whether you can do it for two or three. Is that the stuff you're made of?'[63]

And when Paul tells him that he could do it for one if St George is that one the Master explains that the ultimate implacable judge is the writer's artistic conscience: 'The "one" is of course one's self, one's conscience, one's idea, the singleness of one's aim.' Paul, forced to recognize that the logic of the lesson includes the abandonment of love (and he is by now quite in love with Miss Fancourt) cries out:

'The artist—the artist! Isn't he a man all the same?'
St. George had a grand grimace. 'I mostly think not. You know as well as I what he has to do: the concentration, the finish, the independence he must strive for from the moment he begins to wish his work really decent. Ah my young friend, his relation to women, and especially to the one he's most intimately concerned with, is at the mercy of the damning fact that whereas he can in the nature of things have but one standard, they have about fifty.'[64]

What recompense is there for all this sacrifice? One answer is: a passion that includes all the rest—the passion of the artist to create. And ultimately this passion gives rise to a fuller life, life in the greatest sense. Henry St George says to Paul Overt:

'Let me see before I die the thing I most want, the thing I yearn for: a life in which the passion—ours—is really intense. If you can be rare don't fail of it! Think what it is—how it counts—how it lives!'[65]

In the final section of the tale the beautiful, intelligent, artistically interested, young and free Miss Fancourt, who has seemed to be sympathetic to the idea of artistic perfection, and whom Paul Overt renounces, or at least leaves for a time to go abroad to write his novel, is married to the Master, whose first wife has died. Paul feels that he has been duped. For had not the Master told him that he really must abandon the young lady? However, we are assured that he has produced his finest work of art to date. And the rightness of the Master's lesson is shown in several ways. Miss Fancourt's own judgement is 'placed'. She is extraordinarily happy, and her happiness is almost a form of stupidity, for it precludes her from understanding the artistic thinness of Henry St George's more recent works—all but the first three mentioned at the start of the tale. For all her apparent intelligence and discrimination she cannot see how he has fallen away from his own artistic standards. And the Master's personal happiness is a confession of artistic failure.

If in 'The Lesson of the Master' James suggests that the life of the artist is only possible—for the real artist seeking to do the finest work—through a life which renounces all the normal human pleasures and compensations: wife, children, wealth and solid comfort—the Goncourts in *Charles Demailly* seek to show the necessity of this renunciation and the inevitably tragic and destructive results to the artist who forgets it.[66] Charles himself is given words which recall those of Flaubert quoted above and which are similar to the trend of James's thought in his tale:

'Le mariage nous est défendu . . . Parce que nous ne pouvons faire des maris . . . Un homme qui passe sa vie à attraper des papillons dans un encrier est un homme hors la loi sociale, hors le règle conjugale . . . D'ailleurs, le célibat est nécessaire à la pensée.

(Marriage is forbidden to us . . . Because we cannot be husbands . . . A man who spends his life in catching butterflies in an inkwell is a man outside the laws of society, outside the conjugal norm . . . Besides celibacy is necessary for thought.')

And when he examines the claims of paternity they lead him to this conclusion: 'Nous avons bien mieux; nos enfants, ce sont nos oeuvres!'[67] ('We have much better. Our children are our works!') Charles's tragedy is that he forgets this. His love is for an actress who seems to embody the very conception he is seeking to render in a work of his own. This explanation for his love serves two purposes. Not only does it provide a creditable explanation of why he would select this particular woman and the way he would represent her to his own imagination, it also, by implication, makes clear the difference between the writer's proper involvement with the creatures of his imagination which are drawn from life and his improper attachment to creatures of this world which seem to reflect his imaginative world. As a writer he sees life in terms of literature, yet there is a vital difference between the two and the sorts of attachment that each demands, and his confusion of the two, in a moment of temporary forgetfulness, is the source of his ultimate defeat and destruction—both as artist and as man. The reverse, the transformation of life into art, was earlier proclaimed by Charles himself: 'D'autres disent: Voilà une femme! Nous disons: Voilà un roman!'[68] (Compare Paul Overt's initial reaction to Marian Fancourt.)

Marthe, whom Charles marries, turns out shallow and stupid, tasteless and undiscriminating, unable to appreciate the true nature of his activity as an artist, and capriciously destructive, betraying him to his enemies. Her inability to appreciate the artist's search for perfection is shown most significantly when she urges Charles to collaborate with the vaudevilliste, Voudenet. To suggest this to him is to misunderstand entirely both the nature of his art and the artistic process. For Marthe, Voudenet's methods are justified by the amount of money he makes, although his plays may not be literature. Such a wife for an artist would be bad enough in the compromises to which she would force him. But the Goncourts give her an active role in Charles's final destruction. She has a part in a play—'Le Diable au foyer'—and decides to re-enact this role in her own life.

An interesting comparison may be seen here: James is careful to present his Henry St George as *not* complaining of his wife to either Paul or the youthful and attractive Marian Fancourt. Charles has only a few, and easily overcome, scruples in making known his disillusionment to his friend Chavannes. Everyone acts more amiably, agreeably, and with a suggestion of greater satisfaction and pleasure in James's story. After his second marriage to Marian Fancourt, St George says he will write no more, but he does seem to enjoy life; Charles Demailly, before the end of the novel, has not only ceased to be a writer, but his life is ruined. As in *The Princess Casamassima*, James provides a more powerfully illustrative case than the French writers treating the same subject. Marthe is petty, mean, shallow and vindictive. But there is every reason why a Mrs St George and even more a Marian Fancourt should really appreciate an artist's calling and share in his effort. Yet even these women cannot.

Henry St George tries to act in the interest of the young writer and the cause of literature; Charles is more involved, and mangled as a human and suffering being. Art transforms existence and James seems to suggest that it should enhance it by providing characters that it might be hard to find in real life even in a tale that deals with the deterioration of an artist. James indeed centres our attention on Paul and on how the Master's words and example work on him rather than on the Master's deterioration itself. This deflection of interest away from the Master onto the admiring, and at times perplexed, younger writer provides just the right shade of interest in artistic success, represented in Paul Overt, and places the failure of Henry St George in a contributory rather than principal light.

It is accepted by the Goncourts that the artist has a different nervous organization from the non-artist. Charles's excessive impressionability is explained by his being the last member of a family that itself is the result of the union of two delicate and sickly races. However, this acute sensibility is seen as an indisputable mark of civilization, for civilization develops our consciousness whereas in the primitive state man develops his physical powers. Civilization exacts a high price from us, for it is an alteration of man's original nature. In the Goncourts' phrase: 'C'est un des phénomènes de l'état de civilisation *d'invertir* la nature primitive de l'homme.' Charles is a remarkably unhappy example of this. But however unhappy this condition it is the very basis of his being an artist. He feels and has presentiments of events, thoughts and other people's states of mind before they are expressed and even when they are not expressed. He can feel the happiness, love and friendship enjoyed by others and apparently denied to him. He may envy the happiness of others, but on the other hand those that do not feel and understand art are not to be envied but pitied, even despised. To despise the non-artistic is not James's mode: he is ironic and satiric about them instead, especially in such tales as 'The Death of the Lion', 'The Next Time' or 'The Figure in the Carpet' where writers are fêted and idolized but no one understands what they are writing.

For the Goncourts the proper observation of forms, shapes

and colours and an acute awareness of transient appearances of an object in all its particularity is the mark of an artistic consciousness. The external world has great importance in itself and as a source of emotion. James certainly makes us feel and respond to the visual world and develops different prose techniques to convey his impressions. However the Goncourts give an intensity to their nervous susceptibility that is absent from any of James's writings. As a result of his particular constitution things have a particular importance for Charles. His mood and disposition are constantly affected by the impressions he receives. For Paul Overt the thrills and throbs of existence are delightful; for Charles they are mainly disagreeable. He is more often disturbed and annoyed by the effect things make on him than pleased or soothed. The ability to *see* things, to notice the colour of paper or the shape of a table is *le sens artiste*. (Miss Barrace in *The Ambassadors* remarks on how everyone in Paris is intensely aware of the visual world, how they all run to mere eye.) This gift of seeing things intensely is peculiar to the artist and puts, for the Goncourts, an inevitable wedge between him and his public which does not notice the way things look and is not interested in the search for the *forme artiste* which will best convey it.

The Goncourts and James both agree that the writer has one devotion only: his work. As a result, for the Goncourts, the writer is always noting his actions, his motives and his feelings so that he can render them more accurately: life is his subject matter and he drains it of the common enjoyments by his very observation and analysis of it:

'Il s'analyse quand il aime, et, quand il souffre, il s'analyse encore . . . Son âme est quelque chose qu'il dissèque . . . Nous ne vivons que nos livres . . . Nous parlons d'amour comme les autres, nous mentons, nous n'aimons pas. Notre tête, notre vie, a le doigt sur le pouls de notre coeur.'[69]

(He analyses himself when he is in love, and when he is suffering he still analyses himself . . . His soul is something he dissects . . . We only live our books . . . We talk of love as others do; we lie, we do not love. Our mind, our life, has its finger on the pulse of our heart.)

This echoes James's remark in 'The Author of *Beltraffio*': all life for Mark Ambient is the subject of literature. But for

James this relationship seems to present itself as less destructive of the human being, and more inspiring and enhancing of the pleasures of life, even if derived in a special way. In commenting upon the Goncourts, Daudet and other French writers he knew he often remarked on how they found art such an agony; for him it seems to have been always a more pleasurable activity and he never sympathized with their excessive nervous susceptibilities.

VII

In *Charles Demailly* the actions of certain journalists are part of the destructive forces undermining Demailly's career as a writer. Newspapers, publicity, the great public, and the vulgar act of prying into the private lives of people and creating personalities and celebrities, of making copy out of trivialities or confidences, of exploiting hospitality to feed the insatiable curiosity of readers—these are themes that James treated more than once. Henrietta Stackpole, we recall, cannot understand that the Touchetts do not want to be publicized. And James dealt amusingly with the consequences of publicity, unwanted and scandalous, in *The Reverberator* (1888), the name of the great public organ of virtue and information for which Mr Flack acts as correspondent. His insensitive exploitation of Francie Dosson's confidence—and her own willingness to tell him— nearly destroy her marriage to Gaston Probert. However, in 'The Death of the Lion' James treats specifically of the relationship between the artist and journalism, which creates celebrities and treats of personalities rather than of works, and of the consequences for the artist of journalistic celebration. The note in James is not nearly so acrimonious or bitter as it is in the Goncourts or Balzac's *Illusions perdues*: the devices used by the journalists are not so mean, petty, spiteful or personally vindictive, but the destruction is none the less as final. In James's story too it is not the journalists alone who bring about the final collapse of Neil Paraday; the unconscious, selfishly egotistical world of society hostesses, in which the artist is a sort of performing freak paraded for the benefit of their leisure hours, is as much a cause of the destruction. But it is the newspapers that launch him, that make him a celebrity to be fêted and sought after. In James's story the tone is ironic and lightly satirical and without overt hostility towards journalists or fashionable society, but the significance of the tale is serious indeed: the comedy is high comedy and the outcome is tragic in terms of Paraday's life and work.

But if James's tone is lighter, if the satire is less vitriolic, than that of the Goncourts, the truth he conveys is none the less as deep, perhaps deeper than theirs, for James is showing how the very act of celebration is inimical to the author and not based on any real interest in or appreciation of literature. More and more in the stories of the 1880s and 1890s James is seeing the significance of Flaubert's remarks about the public's hatred of literature—and feeling the effects on his own acceptance as a writer—and exploring the significance of the dedication to art, the religious devotion to form as the artist's true way of living to the fullest. This helps further to explain why, even without a fondness for the wares of the furious band of Realists, he found them eminently serious and returned to their works again and again, and reassessed afresh the significance of Balzac, Flaubert, Daudet and Zola.

If we have come to accept that the morality of a work of art lies in its total structure and overall meaning and that style in itself is a mode of vision and not just a pleasant way of telling the tale, we owe this in no small part to the writers of the 'L'Art pour l'Art' movement. Their use of the visual arts as a vocabulary for discussing literature sprang partly from a desire to free literature from overt moral or social purposes— from literature that was Catholic or Socialist propaganda, however disguised. And James, as we have seen, took over many of the same metaphors in his defence of the seriousness of the novel as a work of art, and not just a pleasant story. The interest of these writers in the visual arts led them to a greater intensity in visual presentation and the rendering of the material aspects of things, a mode of perception that James too developed. In an early work we see him adapting a vocabulary that is modelled on that of Gautier:

The air stood still to take it; the green glittered within the green, the blue burned beyond it; the dew on the forests gathered to dry into massive crystals. and beyond the brilliant void of space the clear snow-fields stood out like planes of marble inserted in a field of lapis-lazuli.[70]

And the influence of Gautier and his sense of the picturesque and plastic qualities of a scene, even one of human misery, can be seen in a description of Venice. James carefully avoids any social commentary or economic-political analysis. He here differs very markedly from Twain's reactions to Rome or Florence; in those cities Twain could not resist pointing the correct philosphic—and democratic moral. James always resisted—and so did Gautier.

The misery of Venice stands there for all the world to see; it is part of the spectacle—a thorough-going devotee of local colour might consistently say it is part of the pleasure.[71]

James does not deny the misery, nor does he delight in it; but he is able to see in it an artistic value and he does not arraign the Venetian State for allowing it.

Later his visual interests were to express themselves in the same delight in the play of light on the surface of things which is so strong a characteristic of the school of Gautier.

The lamps were on brackets, at intervals, and if the light was imperfect it was genial. It fell upon the vague squares of rich colour and on the faded gilding of heavy frames; it made a sheen on the polished floor of the gallery.[72]

If, as Viola Hopkins suggests, 'James's word order and syntax were attuned to the conveying of sensation',[73] this is owing in no small part to what he learned from numerous French examples: Gautier, Flaubert, the Goncourts and Daudet being the most important. But James's most profound connection with the 'L'Art pour l'Art' movement is in his own devotion to form and style and his understanding of the indissoluble link between the subject and its expression. His 'aestheticism' takes the form of a pursuit of more complicated and intricate manners of 'rendering', of creating new forms of presentation. This is evident in his concern for compression and economy in his stories about artists and in the careful choosing of his narrative manner. Concentration, elimination and the total subordination of parts to the whole: these are the chief characteristics of James's developed 'aestheticism', which was to find its culmination in *The Golden Bowl.*

7
A Little Band of Realists
and *The Ambassadors*

Strether's education, moral as well as aesthetic, begins the moment he steps off the boat, and it is only because it begins with gloves, neckties, velvet ribbons and a lady of fashion that it *can*, James would have us believe, later develop into the fuller discrimination of behaviour and morals which forms the centre of the book. This is of fundamental importance: what Strether discovers is a civilization that is full of 'types', where people are in the habit of 'placing' others into numerous social categories and not simply classifying them as male and female—the only social types which, he reflects at one moment, seem known to Woollett, Mass., Strether's home town. It is also a civilization that cultivates the visual sense, and Strether, the middle-aged editor of Mrs Newsome's review, experiences upon his arrival the great freedom of being able to devote himself, for the first time in his life, it appears, to the immediate and the sensible. That this should happen primarily in Paris is the appropriate recognition by James not only of the character of French civilization but also of developments in French literature in the latter part of the nineteenth century.

The civilization which leads to Strether's abandoning his original role and espousing the cause of the woman he has come to save Chad Newsome from, so that instead he tries to save Chad for her and prevent him from returning to Woollett— this civilization is a composite in which the visual, the immediate and the sensible, the forms of life, its accumulations, its tastes and its discriminations in the minutiae of dress, manners and appearance, are necessary parts. Through them Strether is initiated into further discriminations and comes to see them as essential elements in the life that Woollett does not and cannot properly evaluate. The immediate and the sensible are valuable, not only for their own sake, but because they are part of a wider pattern of life where their full and proper value is correctly distinguished.

James's handling of the red velvet ribbon worn by Maria Gostrey the night she and Strether dine together before going to the theatre (Book II, Chapter 1), and of the thoughts that it excites in Strether's mind, shows too the consistency of the texture of images and description, and the insights that a properly constituted observer can gain from the smallest facts of dress and behaviour. All of James's 'minds' are highly complex recorders, filled with literary and historical memories, bent upon analysis, provided with numerous categories and fine distinctions. They act upon their environment as much if not more than it acts upon them.

One of the earliest metaphors for the relationship developing between Miss Gostrey, the ex-patriate American woman living in Paris whom he has encountered on the ship coming over, and Strether is that of 'the laid table of conversation'. In this passage we are present at that social act in one of its most refined forms: an intimate yet public dinner at a small table, lighted candles covered with pink shades, and the soft fragrance of his lady companion wafting pleasantly across to him. And the whole, as so often in this novel, is compared to a 'picture' with various fine 'touches' in it. Hence the ribbon has, first of all, an aesthetic rightness about it—it gives 'value' to all the other elements in her face. And this very aesthetic rightness, this added charm, beauty and taste, is what leads not only to comparisons, on Strether's part, with Mrs Newsome but to an appreciation of the whole alien order of which Maria is herself such an admirable representative. Consequently Maria's ribbon is the key to a comparison of two societies, and this in turn illustrates the extraordinary complexity of 'perceptions' in Jamesian characters.

A more important scene is that in Gloriani's garden. It is here that Strether delivers himself of his oft-quoted speech: 'Live—only live!' But why *here*—and one may ask why *then*? Why not somewhere else, at some other time, to someone else? And what is so remarkable about this speech? Really, very little. Detach the speech from the book and it is insignificant. But any one passage of James's prose, in the later novels, and particularly the remarks of his characters, except those pungent 'Americanisms' of a Waymarsh or Jim Pocock—and the fact that they are exceptions is of the first importance in properly 'placing' these characters—reaches out to others in the novel, touches and connects, refers us back to the accumulated impression the novel has made, the total experience that it has so far given us. This is what makes it so difficult to analyse or summarize or even keep in the memory as a totality, a living experience. The difficulty of holding simultaneously in the mind all the elements of the novel lies not only in its length as opposed to, say, a Shakespeare play, but in the 'subjects' dealt with, and, for it is the same thing, the manner in which these elements are presented. This is one of the ways James achieved a form which holds and preserves substance. By creating such a style he achieved one of the aims of both Flaubert and the 'L'Art pour l'Art' movement: a self-sustaining work of art.

So part of the answer to the question just posed about the words 'Live—only live!'—why at this time, in this place?—lies in the preceding four books. But there are more local and immediate reasons and artistic justifications, even if, in the Jamesian novel, everything does 'hang' together so that no one event can be taken as privileged—they all are. There is no climax—only a series of climaxes. And the web of experience is such an interconnection of elements that there is no event—or impression—in this novel that is not the result of all the others. This is why one of James's favourite expressions is 'There we are'.

In the garden Strether has impressions of many things. And in his presentation of the different order of things perceived James indulges in one of his characteristic tricks of vocabulary: his use of 'impression' both to mean something that can be perceived by the senses, some object or some aspect of an object, its glint or shimmer, and to mean some abstract quality that Strether also 'perceives', and the significance—moral, social, aesthetic—of an object or its attributes. Abstract qualities are rendered into sensuous impressions, and sensuous impressions are perceived as they indicate abstract qualities. Thus: 'His fellow guests were multiplying, and these things, their liberty, their intensity, their variety, their conditions at large, were in fusion in the admirable medium of the scene.' These *things*, all of them abstract qualities—liberty, intensity, variety—are as perceptible as colours or the play of light and this is suggested by their *fusion* in the *medium*. They are somehow discrete elements as much as the dress people wear.

There are several features to notice in the description of the garden itself (Book V, Chapter 1, paragraph 3).[1] We pass from the perception of abstract qualities to the impression of the house itself. But this impression itself is an *effect*—brought about by the totality of certain discrete sensuous impressions (in a narrower and more specialized sense of 'impression'). What James is after is not the causes of an impression—as in Balzac— but the total result so that the individual items, as constituted in the usual quasi-referential mode of description, can be dispensed with.

The place itself was a great impression—a small pavilion, clear-faced and sequestered, an effect of polished parquet, of fine white panel and spare sallow gilt, of decoration delicate and rare, in the heart of the Faubourg Saint-Germain and on the edge of a cluster of gardens attached to old noble houses.[2]

If these are the physical elements that go to make up the house —and we note how often attributes are detached from their objects, how unrelated each item is to any other in any spatial way, how generalized some of the items are—decoration, for example—the garden itself is important for its social significance. And here we touch upon one of James's prevailing habits of mind—the assimilation of the natural world into the human, and particularly the social and aesthetic, or the social as it also embodies aesthetic ideals and standards. And this way of seeing things provides a further example of the prevailing influence of ideas and attitudes James assimilated from the 'L'Art pour l'Art' writers.

It was in the garden, a spacious cherished remnant, out to which a dozen persons had already passed, that Chad's host presently met them; while the tall bird-haunted trees, all of a twitter with the spring and the weather, and the high party-walls, on the other side of which grave hôtels stood off for privacy, spoke of survival, transmission, association, a strong indifferent persistent order.[3]

And then the garden is compared to a 'chamber of state', next to 'a great convent': the images are intensely European, historic, redolent of past traditions and societies, of beliefs and political systems different from Strether's own. James indeed goes on to present a composite impression, one that fuses the present and the past, the old garden and its associations, vague yet persistent, so that time is recreated and held in the mind of the present observer. All the values of the past are made a part of the immediate sensuous impression by the activity of Strether's mind.

Strether had presently the sense of a great convent, a convent of missions, famous for he scarce knew what, a nursery of young priests, of scattered shade of straight alleys and chapel-bells, that spread its mass in one quarter; he had the sense of names in the air, of ghosts at the windows, of signs and tokens, a whole range of expression all about him, too thick for prompt discrimination.[4]

Thus when James in the next sentence refers to 'this assault of images' we are thrown back upon the whole mass of preceding impressions, whether of sensuous origin or deriving from Strether's imagination, or those impressions that are the abstract interpretative categories of the experience, e.g. 'transmission'. It is in such a complex setting as this that Gloriani's expression seems to probe him to his deepest depths and makes him feel that 'in the matter of his accepted duty he had positively been on trial.' So it is the experience of Gloriani's garden, in its accumulated and constantly suggestive impressions, that gives the meaning to Strether's words 'Live—only live!'—without that setting, without our gradual awareness of what the house and the garden signify, these words are of little import.

A third example of the complex use James makes of impressions is provided by Strether's reactions to Chad's flat in the Boulevard Malesherbes. His first sight of it is essential to the process of interpretative appreciation which brings about Strether's reversal of roles: from being the ambassador sent out to plead with Chad to return home to becoming the one who insists upon his obligation to stay. Why is that *troisième* so important? Because it speaks of distinction, taste, judgement, refinement. It shows what Chad has become. James does not assert, as Balzac does, that a house always embodies the qualities of the person inhabiting it; he simply uses the house and Strether's reflections on it as making it clear to Strether, and hence to us, what has happened to Chad. It is the peculiar combination of Paris and Strether's imagination that is significant: his imagination reacts before he can stop it. In such a context imagination seems to mean all our powers of interpretation, evaluation and historical association. But it is this imagination that makes the scene produce its meaning; a meaning that is not compatible with his preconceived ideas or the original purpose of his visit:

What service was it to find himself making out after a moment that the quality 'sprung', the quality produced by measure and balance, the fine relation of part to part and space to space, was probably—aided by the presence of ornament as positive as it was discreet, and by the complexion of the stone, a cold fair grey, warmed and polished a little by life—neither more nor less than a case of distinction, such a case as he could only feel unexpectedly as a sort of delivered challenge?[5]

It is because Strether possesses an imagination that can grasp the meaning of appearances, and because of the value for him of the appearances as elements in the meaning of life, that nothing he sees is lost upon him, and that the way things and people appear—red velvet ribbons or sharp parasols—is an essential element in the new visions Paris presents. He changes his moral evaluations of both Chad and Mme de Vionnet, the beautiful and autocratic Frenchwoman whom Woollett sees as preventing Chad's return to America and duty, because of the surface perfections of their lives. And it is *because* Strether can perceive things in their complexity that his moral outlook is expanded. In that change moral and aesthetic criteria are intimately mingled. This is evident in the way Chad's appearance is discussed. Chad makes a dramatic entry into the box at the theatre where Maria Gostrey and Strether are expecting Little Bilham, the young 'artist man' Strether met when he first went to Chad's flat and found him rather than Chad in possession. His appearance is so altered, and altered for the better, that Strether at first fails to recognize him: his very manner of entering the box denotes accomplishments and refinements unconnected with the former Chad. During their conversation after the theatre Chad repudiates the notion that he is kept in Paris by a woman, so he is, for Strether, 'free'. But one look at him has convinced Maria that Chad is not 'free'. Maria tries to help Strether understand the reason for the change in Chad's behaviour and what it implies in human terms:

'There must, behind every appearance to the contrary, still be somebody—somebody who's not a mere wretch, since we accept the miracle. What else but such a somebody can such a miracle be?'

He took it in. 'Because the fact itself *is* the woman?'

'*A* woman. Some woman or other. It's one of the things that *have* to be.'

'But you mean then at least a good one.'

'A good woman?' She threw up her arms with a laugh. 'I should call her excellent!'[6]

Maria Gostrey's use of 'good' is ambiguous. The exploiting and developing of these ambiguities is essential to Strether's final acceptance of new measures, new values and new discriminations. What Strether comes to see is that there is a multitude of ways of being 'good' which are not covered by the moral categories of Woollett.

For if the woman behind Chad is 'good' how are we to understand her goodness? Partly, if not principally, through the 'good' effects she has had on Chad. And what are these? His developed tastes, his greater ease, his courtesy, his improved manner, his beautiful home, his lovely things. This goodness is then one that expresses itself in pleasing effects and in a greater awareness of the beauty of things and in the importance of style and manner. These are not normally thought of as moral attributes. But in James's novel this is precisely what they are, and aesthetic values take on a moral importance. Little Bilham keeps up the ambiguity of Chad's goodness in his conversation with Strether when he tells him that he is not sure that Chad 'was really meant by nature to be quite so good.' For one part of Chad's goodness is the way he will or won't treat the woman who has done so much to change him. Maria Gostrey has already told Strether that Chad wants to 'sink' the woman and in reply to Strether's dismay at his wishing to do this after all she has done for him she replies that 'He is not so good as you think.' So Chad is not, as Little Bilham tells him, used to being so good—that is, both in being so improved, so polished and so accomplished, and in acting so much for the benefit of and out of consideration for another person.

Similarly when Strether a little later in the same chapter asks Little Bilham: 'Why isn't he free if he's good?' he receives a richly ambiguous reply: 'Because it's a virtuous attachment.' It is virtuous because it has done so much for Chad, it has transformed him into a socially complex and discriminating person, added new tastes and given him new senses and refined his intelligence—changes which are represented to us as highly desirable and worthy of respect. And it is virtuous because it has developed in Chad a sense of new obligations towards such a person which he would not, we are led to see, have recognized before, and which he may not now even be 'good' enough to keep up. At the bottom he may yet be coarse enough to 'sink' her. Without ever formulating these discriminations in quite this abstract way Strether comes to understand the complex nature of moral goodness as it is conceived by Maria Gostrey, Little Bilham and Mme de Vionnet, a moral goodness that is inseparable for them from certain other perceptions and discriminations which are not normally thought to be 'moral' at all, but which are part at least of what is 'good' in life and in individual men and women. The wide-ranging social transformations effected in Chad and in the new range of perceptions and distinctions made by Strether have for their object, as often as not, visual experiences or elegances of dress and manner, or fine points of taste and decoration. For these too are part of Strether's moral education, a part that for some reason those who comment on James seem most often to prefer to ignore, perhaps because for them these cannot be serious objects of intelligent discourse about 'goodness'. But they are for James and for Strether.

Strether meets Mme de Vionnet and her daughter, first at Gloriani's, then in her own house, and lastly one evening at Chad's. Mme de Vionnet is expressed in these settings, particularly in the world of her own house, and in how she acts at Chad's; furthermore there is the continuing miracle of Chad's transformation. So he now sums up his impressions for Little Bilham:

'She's a tremendously clever brilliant capable woman . . . an extraordinary charm on top of it all—the charm we surely all of us this evening know what to think of. It isn't every clever brilliant capable woman that has it. In fact it's rare with any woman. So there you are,' Strether proceeded as if not for little Bilham's benefit alone. 'I understand what a relation with such a woman—what such a high fine friendship—may be. It can't be vulgar or coarse, anyway—and that's the point.'[7]

Little Bilham of course concurs and adds that this relationship is 'the very finest thing' he has ever seen, 'and the most distinguished'. Strether's appreciation of the virtuous influence of Mme de Vionnet upon Chad goes so far as his proclaiming that she has *saved* him—a word that has theological as well as moral implications. Little Bilham reminds him that is what he—Strether—has presumably come out to do; to 'save' Chad. Here Strether makes an important distinction, that complicates and enriches the meaning of 'save' and 'virtuous' both, for it associates manners and morals, social graces and moral qualities into one total appreciation of a person's worth. Strether is on his way to concepts not dreamed of by Woollett.

'I'm speaking—in connection with her—of his manners and morals, his character and life. I'm speaking of him as a person to deal with and talk with and live with—speaking of him as a social animal.'[8]

The distance—in his moral appreciations—that Strether has travelled, and the new sense he has of the varieties of moral goodness, is made clear in a scene of high comedy between him and Sarah Pocock, Chad's firmly positive and moral American sister. Sarah fails to see any of the changes that have taken place in Chad, or at least to see them as valuable. The pertinent fact, for her, is that Chad has established a liaison, and that, for her, his responsibilities unquestionably lie at home. It is because she has not *seen* Paris as Strether has seen it, has not experienced it as he has—for she doesn't look for the same experiences, is incapable of formulating or consciously receiving impressions in the same way as he does—that she fails to recognize the changes that have taken place in him. As she tells Mme de Vionnet soon after her arrival: ' "You know I've been to Paris. I *know* Paris" . . . in a tone that breathed a certain chill on Strether's heart.'[9]

The whole of the superb dialogue between Strether and Sarah (Book X, Chapter 3) is designed to bring out the fundamental distinctions in their comprehension both of what has happened to Chad, and in their understanding of key moral terms. To Strether's plea that charming Mme de Vionnet has been a beneficent influence on Chad she has a rigid reply: 'Do you consider her even an apology for a decent woman?' Strether suggests that Mme de Vionnet would have represented something 'rather new and rather good' to her. Unfortunately, for Strether, this distinction is lost upon Sarah; for whom 'new' means only something lurid and immoral. 'Rather new? I hope so with all my heart!'[10] Indeed for Sarah, there is but one question: what is the nature of the relationship between Chad and Mme de Vionnet? If it is not decent, not 'virtuous' in the Woollett sense, if it is, as she expresses it, a thing one cannot even speak of, then there is an end to the question of any 'good' influence Mme de Vionnet might be thought to have Sarah is so rigid because she has no imagination, there is no room in her for surprise, and her moral scheme has been worked out in advance. Hence neither Paris nor Chad's transformation has anything to offer her.

Strether's last phase is the recognition of the intimate nature of the union between Chad and Marie de Vionnet, the acceptance of this relationship as beneficent and one that Chad would be a brute to break off. Woollett was right all along about the material fact—but the material fact is simply no longer the same for its categories of interpretation distort its significance. The description, full of suggestions, associations, interpretations as it is, of Mme de Vionnet's room is essential for Strether's final judgement of her and Chad. For we see it as he experiences it; it is not a neutral or 'objective' description but one where the objects are felt and appreciated in a particular way. And because it is so felt and appreciated Strether can at the end see their—Chad's and Mme de Vionnet's—'lie' as part of their good taste. There are elements in the description that render the particular sensuous quality of the room: the play of light and shade, the swaying curtains, the plash of a fountain outside. But this last mingles with other sounds which excite Strether's historical imagination so that when Mme de Vionnet enters she is absorbed into a context that makes her resemblance to Mme Roland a definite quality of her appearance. The effect of her reflection in her parquet floor, the gleam of glass and gilt, all the objects in the place lend to an overwhelming impression that she is part of something ancient and unique.

He knew in advance he should look back on the perception actually sharpest with him as on the view of something old, old, old, the oldest thing he had ever personally touched; he also knew, even while he took his companion in as the feature among features, that memory and fancy couldn't help being enlisted for her.[11]

It is because she fits into such a continuity, because her own tact and taste have created such an impression—and while she is the product of such a past and an expression of its values she is also the recreator of their finest nuances—that she is a person able to transform Chad. It is because her 'objects' and everything round her express these continuities and connections that what she has done is right, and Strether comes to fit even the most 'crude' fact of her liaison with Chad into a pattern of significances that completely alters its meaning from that given to it by Sarah and Woollett, although we are left in no doubt as to his disappointment that their relationship was not as fine as he had imagined it. Nevertheless the manner has completely transformed the moral significance of the actions: indeed the manner has become the basis of the moral significances. And that manner is an integral part of perceptions, choices, tastes and discriminations that are elements of a long tradition and are expressed in the smallest differences in physical objects.

It is in giving such an important place to aesthetic and visual appreciation as a means of developing moral discriminations and evaluation of character that James shows in *The Ambassadors* his deep affinity with the 'L'Art pour l'Art' movement. Moral perceptions in the later James are closely associated with aesthetic perceptions. This is both because of the moral value, as we have seen, of aesthetic perceptions, and because the moral and aesthetic senses are merely one. Morals are expressed in terms that are often aesthetic, and the moral sense is a developed aesthetic sense of discrimination.

II

Throughout *The Ambassadors*, by his presentation of the visible world, James suggests a whole culture and civilization in which new values and standards are to be learnt. This interest in the sensuous world and the manner in which it is perceived has deep connections, not only with the world of Paris as James envisages it, but also with developments in French literature with which James was intimately acquainted.[12]

There are obvious difficulties in trying to compare the stylistic techniques of authors writing in two different languages, and it would be futile to attempt to prove a dependence on the part of James upon French models. Rather it is here suggested that there are certain developments in the French literature of his time which help to explain James's lifelong interest in French literature, in its 'doing' and 'rendering', even when he finds what has been rendered inadequate in its penetration of human conduct or its moral implications and tendencies unpalatable or unsavoury. A number of his critical writings show his awareness of and interest in the way French writers rendered the aspect of things. For example, in an article on Daudet in 1883, twenty years before the appearance of *The Ambassadors*, James wrote:

To Daudet, at any rate, the familiar aspects of Paris are endlessly pictorial, and part of the charm of his novels (for those who share his relish for that huge flower of civilization) is in the way he recalls it, evokes it, suddenly presents it, in parts or as a whole, to our senses. The light, the sky, the feeling of the air, the odours of the streets, the look of certain vistas, the silvery, muddy Seine, the cool grey tone of colour, the physiognomy of particular quarters, the whole Parisian expression, meet you suddenly in his pages, and remind you again and again that if he paints with a pen he writes with a brush.[13]

A comparison of three passages from James, Balzac and Flaubert will be illuminating. The first is from the opening paragraph of James's 'Madame de Mauves' (1874).

The view from the terrace at Saint-Germain-en-Laye is immense and famous. Paris lies spread before you in dusky vastness, domed and fortified, glittering here and there through her light vapors, and girdled with her silver Seine. Behind you is a park of stately symmetry, and behind that a forest, where you may lounge through turfy avenues and light-checkered glades, and quite forget that you are within half an hour of the boulevards.[14]

The passage from Balzac comes from the closing scene of *Le Père Goriot*:

Rastignac, resté seul, fit quelques pas vers le haut du cimetière et vit Paris tortueusement couché le long des deux rives de la Seine, où commençaient à briller les lumières.' Ses yeux s'attachèrent presque avidement entre la colonne de la place Vendôme et le dôme des Invalides, là où vivait ce beau monde dans lequel il avait voulu pénétrer.[15]

(Rastignac, left alone, took a few steps towards the top of the cemetery and saw Paris lying crookedly along both banks of the Seine, where the lights were beginning to shine. His eyes fixed themselves almost avidly between the column of the Place Vendôme and the dome of Les Invalides, where lived that fashionable society into which he had wished to penetrate.)

And here is the description of Rouen in Chapter 5, Part Three of *Madame Bovary*:

Descendant tout en amphithéâtre et noyée dans le brouillard, elle [Rouen] s'élargissait au delà des ponts, confusément. La pleine campagne remontait ensuite d'un mouvement monotone, jusqu'à toucher au loin la base indécise du ciel pâle. Ainsi vu d'en haut, le paysage tout entier avait l'air immobile comme une peinture; les navires à l'ancre se tassaient dans un coin; le fleuve arrondissait sa courbe au pied des collines vertes, et les îles, de forme oblongue, semblaient sur l'eau de grands poissons noirs arrêtés.[16]

(Falling away like an amphitheatre and lost in the fog, it [Rouen] spread out, confusedly, beyond the bridges. The open country rose up again in a monotonous sweep until it touched, in the distance, the uncertain base of the pale sky. Seen thus from on high the whole landscape had the motionless air of a painting; the ships at anchor were huddled up in a corner; the river rounded its curve at the foot of green hills, and the islands, oblong in shape, appeared like large, dark fish lying dead still on the water.)

There are three characteristics that all of these passages obviously have in common: they are synoptic, synthetic, and objective. In each case we are given a view of the whole city laid out in front of us. In each case what is seen is not dependent upon who the observer is—it is there for us, or any one else, as much as it is for Rastignac, Emma, or Longmore. And the description carefully delineates the objects and draws their boundaries so that the components of the picture are seen *as objects* with definite spatial relations existing between them. Thus in James's description we have Paris '*domed* and *fortified*'— a view that incorporates a multitude of individual impressions into a general picture, which summarizes and concludes, which decides what it is that one sees and gives a comprehensive definition of the totality of the impressions that would constitute the immediately perceived. And 'girdled' does not so much tell us what the Seine looks like as what it does, what its relationship is to the other objects seen. It is an image which defines a relationship and limits the perceived by intellectualizing the sensuous. To be noted is James's persistent definiteness about the relationships of other objects: '*behind* you is a *park* of stately *symmetry*, and *behind* that a *forest* . . .' What has been seen has been summarized and catalogued; order has been imposed upon the immediate and we see objects grouped and partaking of a collective identity. These same considerations apply to Balzac's description: we see Paris spread out before us— 'tortueusement couché le long des deux rives de la Seine' ('lying crookedly along both banks of the Seine'). The column of the Place Vendôme and the dome of the Invalides are public monuments, named in their public functions and their generality, not seen in their immediacy in sensuous perceptions. They are chosen for their relation to the desires of Rastignac, but this changes nothing in the *way* they are perceived or the way that perception is presented to us. Flaubert also abstracts and generalizes: the city descends 'en amphithéâtre', the countryside is seen beyond as it stretches away to the horizon, and is seen as a countryside, in its collective nature. The ships are seen as a group, and the islands are distinct, with a definite and sharply outlined shape; they are recognized by the narrator immediately as islands. Flaubert also seeks to synthesize and summarize the perceived into recognizable wholes or groups in order to achieve symmetry, order and pattern.

The following passages are from *Renée Mauperin* by the Goncourts.

L'eau battait la poitrine de la jeune fille, s'élevait dans sa robe de laine jusqu'à son cou, lui jetait par derrière une petite vague qui n'était, un moment après, qu'une goutte de rosée prête à tomber du bout de son oreille.[17]

(The water beat against the breast of the young girl, rose within her woollen gown up to her neck, threw behind her a little wave, which a moment later was but a drop of dew ready to fall from the tip of her ear.)

La lumière jouait sur ses joues. L'ombre chatouillait sa bouche aux deux coins; et ses lèvres, rapprochées d'ordinaire dans une petite moue hautaine, laissaient à demi voir, desserrées et entr'ouvertes, le sourire de son âme. Un reflet éclairait son menton; à son cou, un collier d'ambre semblait jouer à chaque mouvement de sa tête. Elle était charmant ainsi, les traits perdus dans la clarté qui tombait des lustres, le dessin du visage effacé dans un bonheur d'enfant comme dans du soleil.[18]

(The light played on her cheeks. Shadows delicately touched the two corners of her mouth, and her lips, usually drawn up into a little haughty pout, relaxed and parted, half-revealed the smile of her soul. A reflection lighted up her chin; on her neck an amber necklace played with each movement of her head. She was charming thus, her features lost in the light which fell from the chandeliers, the design of her face blotted out in a child-like happiness as in the sunlight.)

The aim of each of these last two descriptions seems to be to catch the movement, the flux in the very nature of things and of our perception of them, and to fix our attention upon the momentary and the transient, seen in some minute and surprising detail. Water, wind, sunlight, the waving of trees, the reflections in a river, a sudden illumination of light breaking through the clouds, the moon picking up a detail—these are subjects that abound in the *insolite*, the ever-changing, the suddenly delicate and fragile. In the first example we are taken away from the vision of the river and the waves and our attention is directed towards a minute detail, held before us for its own sake as well as for the intimation it provides as to the nature of waves and their temporariness: 'une goutte de rosée prête à tomber au bout de son oreille' ('a drop of dew ready to fall from the tip of her ear'). In the second example we are brought to a close examination of the effect of light and shade on Renée's face. The effects are precisely, scrupulously noted for their own sake: 'Un reflet éclairait son menton; à son cou, un collier d'ambre semblait jouer à chaque mouvement de sa tête.' ('A reflection lighted up her chin; on her neck an amber necklace played with each movement of her head.') In these descriptions by the Goncourts we are on the watch for the way in which appearances alter; we follow the progressive coming to be of each particular impression. The view of Paris from Saint-Germain-en-Laye in 'Madame de Mauves' is a general one; Rouen in *Madame Bovary* is seen not just on one particular morning but as it is on a number of mornings as Emma arrives there. But the Goncourts are trying to catch the transient, fugitive appearance of things and the description moves through the stages that succeed each other in the medium that is being described, as these appearances are being created.

This is clearly apparent in this passage from Daudet's early *Fromont Jeune et Risler Ainé* (1874).

Là-bas, au dessus de Paris, qu'on entendait gronder sans le voir, une buée s'élevait, lourde, chaude, lentement remuée, frangée au bord de rouge et de noir comme un nuage de poudre sur un champ de bataille . . . Peu à peu des clochers, des façades blanches, l'or d'une coupole, se dégagèrent du brouillard, éclatèrent en une splendeur de réveil. Puis, dans la direction du vent, les mille cheminées d'usine, levées sur ce moutonnement de toits groupés, se mirent à souffler à la fois leur vapeur haletante avec une activité de steamer au départ . . .[19]

(Over there, above Paris which could be heard grumbling without being seen, a mist arose, heavy, hot, slowly shifting and fringed at the edge with red and black like a cloud of smoke above a battle-field . . . Little by little steeples, white façades, the gold of a cupola, emerged from the haze and burst in a magnificent awakening. Then, in the direction of the wind, a thousand factory chimneys, raised above this surge of bunched roofs, began all at once to breathe forth their panting vapour with the haste of a departing steamer . . .)

We notice how the verbs and adverbial phrases emphasize this progressive unfolding of visual or other sensory impressions: 's'élevait . . . peu à peu, se dégagèrent . . . éclatèrent, puis . . . se mirent,' etc. This description also achieves something else. Our attention is not directed towards a comprehensive view of Paris, but towards certain aspects of it. It is not the city we discover lying below the mist but the *buée* itself that we see with its particular colours. Nor do we notice some specific building or the relationship existing between any of them, but the sudden, discontinuous flash of a steeple, a white façade, the gold of a cupola. The external world is fragmented, reduced to its aspects, perceived immediately as fragments—the 'attributes' are more important than the 'substances' in which they adhere, and are sometimes free from any 'substance' at all.

Here is another description from *Renée Mauperin*.

La campagne, le faubourg et la banlieue se mêlaient sur les deux rives. Des lignes de peupliers se montraient entre les maisons espacées comme au bout d'une ville qui finit. Il y avait des masures basses, des enclos de planches, des jardins, des volets verts, des commerces de vins peints en rouge, des acacias devant des portes, de vieilles tonnelles affaissées d'un côté, des bouts de mur blanc qui aveuglaient; puis des lignes sèches de fabriques, des architectures de brique, des toits de tuile, des couvertures de zinc, des cloches d'ateliers. Des fumées montaient tout droit des usines, et leurs ombres tombaient dans l'eau comme des ombres de colonnes. Sur une cheminée était écrit: *Tabac*. Sur une façade en gravois, on lisait: *Doremus, dit Labiche, relayeur de bateaux*. Au-dessus d'un canal encombré de chalands, un pont tournant dressait en l'air ses deux bras noirs. Des pêcheurs jetaient et retiraient leurs lignes. Des roues criaient, des charrettes allaient et venaient.[20]

(The countryside, the factory area and the suburbs merged together along both banks. Lines of poplars appeared between scattered houses, as where a town comes to an end. There were mean hovels, board fences, gardens, green shutters, wine shops painted red, acacias in front of doors, ancient arbours collapsed on one side, bits of white wall which blinded you; then the sharp lines of the factories, brick edifices, tiled roofs, zinc roofings, workshop bells. Smoke rose straight up from the factories and their shadows fell on the water like the shadows of columns. On one chimney was written: *Tobacco*. On a plastered façade could be read: *Doremus, (Labiche), Boat Station Master*. Above a canal cluttered with barges a swing-bridge raised its two black arms in the air. Fishermen threw out and pulled in their lines. Wheels creaked, carts came and went.)

The trees are first seen in lines between the houses spaced out along the road. There then follows a series of nouns—'masures', 'enclos', 'jardins', 'volets', 'commerces de vin', 'acacias' ('hovels', 'fences', 'gardens', 'shutters', 'wineshops', 'acacias'). The relationships between the objects designated are imprecise and the effect is kaleidoscopic. Sometimes we see large wholes— 'des masures'—sometimes a part of a larger unity—'des volets verts'—and at others only a small but arresting sight—'de vieilles tonnelles affaissées d'un côté' ('ancient arbours collapsed on one side'). Everything is thrown in pêle-mêle, all perceptions on the same level. We see, suddenly, names of businesses or of their proprietors. Noise comes from somewhere—'des roues criaient' ('wheels creaked'). And our eye is caught (in an unquoted part of the same passage) by 'des cordes de halage (qui) rasaient le chemin rouillé'. ('. . . tow-ropes (which) scraped the rusty path.') We have neither a synoptic nor a synthetic vision of the landscape through which the Seine flows near Renée's house, but one which disintegrates the scene into a number of sharply rendered and transitory appearances.

We can see something similar in *The Ambassadors*. Strether is in Sarah Pocock's hotel room where Mme de Vionnet, who has come to her, is about to take her leave.

The glazed and gilded room, all red damask, ormolu, mirrors, clocks, looked south, and the shutters were bowed upon the summer morning; but the Tuileries garden and what was beyond it, over which the whole place hung, were things visible through gaps; so that the far-spreading presence of Paris came up in coolness, dimness and invitation, in the twinkle of gilt-tipped palings, the crunch of gravel, the click of hoofs, the crack of whips, things that suggested some parade of the circus.[21]

This passage is typical of the book and gives it its peculiar tone and atmosphere. The sentences disclose an order of discovery, and what is discovered amounts often to fragmentary and discontinuous impressions. To some it may appear that there is something insubstantial and vaporous about Strether's Paris, that it is not particularized and embodied sufficiently for us to believe in it. In the way that Balzac, Flaubert and Zola make their places substantial this is true. But James is obviously up to something else. And his procedure is closely allied to the other elements in the novel, in the depiction of a mind at work, so that objects do not stand apart from it as separate entities.

In addition to the discontinuous and fragmentary nature of the scene described we can see two further features in this example that ally it to the procedures of Daudet and the Goncourts. First there is the expression of qualities as nouns— 'coolness', 'dimness'. (This itself is but part of the general use of abstractions throughout the novel.)[22] In his study of the instantaneous in French novels Jacques Dubois gives many examples of this practice,[23] and suggests that the device is used by French writers to achieve much the same effects as we can notice in James's prose.

Qu'apercevons-nous? Que l'action exprimée dans les diverses propositions s'exerce depuis des aspects, sur des aspects ou par rapport à des aspects comme depuis, sur ou par rappart à de vrais objets. Ces aspects tendent par conséquent à bénéficier d'une plus grande réalité, d'une espèce de solidité, en devenant comme des choses. Ayant été nommés, dénombrés, portés au premier plan, ils s'objectivent.[24]

(What do we perceive? That the action expressed in the diverse statements is exerted from aspects, on aspects, or in relation to aspects, as from, on, or in relation to real objects. Consequently these aspects tend to benefit from a greater reality, from a kind of solidity, in becoming like things. Having been named, enumerated, carried to the forefront, they become objectified.)

Throughout *The Ambassadors* we can notice too another feature which is similar to what may be found in the prose of Daudet and the Goncourts: the long sentence composed of many parallel phrases of equal importance, each one expressing a particular sight or sound, but not composing a definite object, or suggesting any spatial relationships between the various aspects. The result is that we do not have a firmly defined picture created for us as in the earlier passages quoted from Flaubert, Balzac or James himself.

Let us now examine two scenes, one from Daudet and another from James of luncheons along the banks of the Seine.

L'hôtesse apportait dans une casserole toute dorée au feu une tanche superbe, pêchée par Romain dans la réserve réglementaire à deux cents mètres en amont et en aval de son écluse; et le fumet de ce plat campagnard, les explications de l'éclusier, l'appétit gagné par la course sur l'eau, firent diversion à cette sinistre légende locale, vite évaporée d'ailleurs au vent frais qui venait de la Seine et la rebroussait toute, devant la terrasse, en mille petites écailles d'argent, dont le mouvement et la clarté moiraient de reflets dansants les verres, les carafes, la nappe jaune et rude.[25]

(The landlady brought, in a casserole all browned in the oven, a magnificent tench, caught by Romain in his statutory preserve of two hundred metres above and below his lock. And the delicious aroma of this country dish, the explanations of the lock-keeper, the appetite gained by the outing on the water, took their minds off that sinister local legend, soon evaporated furthermore in the fresh wind which came from the Seine and combed it all in front of the terrace into a thousand silver flakes, whose movement and brightness made moires dance in reflections on the glasses, the carafes, and the coarse yellow table-cloth.)

How could he wish it to be lucid for others, for any one, that he, for the hour, saw reasons enough in the mere way the bright clean ordered water-side life came in at the open window?—the mere way Madame de Vionnet, opposite him over their intensely white table-linen, their *omelette aux tomates*, their bottle of straw-coloured Chablis, thanked him for everything almost with the smile of a child, while her grey eyes moved in and out of their talk, back to the quarter of the warm spring air, in which early summer had already begun to throb, and then back again to his face and their human questions.[26]

What we see in both of these passages is a plurality of centres of attention and a movement between them. Daudet brings both the table with its fish and the river into his sentence and each has its own descriptive aspects which are inserted into the narrative. In James's sentence we are aware of the table, the summer on the Seine outside and Mme de Vionnet's own perceptions and wandering attentions. Between these elements there is a constant to-ing and fro-ing. In both cases we have the effect of a particularly vivid and experienced moment. For this too is a common element in the later works of James and in those by Daudet and the Goncourts—the attempt to give us, through different means, the sense of living a unique moment. The very fragmented and discontinuous nature of the description is part of this effect.[27]

In the James passage we notice something else as well; Strether's mind as an element in the situation. We are attentive to everything in this passage because Strether is noticing it, reflecting upon it and trying to assess its value. Such procedures are not unknown to the Goncourts and Daudet; they often mingle the reflections of their characters with the description of objects or the narrations of events. James, however, is far more consistent in doing so, and makes such a use of point of view a central feature of his later technique. But subjectivity of experience and immediacy can be gained in other ways than through the constant presence of an interpreting mind. No French author of the later nineteenth century developed the ever-present recording mind to the extent that James did— but they took some steps on the way and they developed modes of expression and manners of description and narration that often accomplished similar effects.

How is a description altered when what is to be shown is not only the external world but also, at the same time, the mind of one of the characters in the process of perceiving it?

C'est une femme. Jeune, vieille, laide, jolie? Le roi,—affaire d'habitude,—jette un regard de ce côté. Rien ne bouge que les deux ailes d'une petite toque qui se renversent, ont l'air de se replier pour le sommeil. 'Elle dort, . . . faisons comme celle . . .' Il s'allonge, s'enveloppe d'une couverture, regarde encore vaguement des silhouettes d'arbres et de buissons, confuses, moelleuses dans l'ombre, qui semblent se jeter l'une sur l'autre au passage du train, des poteaux à disques, des nuages affolés dans un ciel tiède; et ses paupières devenues lourdes vont se fermer, quand il sent la caresse sur son visage d'une chevelure fine, de cils abaissés, d'une haleine de violette, de deux lèvres murmurant sur ses lèvres: 'Méchant! . . . sans me dire adieu! . . .'[28]

(It's a woman. Young, old, ugly, pretty? The King—force of habit—casts a glance in that direction. Nothing stirs except the two folds of a little toque which fall back and have the air of curling up for sleep. 'She sleeps . . . let's do likewise . . .' He stretches out, wraps himself up in a blanket, vaguely looks out again at the silhouettes of trees and bushes, indistinct and velvety in the shadows, seeming to throw themselves one upon the other at the passing of the train; signals, wildly racing clouds in the soft sky; and his eyelids, grown heavy, are about to close when he feels the caress of soft hair on his face, of lowered eyelashes, a breath of violets, and two lips murmuring on his lips: 'Naughty! . . . without saying good-bye to me! . . .')

Compare this scene with that in *The Ambassadors* when Strether views Chad's balcony for the first time.

Since, accordingly, at all events, he had had it from Mrs Newsome that she had, at whatever cost to her more strenuous view, conformed, in the matter of preparing Chad, wholly to his restrictions, he now looked up at the fine continuous balcony with a safe sense that if the case had been bungled the mistake was at least his property. Was there perhaps just a suspicion of that in his present pause on the edge of the Boulevard and well in the pleasant light?[29]

Here narrative, description and reflection are all intermingled. But more than this: where Strether is and what he sees is presented intermittently, because we are given these things as he becomes aware of them. We never in fact have a clear description of the house and the balcony as independent entities, outside Strether and apart from him, gathered together in one description for him or the reader to know at once. The elements are not synthesized into a solid object. The whole of the passage illustrates the movement involved, the discontinuous nature of Strether's awareness of what it is that he 'sees'. He makes out certain aspects, but the way the house is built, the very colour of the stones, the open window and the young man appearing on the balcony are all dependent—so far as we come to know them at all—on Strether's perceptions, and these are constantly intermingled with his reflections and assessments. As in the work of Daudet and the Goncourts the effect is that the external material world is made subjectively dependent, and hence seems both less stable and less 'really' present. Balzac overwhelms us with the intensity of the house; James, in his late work, overwhelms us with the intensity of the consciousness filled with its own perceptions and interpretations of the house. And we can see, to a lesser degree, the same things happening in the extract quoted above from Daudet's *Les Rois en exil*. The description is broken up and scattered about. There is a constant irruption into the narrative or description of the reactions or thoughts of one of the characters.[30] It is a habit with Daudet to place himself, as author, in the position of one of his characters so that we see what happens as the character's consciousness passes through various stages. The extract quoted particularly shows this process of knowing a fragment of the external world through a consciousness as it lives through a certain period of time, so that the very sense of a lapse of time is part of our total impression.

Throughout *The Ambassadors* we are given experiences, not in the form that *anyone* would receive them, but in the form that they are perceived by a specially sensitive and consciously articulate mind. What is there *could* be perceived by others than Strether, but the important fact is that for the most part it is not. Only Maria Gostrey—and to a lesser extent Little Bilham—help him and save him from solipsism. (It is because there is no reliable corroborator for the governess in *The Turn of the Screw* that fantastic theories have been enunciated concerning that story.) The novel is not about what Chad and Mme de Vionnet *did* but about Strether's gradual apprehension of the nature of their liaison—in all of its aspects and not merely it sexual. We are less interested in the facts than in the way his mind apprehends those facts.

This permits, indeed entails, a great loosening of the narrative structure and the incorporation of a multitude of impressions both within a chapter and within each individual sentence. Hence sentence length and syntax are stretched to permit such incorporation. Our attention is focused on elements that would appear to have little to do with the narrative of the story as conceived of as a series of actions, and their consequences, committed by a number of characters.

In a work such as *The Ambassadors* and in the work of James's French contemporaries we see objects being presented to us in fragments so that the external world appears less solid and less reliable than the mind that perceives it. The importance of an object lies not in the assistance it gives to the action, or in its being a sign of a particular place or a symbolic summarization, but in its being something that appears to someone at a particular moment and forms part of that person's consciousness. *The Ambassadors* emphasizes in manifold ways the importance of appearances and the value of the immediate, the sensible, and the joy of taking things as they come. For James, Daudet and the Goncourts the presence of a mind, although indicated in different ways, is an essential part of their presentation of the immediate and the sensible. All, in their different ways, aim both to give us the sense of the way things appear to an observer and to reproduce the sense of a certain lived time. They are all 'realists' in their concern to give us the feel of the experienced moment. Strether himself expresses this, and the way his total appreciation of things is affected, thus:

'Everything has come as a sort of indistinguishable part of everything else. Your coming out belonged closely to my having come before you, and my having come was a result of our general state of mind. Our general state of mind had proceeded, on its side, from our queer ignorance, our queer misconceptions and confusions—from which, since then, an inexorable tide of light seems to have floated us into our perhaps still queerer knowledge.[31]

And if we expand the implications of this passage, it may be taken to express an important truth about James's relation to French authors, for *The Ambassadors* is a subtle tribute to the living influence that French literature continued to be for James.

8
The Culmination: *The Golden Bowl*

Of all James's works *The Golden Bowl* (1904) exemplifies most his ability to assimilate and transform French influences. Not the least important of these is that of Balzac, though on the surface nothing could be less Balzacian. Yet in *The Golden Bowl*, as indeed in all the late novels—*What Maisie Knew, The Wings of the Dove, The Ambassadors* and the others—James achieves, in his own characteristic fashion, one of the Balzacian virtues he most consistently praised: intensity of presentation. In one of his earliest critical essays he had praised Balzac for packing his frame as tightly as he could so that it nearly burst from the pressure of what had been forced into it. Balzac accumulated apparently overwhelming evidence for the physical existence of both things and people. However, as was noted in Chapter 2, these details not only support physical reality but often bear a symbolic value as well. James packs his frame just as tightly— but with the facts of consciousness, the characters' awareness of each other, with subtle feelings, acute and minute analyses of states of mind and moral discriminations. And the intensity of his illusion is as great: as the specificity of presentation is brought more and more within the characters' minds we become more and more convinced that James has totally exhausted the treatment of his subject. What more *could* Maggie Verver think? Her consciousness already seems to overflow. Further- more, it is part of James's art that he keeps the reader's mind constantly stretched so that what the characters find out is both ample and sufficient but yet not predictable. When we have followed the steps we have seen the full working out of all the possibilities of the initial situation and its completion. It is only retrospectively that we feel the inevitability of what has been thought and done. The intensity is of a different order and achieved by different means, but it accomplishes what for James was a high requirement of art: the illusion of life through the multiplicity and accumulation of the evidence of the living quality of the characters. This intensity of illusion was something he recognized and respected in Balzac, Flaubert, Maupassant and other French writers however they might differ from him in other respects.

In these last novels James creates works in which the elements are highly formalized and stylized and which, consequently, are enclosed and self-contained works of art. Nevertheless he treats of subjects of a Balzacian character: lust, jealousy, hatred, revenge, the search for power and the rapacious quest for wealth. Kate Croy's intensely felt poverty and her dependence on her powerful and wealthy aunt, whose Philistine luxury seems crushing to Merton Densher, drive her to manoeuvre Densher into making love to Milly so that Milly will marry him. Since Milly is dying her immense fortune would go then to Densher. He and Kate will be able to marry and be wealthy —two things which seem impossible to join at the outset of the novel. The intensity of Kate's passion and the machinations she contrives are worthy of a Balzacian heroine. In one of the subtlest and least direct of his novels James deals with elemental passions and their corruption and with the power and attraction of wealth and its pursuit through sexual and emotional exploitation. In a work that seeks to achieve a flawless, self-enclosed, self-sustaining world of art he could deal, it would appear, with more violent and cruder emotions than he could when he employed more conventional narrative techniques in such realistic novels as *The Bostonians* or *The Princess Casamassima*. The less Balzacian or realistic his methods the more Balzacian became his subject-matter.

The Golden Bowl deals with adultery—and more specifically and intensely than any other novel by James, except perhaps *What Maisie Knew*. But there adultery is treated obliquely through Maisie and its effects on her, whereas it is central to the lives of the Prince, Charlotte and Maggie in *The Golden Bowl*. Yet in no other novel is there less sense of anything outside it, less indication given to the reader of a world beyond the enclosed world created by James's prose. Everything— every word, gesture, sentence, image, phrase, incident—is part of this world, refers only to what happens within it. Matcham, Gloucester, Portland Place, Eaton Square, Cadogan Place, Fawns are names, whether denoting real or fictitious places, whose relevance is strictly limited to the novel. But the subject is human: love, devotion, fidelity, infidelity, sacrifice, pain, filial and paternal attachment, and the working out of a marriage. It is necessary to emphasize this; for the very artifice of the novel might seem to deny it. The presence of the human subject-matter shows that this artifice is, on the contrary, a means of achieving an intensification of life.

James's characteristic aestheticism, as was remarked earlier, took the form of a search for an indissoluble link between form and subject-matter, of a personal style which was in itself a way of seeing and interpreting the world. His emphasis on the supremacy of form shows itself most in the means he developed for achieving economy, concentration, elimination and the total subordination of the parts to the whole. Thus Henrietta Stackpole and Maria Gostrey are *ficelles*. The latter's function is to help Strether in his understanding of the Parisian world. She is also a 'value' in the overall picture. That James has succeeded in clothing her with substantial human attributes comes out in the reactions of those readers who find that she has been too much sacrificed to the pattern—her having to 'lose' Strether fits the structural demands but is felt to cost too much in human terms.

It was noted earlier how what Emma Bovary observes at the Château de la Vaubyessard is relevant to her interests and state of mind, how Flaubert subordinates the paintings and the dinner service to her reflections or to their importance to her in estimating the grandeur of the occasion and the meanness of her usual life. In *The Golden Bowl* James has employed these same techniques but has carried them much further. For there are a number of ways in which *The Golden Bowl* achieves its sense of rounded completeness and self-enclosure. For example, the external 'real' world—the transient, the particular feel and sense of the moment—is always worked into the overall texture of the book, without ever denying, as has been noted in the foregoing discussion of *The Ambassadors*, its unique quality. This subordination is accomplished by various means. One is the filtering of the impressions of physical objects through the consciousness of one of the characters. What is seen is both part of the observable world and part of the mind through which it is presented to us. An example is the Prince's impressions of the objects in the Bond Street windows at the opening of the novel. But this restricted 'point of view' is insufficient in itself to achieve the subordination of the parts to the whole. There is nothing accidental, fortuitous or casual about what the Prince is made to observe. The Prince has been reflecting on how modern London represents more truly the notion of an Imperium than his own contemporary Rome. What he notices are 'objects massive and lumpish, in silver and gold, in forms to which precious stones contribute, or in leather, steel, brass, applied to a hundred uses and abuses.'[1] These are tumbled together as if they were the loot of the far-off victories of the Roman Empire. But what he sees is even further incorporated into the pattern of the novel; he is one of Mr Verver's spoils, one of the acquisitions of his Empire. And other images throughout the novel will recall and echo these opening observations of the Prince, this sense of multiplicity of precious and heavy objects.

A further example of how James fits the particular incident into the general themes and patterns of the novel may be seen in Part II, Chapter 6. Adam Verver visits Brighton with Charlotte Stant. Whilst they are there they go and see a Mr Guterman-Seuss who has some rare damascene tiles to sell. The expedition and purchase themselves contribute to one of the thematic patterns of the novel: Mr Verver's passion for collecting and the immense wealth he represents, with all the effects this has on the other characters. But the purchasing and bargaining are further subordinated to the feelings of Adam Verver and the effect that Charlotte's presence has on him, 'every inch of the rest of him [that not concentrating on the business deal] being given to the fore-knowledge that an hour or two later he should have "spoken" '.[2] So the whole incident is placed within the fundamental structure of the novel: the two marriages and their inter-relationships. Maggie's friend Charlotte has been called upon to protect Adam Verver from fortune-hunting and predatory women, and now he feels that she would make the best protection by becoming permanent and would best help to restore the former harmony between himself and his daughter Maggie, releasing the latter from the anxiety of having abandoned him by her marriage to the Prince. The whole incident is coloured by these considerations and the tiles and the details of the purchase recede into the overall structure of the book. In the same way Brighton as a place is never 'gone into' as James tried to 'do' Northampton, Mass. in *Roderick Hudson*. The Goncourts' *sense artistique* would here have got the better of their *forme artistique*: they would have delighted in the tiles as beautiful and precious objects. In this novel on the contrary the physical world is a 'value' as it heightens the characters' consciousness of themselves or of others.

By the time *The Golden Bowl* was written James could make use of his sense of the comedy of manners as well as his ability to create pointed dialogue and dramatic scenes in a wide complex that entirely subordinated them without destroying their surface reality. It has already been seen how this use of conversation is related, in *The Wings of the Dove*, to the Flaubertian search for a unified and harmonious language. The conversation in *The Golden Bowl* has the tone of easy social chat, at times even of flirtatious badinage. But James makes a thematic use of this superficial tone, and the exaggerations of a refined and consciously cultivated social usage. One way in which he achieves this integration is to indicate that the characters themselves are not fully conscious of all the implications of what they are saying. Such for example is the case with Maggie's teasing remark to the Prince: ' "Oh," she had returned, "You shall not be buried, my dear, till you're dead. Unless indeed you call it burial to go to American City." '[3] It is not until much later that we realize that this foreshadows Charlotte's fate. But conversation forms part of the total structure of the novel in other ways. It is linked to the narrative and to the consciousness of the characters through the use of key terms and images, and through the suggestion of some of the principal themes. The public history of the Prince and his value as a piece in her father's collection is made light of by the Princess: but it is a note that recurs throughout the novel and it helps to define Adam Verver's attitude towards him and gives an indication of why he is acceptable as a son-in-law. The Princess's reference to their being pirates takes us back to the opening paragraphs of the novel where the Prince is walking along Bond Street and noticing all the spoils of Empire in the shop windows, and knits all comments into a closer fabric. The difference between the Prince and the Princess comes out in the tone of the Prince's remarks about his veracity and the Princess's reaction to it. The tone is an indication of a central difference in their values, as is the question itself.

Of course conversation, when properly used, is always part of the action, a development of character in a situation and a preparation of other situations. But nowhere outside a Jamesian novel are the dialogue and other elements of the novel so interdependent; nowhere else does the talk have less the air of being casual and free. James never used it merely to indicate time, place or circumstance. James's conversation is both elliptical and allusive. And part of this allusiveness comes through the use of images that are employed in the conversation and then in a character's reflections about it. For example, the Prince sees himself in a bath of American good faith, scented with an essence poured from a gold-topped phial, the gold-topped phial recalling all the remarks about precious and rare objects. And these reflections go on to connect with one of the central and recurring themes: the credulity of Maggie and her father, their generosity, their faith and disbelief in guile or possible betrayal.

James furthermore weaves the conversation into the total structure of the book by writing it in such a way that much of it cannot be understood on its own or on its first occurrence. All of the early passages are full of forebodings, of hints of danger from the Prince, his fear of himself and his awareness of his burdensome past. So an apparently light-hearted remark by Fanny Assingham: ' "Oh, you deep old Italians" ' is pregnant with meanings and implications which are only finally worked out during the course of the novel. The conversation therefore implicitly ranges backwards and forwards from its present context. We are made aware of this by its elliptical nature and by the way the characters look at each other, colour, start, pull up. What they *say* does not seem to call for such reactions; so what they *mean* must be much more than appears superficially. That the characters find it necessary to assume an easy tone and feel that they must choose their words carefully as well as take on a manner towards each other are all important indications which colour the otherwise light conversation. The kind of concentration and economy that James can achieve is brilliantly exemplified in Book I Chapter 3 when Charlotte says to the Prince: ' "You see you're not rid of me." ' The context of the remark makes the images in which the Prince has been thinking of her and the accumulated 'he knew's which immediately precede her challenge and which indicate all his former acquaintance with her reverberate with intense meaning.

Making use then of clumsy terms of excess, the face was too narrow and too long, the eyes not large, and the mouth on the other hand by no means small, with substance in its lips and a slight, the very slightest, tendency to protrusion in the solid teeth, otherwise indeed well arrayed and flashingly white. But it was, strangely, as a cluster of possessions of his own that these things in Charlotte Stant now affected him; items in a full list, items recognized, each of them, as if, for the long interval, they had been 'stored'—wrapped up, numbered, put away in a cabinet. While she faced Mrs Assingham the door of the cabinet had opened of itself; he took the relics out one by one, and it was more and more each instant as if she were giving him time. He saw again that her thick hair was, vulgarly speaking, brown, but that there was a shade of tawny autumn leaf in it for 'appreciation'—a colour indescribable and of which he had known no other case, something that gave her at moments the sylvan head of a huntress. He saw the sleeves of her jacket drawn to her wrists, but he again made out the free arms within them to be of the completely rounded, the polished slimness that Florentine sculptors in the great time had loved and of which the apparent firmness is expressed in their old silver and old bronze. He knew her narrow hands, he knew her long fingers and the shape and colour of her finger-nails, he knew her special beauty of movement and line when she turned her back, and the perfect working of all her main attachments, that of some wonderful finished instrument, something intently made for exhibition, for a prize. He knew above all the extraordinary fineness of her flexible waist, the stem of an expanded flower, which gave her a likeness also to some long loose silk purse, well filled with gold pieces, but having been passed empty through a finger-ring that held it together. It was as if, before she turned to him, he had weighed the whole thing in his open palm and even heard a little the chink of the metal. When she did turn to him it was to recognize with her eyes what he might have been doing. She made no circumstance of thus coming upon him, save so far as the intelligence in her face could at any moment make a circumstance of almost anything. If when she moved off she looked like a huntress, she looked when she came nearer like his notion, perhaps not wholly correct, of a muse. But what she said was simply: 'You see you're not rid of me. How is dear Maggie?'[4]

James at times pays a price for this subordination of dialogue to the total design: the conversation can seem false to reality in its attempts at intensity and consistency. Adam Verver in thinking about the Prince finds his specific charm in his lack of angularity—a commonplace enough metaphor and not one to surprise us in the mind of Adam Verver. But when he addresses the Prince he does so in the terms of one of James's earlier similies: that the Prince is a great Palladian church. He then elaborates this comparison in a style that is similar to that used in the narrative and which is extremely complex.

'You're round, my boy.' he had said, '—you're *all*, you're variously and inexhaustibly round, when you might, by all the chances, have been abominably square. I'm not sure, for that matter', he had added, 'that you're *not* square in the general mass—whether abominably or not. The abomination isn't a question, for you're inveterately round—that's what I mean—in the detail. It's the sort of thing in you that one feels—or at least I do—with one's hand. Say you had been formed all over in a lot of pyramidal lozenges like that wonderful side of the Ducal Palace in Venice— so lovely in a building, but so damnable, for rubbing against, in a man, and especially in a near relation. I can see them all from here—each of them sticking out by itself—all the architectural cut diamonds that would have scratched one's softer sides. One would have been scratched by diamonds—doubtless the neatest way if one was to be scratched at all—but one would have been more or less reduced to a hash. As it is, for living with, you're a pure and perfect crystal.'[5]

Although James has created a context where metaphors of this seem appropriate, what we have learned of Adam Verver has not prepared us for such extended flights of fancy. We find it difficult to imagine Mr Verver, a retired business-man, actually speaking like this. His language, we feel, would have been more like that of Christopher Newman in *The American* or even that of Mr Leavenworth, the rich American in *Roderick Hudson* who orders an enormous and pretentious statue for his palatial home in the Middle West. This kind of realism, inspired by Balzac, he has abandoned for the unification and harmony of language inspired by Flaubert.

James, in carrying out his search for a totally integrated work of art in *The Golden Bowl*, develops grandiose metaphors. The objects which serve as a base for these metaphors do not have an independent life. Images tend to refer to other, previously suggested, images, or to be taken from the same area of discourse. Therefore one gets the continuous effect of each item referring to another in the same world. Furthermore much of the imagery is taken from the highly sophisticated, or at least expensive, way of life of the characters. James never goes outside this world to invoke natural images: the imagery is determined by the initial interests or characteristics of the actors. The elaborate pagoda image at the beginning of Part II, standing as it does for the way Maggie has arranged to be both married to the Prince and yet as much as ever her father's daughter, fits admirably into the world of a collector's spoils.

James transforms the London world of the nineteenth century into a self-sustaining world of art. This is shown by the way he represents and interprets the Prince throughout the novel.

The Prince's dark blue eyes were of the finest, and, on occasion, precisely, resembled nothing so much as the high windows of a Roman palace, of an historic front by one of the great old designers, thrown open on a feast-day to the golden air. His look itself at such times suggested an image—that of some very noble personage who, expected, acclaimed by the crowd in the street and with old precious stuffs falling over the sill for his support, had gaily and gallantly come to show himself: always moreover less in his own interest than in that of spectators and subjects whose need to admire, even to gape, was periodically to be considered. The young man's expression became after this fashion something vivid and concrete—a beautiful personal presence, that of a prince in very truth, a ruler, warrior, patron, lighting up brave architecture and diffusing the sense of function.[6]

Mr Verver recurs to those architectural images in describing the relations between the Prince and himself. These images and figures are not decorative; they indicate how people think and define character. It is through such functions, as well as their internal consistency, that they become part of the design of the novel. This architectural imagery is employed later in another function. The Prince's grandeur and his particular moral and social qualities which are suggested by these images are implicitly contrasted with those of Adam Verver when a different type of architectural image is used to designate him: his face we are told, was like a room 'clear-swept and un-encumbered with furniture'. The blandness—somewhat like that of old Mr Wentworth in *The Europeans*—the absence of 'signs' of a sharply marked social 'type', the openness of his character, the lack of historical associations or transmitted experience—these are all suggested by such an image. The Prince, morally, socially and historically, is a more complicated human creature than Adam Verver, and these architectural images, whilst never introducing a 'note' outside the range of interests which the novel treats, help to develop and probe that contrast.

By his use of imagery which is internally consistent, which constantly echoes the principal themes of the novel and which finds a place in the conversations or reflections of the characters James has carried further his emulation of Flaubert's effort towards creating a style which sustains a novel by its own force. There are techniques in *The Golden Bowl* which in themselves have little direct connection with the methods of French writers. However they form part of James's attempt to create a formally perfect work and through that formality create an imaginative world that seems harmonious and self-sustaining. At the same time, by this concentration and economy, he explores the possibilities of human nature. Therefore although James had to create his own methods to achieve the formal perfection he sought, that very effort connects him with the impetus of the 'L'Art pour l'Art' movement and those writers like Flaubert and Daudet who derived much of their own inspiration from it.

One of these techniques is the cutting out of narrative transitions and explanations, either through the highly developed sensitiveness of one character to another or through the use of a summarizing consciousness. An early example of the first, where the sensitiveness of characters to each other is the method of concentration and narrative economy, comes when the Prince visits Mrs Assingham in Book I, Chapter 2. Equally James can use his restricted 'point of view' for much more than 'psychological realism' or for giving the illusion of living characters. For example when Charlotte enters Mrs Assingham's drawing-room (Chapter 3) she knows that her hostess is not alone and behaves as she does because of this knowledge. Her manner is a result of her knowledge and it permits the Prince to 'take her in still better than if she had instantly faced him.' The Prince is conscious of this—of Charlotte's knowledge and of the opportunity she affords him to observe her. So we have all these things at once: her manner, its reasons, its effects on him and his understanding and interpretation of the situation, and its meaning for her as understood by him. The very restriction of point of view permits such economy and concentration, whilst also gaining the 'objectivity' sought by French writers, for the author is not directly present.

Consciousness also acts as a narrative condensation in Adam Verver's meditations about Charlotte whilst walking on the terrace (Book II, Chapter 5). Here all sorts of associations and similarities in the manner and tone of both the Prince and Charlotte are gathered and a strong suggestion of a deep underlying affinity between them made without ever being explicitly stated. These reflections act both as a condensation and as a dramatic prefigurement for the future relations between the two.

The use of more than one 'reflector' in this novel is necessary to get such multiple effects. For that the Prince and Charlotte have loved each other is not known to Adam Verver but is known to the reader. Adam's reflections then are more significant to us because we remember certain previous scenes, unknown to him. But his observations on the other hand help us to appreciate the way that the love between Charlotte and the Prince has affected her and reveal new depths in that connection. No amount of conversation could, in such a short space, give so much, and normal narrative would reveal less of what that conduct means to others, for the observation and interpretation of that conduct by Adam Verver is what gives it importance, not the mere fact that Charlotte seems to have the same tact as the Prince. Adam Verver's awareness deepens the significance of this similarity, not only to him but also to the reader. The technique is inseparable from the significance, and this is precisely what James, Flaubert, the Goncourts and Daudet all aimed to achieve.

Hence in a novel that in many ways is unlike any nineteenth-century French novel one might care to name, James shows his affinities with the most important French literary movements after Romanticism. In his last works he is drawing upon an accumulation of experience, reading and reflection and he transforms the various experiments of French authors into his own distinctive type of fiction. Throughout his life he attempted to give expression to visual impressions and to convey in his prose the immediate and the sensible. At first (in the 1870s and 1880s) his descriptions emulate Gautier when he is dealing with Italian scenes. His early fictional descriptions parallel the manners of Balzac and Flaubert. Later he finds that the experiments of the Goncourts and of Daudet are appropriate for the novel that most attempts to convey the presence of Paris through suggestion rather than through detailed description: *The Ambassadors*.

In *The Golden Bowl* a number of French influences converge, particularly those that derive from Gautier and 'L'Art pour l'Art' via Flaubert. It was a basic tenet of the movement both that art is the means of giving life new significance and that art is what makes life itself worthwhile. In *The Golden Bowl* James, by the very intense artificiality of the formalized and patterned human relationships, is attempting to give them new significance. The world of *The Golden Bowl* is self-contained and self-enclosed—an objective ardently pursued by Flaubert. It is obvious that if Flaubert achieved his aim it was in novels of a different temper and character from those of James. This does not make his example any the less pervasive and stimulating. And within the world that James has wrought the language achieves a new intensity by its unification of vocabulary, tone and manner—another Flaubertian objective. Within this world too the objects are all of a sort, so that we have been cut free from any references that might distract us from the artistic and artificial universe James has created for us. The result is an atmosphere that some find hard to breathe. But it is an atmosphere close to Flaubert and Gautier, an atmosphere where everything lives and breathes by and through art.

In the later novels—*The Wings of the Dove, The Ambassadors, The Awkward Age, What Maisie Knew, The Golden Bowl*—it is not then so much in the themes and subject-matter that James shows how he has assimilated the lessons of French literature, but in his efforts to create works that are internally consistent, self-sustaining, self-enclosed and held aloft by the power of their form and the cadences and imagery of their prose. In his preface to the New York edition of *The American* he wrote:

... the content and the 'importance' of a work of art are in fine wholly dependent on its *being* one: outside of which all prate of its representative character, its meaning and its bearing, its morality and humanity, are an impudent thing.[7]

If James's novels are important as works of art and through their so being have importance for their humanity and morality, this is in no small part owing to the manner in which throughout his career he was able to assimilate and transmute the lessons of the French novelists of his time.

Chronology of James's Life and Works with Special Reference to French Literature

Many of the works with which James was familiar were written either before his birth or when he was still very young. I have listed below the more important works published during James's lifetime by those French writers who were of most interest to him, including George Sand and Prosper Mérimée. Even though I have not dealt with these two in the course of this book, they were important for his early work, and for his conception of the possibilities and the significance of French literature, particularly before his taking up residence for good in Europe. He devoted a number of pages to them both, writing on George Sand as late as 1914.

Besides the abbreviations used in the Notes, Edel III and Edel IV refer to Leon Edel, *Henry James: The Middle Years* and *Henry James: The Treacherous Years*, respectively. *TSP* refers to Virginia Harlow, *Thomas Sargeant Perry, A Biography*, Durham, revised edition 1950. Works mentioned without an author are by Henry James.

1843 April 15. Birth of Henry James in New York. In October his family goes to Europe, living in Paris and London and returning in the late summer or early autumn of 1845 to live for the next ten years in Albany and New York City. In *A Small Boy and Others* James wrote: 'We had somehow waked early to a perception of Paris, and a vibration of my very most infantine sensibility under its sky had by the same stroke got itself preserved for subsequent wondering reference. I had been there for a short time in the second year of my life, and I was to communicate to my parents later on that as a baby in long clothes, seated opposite to them in a carriage and on the lap of another person, I had been impressed with the view, framed by the clear window of the vehicle as we passed, of a great stately square surrounded with high-roofed houses and having in its centre a tall and glorious column. I had naturally caused them to marvel, but I had also, under cross-questioning, forced them to compare notes, as it were, and reconstitute the miracle. They knew what my observation of monumental squares had been—and alas hadn't; neither New York nor Albany could have offered me the splendid perspective, and, for that matter, neither could London, which moreover I had known at a younger age still. Conveyed along the rue St-Honoré while I waggled my small feet, as I definitely remember doing, under my flowing robe, I had crossed the rue de Castiglione and taken in, for all my time, the admirable aspect of the Place and the Colonne Vendôme.'

Balzac: *David Séchard* (third part of *Illusions perdues*).

1843-45 Sand: *La Comtesse de Rudolstadt.*

1844 Balzac: *Les Trois Amoureuses* (in 1845 retitled *Modeste Mignon*); *Splendeurs et misères des courtisanes.*

1845 Gautier: *Voyage en Espagne* (a new version of what in 1843 was entitled *Tra los montes*); *Poésies complètes de Theophile Gautier; Nouvelles.*

1846 George Sand: *La Mare au Diable.*

1847 Mérimée: *Carmen* (revised and enlarged text of a story first published in 1845).

Gautier: *Salon de 1847.*

Balzac: *Histoire des Parents pauvres* (*La Cousine Bette* and *Le Cousin Pons*).

1842-48 *Oeuvres complètes de M. de Balzac*, the co-called 'Furne' edition, 17 volumes. Three further volumes published in 1855 by Houssiaux to make 20 volumes. Another collected edition in 24 volumes was published in 1869-76.

1852 The Goncourts: *Salon de 1852.*

1852 Mérimée: *Nouvelles.*

Gautier: *Italia; Emaux et Camées.*

In a letter to his father, April 11, 1876 James tells of a visit to Flaubert who had talked to him, among other things, of his intimate friend Gautier. He mentions in particular a poem called *Les Portraits ovales* (real title *Pastel* from *Emaux et Camées*). And in his essay about Flaubert in 1902 James still recalls this scene: 'Flaubert's own voice is clearest to me from the uneffaced sense of a winter weekday afternoon when I found him by exception alone and when something led to his reading me aloud, in support of some judgment he had thrown off, a poem of Theophile Gautier's. He cited it as an example of verse intensely and distinctively French, and French in its melancholy . . . He converted me at the moment to this perception, alike by the sense of the thing and by his large utterance of it; after which it is dreadful to have to confess not only that the poem was then new to me, but that, hunt as I will in every volume of its author, I am never able to recover it. This is perhaps after all happy, causing Flaubert's own full tone, which was the note of the occasion, to linger the more unquenched.'

1853   Gautier: *Constantinople.*

1854   The Goncourts: *Histoire de la société française pendant la Révolution.*

1854-55   Sand: *Histoire de ma vie.* In a letter to T. S. Perry of September 20, 1867 James wrote: 'I read recently, by the way, this lady's *Memoirs*, a compact little work in ten volumes. It's all charming (if you are not too particular about the exact truth) but especially the two 1st volumes, containing a series of letters from her father, written during Napoleon's campaigns. I think they are the best letters I ever read.'

1855-58   On June 27, 1855 the James family sets sail for Europe again. Henry has a short spell at a school in Geneva, and then in October 1855 the family moves to London where they live until moving to Paris in the summer of 1856. Of the Institution Fezandié where James went to school he wrote thus in *A Small Boy and Others*: 'I see much of the rest of that particular Paris time in the light of the Institution Fezandié, and I see the Institution Fezandié, rue Balzac, in the light, if not quite of Alphonse Daudet's lean asylum for the *petits pays chauds*, of which I have felt the previous institutions of New York sketchily remind me, at least in that of certain other of his studies in that field of the precarious . . . Paris over parts of which the great Arch at the top of the Champs-Elysées flings, at its hours, by its wide protective plausible shadow, a precious mantle of "tone". . . It was to the big square villa of the rue Balzac that we turned, as pupils not unacquainted with vicissitudes . . . an establishment that strikes me, at this distance of time, as of the oddest and most indescribable— or as describable at best in some of the finer turns and touches of Daudet's best method.' And of the district in general he wrote: 'I positively cherish at the present hour the fond fancy that we all soaked in some such sublime element as might have hung about there—I mean on the very spot—from the vital presence, so lately extinct, of the prodigious Balzac; which had involved, as by its mere respiration, so dense a cloud of other presences, so arrayed an army of interrelated shades that the air was still thick as with the fumes of witchcraft, with infinite seeing and supposing and creating, with a whole imaginative traffic.

The Pension Vauquer, then but lately existent, according to Le Père Goriot, on the other side of the Seine, was still to be revealed to me . . .'

In the summer of 1857 the family goes to Boulogne-sur-mer, and in the autumn and winter after a short return to Paris Henry goes to school there, one of his classmates being C. B. Coquelin, who became one of the most famous actors of his time. James wrote an article on him for *Century Magazine*, January 1887. The family returns to America in 1858.

1856   The Goncourts: *Une Voitue de masques*; *Les Actrices*.
Gautier: *L'Art moderne*.
Flaubert: *Madame Bovary* appeared in *La Revue de Paris*, October-December. Of this appearance James wrote in 'Gustave Flaubert, 1902': 'The author of these remarks remembers, as with a sense of the way such things happen, that when a very young person in Paris he took up from the parental table the latest number of the periodical in which Flaubert's then duly unrecognized masterpiece was in course of publication.'

1857   Flaubert: book publication of *Madame Bovary*, *Moeurs de province*.
The Goncourts: *Sophie Arnould, d'après sa correspondance et ses mémoires inédits*.

1858   Gautier: *Honoré de Balzac, sa vie et ses oeuvres*—biography by Gautier, analysis of *La Comédie humaine* by Taine.

1859-60 In October 1859 the James family once more moves to Europe. This time Henry is educated in Geneva from October 1859 to July 1860. After several months in Bonn the family returns in September 1860 to America.

1859   The Goncourts: *L'Art du dix-huitième siècle*, first of twelve parts, the last appearing in 1875.
George Sand: *Elle et Lui*.
Paul Musset: *Lui et Elle*.

1860-61 In Newport, Rhode Island, James meets the painter John La Farge who introduces him to the works of Balzac and Mérimée. On Mérimée's *La Vénus d'Ille* James wrote in 1898: (Literature, III, July 23) 'This sensitive spirit found itself, one unforgettable summer's day, fluttering deliciously—quite as if with a sacred terror—at the touch of *La Vénus d'Ille*. That was the first flush of a sentiment destined to last for many a year and of which the ashes are not even at present completely cold. *La Vénus d'Ille* struck my immaturity as a masterpiece of art and offered to the young curiosity concerned that sharpest of all challenges for youth, the challenge as to the special source of the effect.' In the same article he goes on to say that 'The poison of the "short story" was evidently in one's blood when *Tamango, Mateo Falcone, L'Enlèvement de la Redoute* had the magic of an edge so fine and a surface so smooth.' He translates the first two but they are refused. (He also attempts a translation of *La Vénus* which is neither acknowledged nor printed.) And he goes on to mention most of the other stories or novellas written by Mérimée. 'The glamour was doubtless in the perception that, somehow, more than any one else in the same line, equally near at hand, Mérimée was an "artist".'

1860   The Goncourts: *Les Hommes de lettres*; *Les Maîtresses de Louis XV*.

1861   The Goncourts: *Soeur Philomène*.

1863   Flaubert: *Salammbô*.
        Gautier: *Romans et contes*; *Le Capitaine Fracasse*.

1864   James's first published story, 'A Tragedy of Error' given a French setting, and a very Balzacian heroine.
        The Goncourts: *Renée Mauperin*; *Germinie Lacesteux*.

1865   Gautier: *Quand on voyage*.

1865-67 James's reviews of this period are mainly of English and American works, but include one of Dumas the Younger's *Affaire Clémenceau*, Hugo, and Eugénie and Maurice de Guérin. He makes constant reference to French writers in his criticism, often citing their examples as models to follow: Balzac, George Sand, Mérimée. Many of his stories of this period and until 1874 show strong marks of the same influences.

1866   The Goncourts: *Idées et Sensations*.
        Emile Zola: *Mes Haines, Causeries littéraires et artistiques*.

1867   The Goncourts: *Manette Salomon*.

1867   Zola: *Thérèse Raquin*.
        Gautier: *Voyage en Russie*.
        In a letter to Thomas Sargeant Perry, which he starts in French, after having mentioned different French authors he has been reading—Victor Cherbuliez, Octave Feuillet, George Sand, Taine, and Sainte-Beuve—James remarks: 'Our vast literature and literary history is to most of us an unexplored field—especially when we compare it to what the French is to the French.—Deep in the timorous recesses of my being is a vague desire to do for our dear old English letters and writers *something* of what Ste Beuve and

the best French critics have done for theirs . . . When I say that I should like to do as Ste Beuve has done, I don't mean that I should like to imitate him, or reproduce him in English: but only that I should like to acquire something of his intelligence and his patience and vigour . . . I feel that my only chance for success as a critic is to let all the breezes of the west blow through me at their will. We are American born—*il faut en prendre son parti*. I look upon it as a great blessing; and I think that to be an American is an excellent preparation for culture. We have exquisite qualities as a race, and it seems to me that we are ahead of the European races in the fact that more than either of them we can deal freely with forms of civilization not our own, can pick and choose and assimilate and in short (aesthetically etc) claim our property wherever we find it.' (Letter of September 20, 1867, *TSP*, pp.284-5.)

1868   More reviews by James of American, French and English literature including ones of Taine, Sainte-Beuve and George Sand.

1868   Alphonse Daudet: *Le Petit Chose*.
        The Goncourts: *Charles Demailly* (second edition of *Les Hommes de lettres*).

1869   The Goncourts: *Madame Gervaisais*.
        Turgenev, *Nouvelles moscovites*, stories translated by Turgenev and Mérimée.
        Daudet: *Lettres de Mon Moulin*.

1869-70 In February 1869 James travels to Europe, visiting England, France and Switzerland, returning to America in April 1870. On this trip he meets William Morris.

1870   Flaubert: *L'Education sentimentale*.
        20 June. Death of Jules de Goncourt.

1871   James first novel, *Watch and Ward*, published serially in *Atlantic Monthly*, shows strong signs of Balzac's influence.
        Zola: *La Fortune des Rougon*.
        Mérimée: *La Chambre Bleue*.
        Gautier: *Tableaux de siège*.

1872-74 In May 1872 James again sets forth for Europe, this time in the company of his sister and aunt. They visit England, France, Switzerland, Germany, Austria and Italy. Henry lives in Rome from December 1872 to June 1873. After travelling during the summer he returns to Italy, this time to Florence in October, to be joined by his brother William. He remains in Florence until June 1874, apart from a short stay in Rome, and after travelling through Switzerland,

Germany, Holland and Belgium, returns to America in the autumn of 1874.

1872   Further reviews by James of French literature and art including a review of Taine's *Notes sur l'Angleterre*, *Nation*, January 23, and another of Gautier's *Tableaux de siège*, *Nation*, January 25, and a review of an English translation of Taine's *Histoire de la littérature anglaise*, *Atlantic Monthly*, April.

Daudet: *Aventures prodigieuses de Tartarin de Tarascon.*

Zola: *La Curée.*

Gautier: *Théatre. Mystère, Comédie et ballets*; *Emaux et Camées*, author's definitive edition; *Henri Regnault*; *Histoire du romantisme.*

1873   'The Madonna of the Future' published in *Atlantic Monthly* in March, 'The Sweetheart of M. Briseux' in *Galaxy* in June.

Daudet: *Contes du Lundi.*

The Goncourts: *L'Art du dix-huitième siècle*, second and expanded edition; *Gavarni, L' homme et l'oeuvre.*

Zola: *Le Ventre de Paris.*

Mérimée: *Dernières nouvelles* and *Lettres à une Inconnue* reviewed by James in the *Independent*, April 9, 1874; this review reprinted in *French Poets and Novelists*, 1878 as 'Mérimée's Letters'.

Review of Gautier's *Théâtre*, etc. for *North American Review*, April, 1873. Reprinted as 'Théophile Gautier' in *French Poets and Novelists*. On this article see James's letter to T. S. Perry, January 1, 1873. He declines writing a 'really exhaustive article' because he has not the materials necessary to hand nor the time, but if he were to do so the quotations would be distributed 'through a tissue of finely-wrought eulogy'. He goes on: 'I should like very much however to say a good word for our rare old Théophile, whom the world doesn't seem to me to hold in a decent esteem.' On January 24 he sends off the manuscript of the article. 'You will see that it is but slightly biographical, as I lacked time and material to make it so; but you will probably find it a prettily enough turned compliment—a sort of monody on his death. I gave it my best care and it is—I may say it—well written.' (*TSP*, pp.288, 289.) James also wrote a review of the *Correspondance of Henri Regnault* (for the *Nation*, January 2), the sculptor about whom Gautier had published a short pamphlet the year before.

1874   Daudet: *Les Femmes d'artistes*; *Fromont Jeune et Risler Aîné*;
        Robert Helmont, Études et paysages.
        Mérimée: *Portraits historiques et littéraires*.
        Gautier: *Portraits contemporains*.
        Zola: *La Conquête de Plassans*.
        'The Last of the Valerii' in *Atlantic Monthly* for January,
        a story inspired by and largely based upon Mérimée's
        La Vénus d'Ille; 'Madame de Mauves' in *Galaxy*, February-
        March. The travel sketches of this period, 1870-74, and
        many of the stories with an Italian setting show strong
        traces of the influence of Gautier and Mérimée.
        Reviews of Flaubert's *La Tentation de Saint Antoine* and of
        the English translation of Gautier's *Voyage en Russie*
        (*Winter in Russia*) in *Nation*; a review of Gautier's *Histoire
        du Romantisme* in the October issue of *North American
        Review*, and an important article on Turgenev in the April
        issue, reprinted in *French Poets and Novelists*; articles and
        reviews on Hugo and Sainte-Beuve. James's review of
        Daudet's *Fromont Jeune et Risler Aîné*, *Galaxy*, August, 1875,
        is on the whole a strong attack on French realism and the
        lengthy treatment of such characters as Emma Bovary
        and the heroine of this novel, Sidonie Chèbe: 'She is a
        person for one to qualify by a single homely epithet, and
        dismiss from one's thought.' He concludes: 'We may say
        of him, on the whole, that he is an artist gone astray.'
        But these views should be compared to his 1883 article,
        reprinted in *Partial Portraits*, 1888.

1875   Zola: *La Faute de l'Abbé Mouret*.
        Edmond de Goncourt: *Catalogue raisonné de l'oeuvre peint,
        dessiné et gravé d'Antoine Watteau*.
        A very important and very productive year for James.
        He writes many reviews and notices, *Roderick Hudson*
        appears serially in *Atlantic Monthly* from January to
        December before being issued as a book, and he publishes
        Transatlantic Sketches. Reviews include one of the English
        translation of Gautier's *Constantinople* and Taine's *Notes on
        Paris*, both for the *Nation*. Longer articles include 'The
        Letters of Madame de Sabran', 'Honoré de Balzac', and
        'The Two Ampères', all to be reprinted in *French Poets and
        Novelists*. On October 20 he leaves for Europe and after a
        short stay in England arrives in Paris on November 11.
        He starts writing a series of articles on Parisian topics for
        the *New York Tribune*. On November 22 he calls on Tur-
        genev who that winter introduces him to Flaubert and his

circle: Edmond de Goncourt, Maupassant, Zola, Daudet and others.

1876   Zola: *Son Excellence Eugène Rougon*.
Daudet: *Jack, moeurs contemporains*. In a letter to T. S. Perry James writes: 'The book to me was dreary and disagreeable, and in spite of cleverness intrinsically weak. I prefer an inch of Gustave Droz to a mile of Daudet. Why the French circle don't like him is their own affair.' Although James was never to think this work of Daudet's his best his opinion of the merits of Daudet were to alter significantly and he soon ceases to refer to Droz.

James continues his letters to the *Tribune* on Parisian and French topics including art, literature and the theatre. 'The Minor French Novelists' published in *Galaxy* is reprinted, in part, as 'Charles de Bernard and Gustave Flaubert' in *French Poets and Novelists*. An article on 'Charles Baudelaire' for the *Nation* is also reprinted in that volume. He writes travel sketches of Chartres, Rouen, and Etretat which are reprinted in *Portraits of Places*, 1883. *The American* appears in *Atlantic Monthly* from June 1876 to May 1877.

On his introduction to Flaubert and his circle James writes to Perry: 'I sometimes see Turgeneff and Gustave Flaubert—excellent old fellows both: I hardly know which, personally, I prefer. Flaubert's person has raised my estimate of his work. There is something even touchingly simple about him.' And in another letter: 'Tu vois que je suis dans les conseils des dieux—que je suis lancé en plein olympe. J'ai vu deux ou trois fois Flaubert (par Tourguéneff avec lequel il est très lié)—et il m'a fait un accueil fort gracieux. C'est un grand gaillard à visage sanguin, à l'encolure d'athlète, mais très simple et très doux de manière, très naïf et très sincère de caractère et pas du tout pétillant d'esprit. Depuis que je le connais j'envisage ses livres tout autrement que je n'ai fait jusqu'ici. Nous causerons un jour de ça. J'ai rencontré chez lui deux fois sa petite *école*—Zola, Goncourt, Daudet, etc. Cela m'a intéressé bien qu'évidemment je ne pousserai pas bien loin dans leur intimité. Ce sont des garçons d'un grand talent, mais je les trouve affreusement bornés. Ils sont pourtant bien amusants, et la première fois que me trouvai parmi eux il me sembla que j'entendais causer pour la 1ère fois.' (*TSP*, January 11, 1876 and February 3, p.291.) ('You see that I am in the counsels of the gods—that I am thrown on to Olympus itself. Two or three times I have seen Flaubert (through Turgenev to whom he is very close) —and he gave me a most gracious welcome. He is a big, red-faced fellow, of athletic build, but very simple and gentle, very naïve and sincere in character and not at all scintillating with wit. Since I have known him, I have seen his books quite differently from before. One day we shall talk about that. Twice at his home I met his little 'school'— Zola, Goncourt, Daudet, etc. This interested me, though of course I will not push my way very far into their circle. They are fellows of great talent, but I find them dreadfully restricted. However, they are very amusing and the first time I found myself among them it seemed to me that I was hearing talk for the first time.') These visits are also recalled in 'Gustave Flaubert, 1902'.

In December 1876 James moves to London.

1877   Daudet: *Le Nabob, moeurs parisiennes*. 'Read at any rate the *Nabob* (A. Daudet). It is both very clever and very poor.' (James to Perry, *TSP*, p.298.)
Edmond de Goncourt: *La Fille Elisa*. Reviewed by James in the *Nation*.
Zola: *L'Assommoir*. 'It is worth it if your stomach can stand it.')(*TSP*, p.295.)
Flaubert: *Trois Contes*.
James publishes a number of essays on French subjects which are later reprinted in *French Poets and Novelists*: 'The Letters of Honoré de Balzac,' 'The Théâtre Français', 'Alfred de Musset' and 'George Sand'. A travel sketch, 'From Normandy to the Pyrenees' is later reprinted in *Portraits of Places*, 1883. Other reviews include one of Turgenev's *Tierres Vierges*.
In September 1877 James revisits Paris and the Théâtre Français. He sees a performance of Dumas the Younger's *Le Demi-Monde* which is to serve as the 'germ' of several of James's later stories, particularly 'The Siege of London', 1883.

1878   James publishes *French Poets and Novelists*, *Watch and Ward*, *The Europeans*, and *Daisy Miller*. His previous autumn's trip issues in a number of essays: 'Paris Revisited', 'A Little Tour in France', 'Italy Revisited', 'Recent Florence'. All of these are reprinted in *Portraits of Places* although not always with the same title.
Zola: *Une page d'amour*. Reviewed by James in the *Nation*.

1879   James publishes *The Madonna of the Future and Other Tales*

and his study, *Hawthorne*. When in June Turgenev comes to England to receive his honorary DCL from Oxford James entertains him to dinner in London and then in the autumn re-visits Paris again and sees Turgenev there.
Daudet: *Les Rois en exil*.
Edmond de Goncourt: *Les Frères Zemganno*.
In a letter from Paris to T. S. Perry James writes: '. . . the literature is pitifully thin. Il n'y a que Zola! I admire him more than you, and mean to write an article for John Morley about him . . . Zola's naturalism is ugly and dirty, but he seems to me to be *doing something*—which surely (in the imaginative line) no one in England or the U.S. is, and no one else here.' (*TSP*, p.304.)

1880   James publishes *Washington Square* which has many affinities with Balzac's *Eugénie Grandet*, and essays on Sainte-Beuve, Eugène Delacroix, and a review of Zola's *Nana*.
May 8. Death of Flaubert.
The Goncourts: *L'Art du dix-huitième siècle*, 3rd and expanded edition.
Zola: *Nana*; *Le Roman expérimental*.
Les Soirées de Médan. A collection of stories by Zola, Maupassant, Huysmans, Céard, Hennique and Alexis. Contains Maupassant's first published work, 'Boule de Suif'.

1881   *The Portrait of a Lady*. James returns to America in October. His *Notebooks* entries from November 25 to February 9, 1882 serve to sum up, for him, the meaning of his European experience and his decision to make England and Europe his home (pp.23-39).
Flaubert: *Bouvard et Pécuchet*.
Edmond de Goncourt: *La Maison d'un artiste*.
Zola: *Le Naturalisme au théâtre*.
Maupassant: *La Maison Tellier*—with dedication to Turgenev.
In a letter from Paris in February James writes to Perry: 'I have also just bought two books—Mérimée's Letters to Panizzi and Zola's *Naturalisme au Théâtre* . . . Zola has his faults and his merits; and it doesn't seem to me important to talk of the faults. The merits are rare, valuable, extremely solid.' American literature on the other hand seems 'written by eunuchs and sempstresses.' It is an age of 'merely material expansion . . . . Art, form, may return, but I doubt that I shall live to see them.' (*TSP*, pp.309-10).
Daudet: *Numa Roumestan*. '*Numa Roumestan* is a masterpiece;

it is really a perfect work, it has no weakness, no roughness, it is a compact and harmonious whole' (*Partial Portraits*, p.197).

1882   On January 29 James's mother dies. In May he returns to England and then in September crosses to France to begin work on a series of travel sketches to be published first in *Atlantic Monthly* in 1883 and 1884, and then as *A Little Tour in France*, 1884. While in Paris he visits Turgenev at Bougival. He publishes a review in *Atlantic Monthly* of Ernest Daudet's *Mon Frère et moi*; *Souvenirs d'enfance et de jeunesse*.
Zola: *Pot-Bouille*.
Maupassant: *Mlle Fifi*.
Edmond de Goncourt: *La Faustin*.
George Sand: *Correspondance*.

1883   *The Siege of London* and the first collected edition, in 14 volumes, of James's novels and stories. *Portraits of Places*. His essay 'Alphonse Daudet', published in *The Century Magazine* in August, states: 'The appearance of a new novel by this admirable genius is to my mind the most delightful literary event that can occur just now; in other words Alphonse Daudet is at the head of his profession.'
James also translates Daudet's Reminiscences of Turgenev for *Century Magazine* in November.
Daudet: *L'Evangéliste*.
Zola: *Au Bonheur des dames*.
Maupassant: *Une Vie*; *Contes de Bécasse*. According to Edel, III, p.109, *Une Vie* is signed and dated in James's hand, 'Boston, June 19, 1883' and *Contes de Bécasse* is inscribed 'Boston, August 1883'.

1884   'Ivan Turgenieff', *Atlantic Monthly*, January: 'The Author of Beltraffio', *English Illustrated Magazine*, June-July; 'A New England Winter', *Century Magazine*, August-September; 'The Art of Fiction', *Longman's Magazine*, September.
In February James visits Paris and meets Edmond de Goncourt, Daudet, Loti, Zola, Coppée, etc. On February 13 he writes to T. B. Aldrich: 'I spent last evening at Alph. Daudet's, and was much impressed with the intense seriousness of that little group—himself, Zola, Goncourt, etc. About Daudet's intensity of effort there is something tragical, and his wasted, worn extraordinarily beautiful and refined little face expresses it in a way which almost brings tears to my eyes. The torment of style, the high standard of it, the effort to say something perfectly in a

language in which everything has been said, and re-said,—so that there are certain things, certain cases, which can never again be attempted—all this seems to me to be wearing them all out, so that they have the look of galley-slaves tied to a ball and chain, rather than of happy producers ... This all proves, what one always feels that (in their narrow circle) terrible are the subtleties they attempt.' (*Selected Letters* pp.109–10).

To Howells on February 21 : 'I have been seeing something of Daudet, Goncourt, and Zola; and there is nothing more interesting to me now than the effort and experiment of this little group, with its truly infernal intelligence of art, form, manner—its intense artistic life. They do the only kind of work, to-day, that I respect; and in spite of their ferocious pessimism and their handling of unclean things they are at least serious and honest. The floods of tepid soap and water which under the name of novels are being vomited forth in England, seem to me, by contrast, to do little honour to our race.' (*Letters* I, p.105).

Later in the year James writes to T. S. Perry about the reception—or rather lack of it—that his essay 'The Art of Fiction' has received in England: 'My poor article has not attracted the smallest attention here and I haven't heard, or seen, an allusion to it. There is almost no care for literary discussion here,—questions of form, of principle, the 'serious' idea of the novel appeal apparently to no one, and they don't understand you when you speak of them.' (Letter of September 26, *TSP*, p.317).

On June 19 James writes to Daudet thanking him for the copy of his novel *Sapho* which Daudet has sent to him. He finds many things to praise in it but his central reservation reminds one of his comments on Emma Bovary: 'En un mot, le drame ne se passe peut-être pas assez dans l'âme et dans la conscience de Jean.' (*Letters*, I., p.109.)

This year also sees the beginning of James's long friendship with the younger French writer Paul Bourget, who is introduced to him by the American painter John Sargeant. Flaubert: *Lettres de Gustave Flaubert à George Sand.* 'It's a filthy world, and if you wish to know some of the thoughts that arise in me, read G. Flaubert's letters to Mme Sand.' (*TSP*, p.316, Letter of March 6.)

Edmond and Jules de Goncourt: *Un Premier Livre. En 18. . .*, preface by Edmond de Goncourt. The original edition (1859), all save a few copies, had been destroyed by the authors because the printers had suppressed certain passages without their consent.

Edmond de Goncourt: *Chérie*.

Zola: *La Joie de vivre*. James mentions this book in letters to both Howells and T. S. Perry.

Maupassant: *Clair de Lune*; *Au Soleil*; *Les Soeurs Rondoli*; *Miss Harriet*.

At the end of the year as James is working on *The Princess Casamassima* he visits Millbank prison to gain information for one of his scenes. He writes to Perry: 'You see I am quite the Naturalist.' (Letter of December 12, *TSP*, p.319.)

1885   *The Bostonians* and *The Princess Casamassima* begin serial publication, the first in *Century Magazine* in February, the second in *Atlantic Monthly* in September. Of *The Bostonians* James writes in his *Notebooks*: 'Daudet's *L'Evangéliste* has given me the idea of this thing. If I could only do something with that *pictorial* quality!' (p.47).

In the autumn of this year James is again in Paris where he visits friends, including Paul Bourget who introduces him to Barbey d'Aurevilly.

Daudet: *Tartarin sur les Alpes*.

Zola: *Germinal*.

Maupassant: *Bel-Ami*; *Toine*; *Yvette*; *Contes du jour et de la Nuit*.

1886   On August 12 James entertains Maupassant to dinner at Greenwich. Included in the company are Edmund Gosse and Count Joseph Napoleon Primoli. This year too sees the book publication of both *The Princess Casamassima* and *The Bostonians*.

Daudet: *La Belle-Nivernaise*.

Flaubert: *Par les Champs et par les grèves* (*Voyage en Bretagne*). An early work written in collaboration with Maxime du Camp. The odd numbered chapters are by Flaubert.

Zola: *L'Oeuvre*.

Maupassant: *Monsieur Parent*; *La Petite Roque*.

1887   'Coquelin' in *Century Magazine* for January.

Flaubert: *Correspondance* (1830-50). Letters published by his niece, the first of four series.

The Goncourts: *Journal des Goncourts. Mémoires de la vie littéraire*, 9 volumes, 1887-96.

Maupassant: *Mont-Oriol*; *La Horla*.

1888   *Partial Portraits*.

The Reverberator. The *Notebooks* entries for this (pp.82-85)

show James thinking often in Balzacian terms: the story is one of his attempts to sketch his age; the antecedents for his heroine must be of the explanatory sort, and the type he has chosen, the Europeanized American, is one that represents a real social and human category. *The Aspern Papers* (including 'Louisa Pallant' and 'A Modern Warning'); 'Guy de Maupassant' in the *Fortnightly Review*, March, reprinted in *Partial Portraits*. 'Pierre Loti' in *Fortnightly Review*, May, and 'The Journal of the Brothers Goncourt' in the same review for October; both are reprinted in *Essays in London and Elsewhere*, 1893. 'A London Life' is published in *Scribner's Magazine*, June-September, 'The Lesson of the Master' in the *Universal Review*, July and August, and 'The Liar' in *Century Magazine*, May-June. The *Notebooks* entry for 'The Liar' (p.62) suggests that the idea for the story comes from Daudet's *Numa Roumestan*.
Daudet: *L'Immortel, moeurs parisiennes*; *Trente ans de Paris*.
The Goncourts: *Préfaces et manifestes littéraires*.
Maupassant: *Pierre et Jean*; *Le Rosier de Madame Husson*; *Sur L'Eau*; *L'Héritage* (includes 'La Parure'). In his preface to 'The Author of *Beltraffio*' for the New York Edition James wrote that 'The origin of "Paste" is rather more expressible, since it was to consist but of the ingenious thought of transposing the terms of one of Guy de Maupassant's admirable *contes*', this *conte* being 'La Parure'.
Zola: *Le Rêve*.

1889   On May 18 James has lunch with Hippolyte Taine on the invitation of Jules Jusserand, French chargé d'affaires and scholar, a friend of James's. In his *Notebooks* (p.101) James records: 'Taine used the expression, very happily, that Turgenieff so perfectly cut the umbilical cord that bound the story to himself.'
The Tragic Muse, *Atlantic Monthly*, January-December. 'Guy de Maupassant', *Harper's Weekly*, October 19. This is reprinted as a preface to an English translation of a collection of Maupassant stories, *The Odd Number*. In October and November James again visits Paris and sees Daudet, Bourget, Francois Coppée and Edmond de Goncourt, visits the Exhibition and frequents the theatres.
Flaubert: *Correspondance*, 2nd series (1850-4).
Maupassant: *Fort comme la mort*; *La Main gauche*.

1890   James translates and writes a preface for Daudet's *Port Tarascon: The Last Adventures of the Illustrious Tartarin*—the only translation he undertook after his youthful and abortive efforts with Mérimée's stories. This is published in *Harper's New Monthly Magazine*, June-November, before being issued in book form in the same year with a slightly expanded preface and with certain passages restored that had been suppressed in magazine publication as likely to offend the religious feelings of readers. James also writes 'Daumier, Caricaturist' for *Century Magazine* for January and *The Tragic Muse* is issued.

Zola: *La Bête humaine*.

Maupassant: *Notre Coeur*; *L'Inutile Beauté*; *La Vie errante*; *Histoire d'une fille de ferme*.

1891   In a letter to Robert Louis Stevenson, October 30 James writes: 'The Frenchmen are passing away—Maupassant dying of locomotor paralysis, the fruit of fabulous habits, I am told. *Je n'en sais rien*, but I shall miss him . . . I saw Daudet last winter . . . who is also *atteint de la moelle épinière* and writing about it in the shape of a novel called *La Douleur*, which will console him by its sale.' (*Selected Letters*, p.177.)

Flaubert: *Correspondance*, 3rd series (1854-69).

Edmond de Goncourt: *Outamara, le peintre des maisons vertes*.

Zola: *L'Argent*.

1893   Towards the end of March James goes to Paris and whilst there dines twice with Daudet in his home in the Rue de Bellechasse.

Flaubert: *Correspondance*, 4th series (1869-80). James writes a review of this for *Macmillan's Magazine* for March. This is reprinted as 'Gustave Flaubert'—for the review is an occasion for James to write generally about Flaubert—in *Essays in London and Elsewhere* of the same year.

Zola: *Le Docteur Pascal*.

In a letter to Morton Fullerton, July 14, James comments on Maupassant's death. 'I don't know what prevented my wiring you a crystalline tear to drop on Maupassant's grave. Or rather, I do. Everything prevented it, including the fact that my tears had been already wept; even though the image of that history had been too *hard* for such droppings.' And in the same letter he remarks of *Le Docteur Pascal*: 'What won't the French write about next. Strange are the loves of a sick sexagenarian and his niece. Yet I love my Zola.' (*Selected Letters*, pp.215 and 216.)

1894   'The Death of the Lion', *Yellow Book*, April.

Zola: *Les Trois Villes. Lourdes*.

1895   In February James writes a letter to Daudet on reading
his new book, *La Petite Paroisse*. 'J'ai lu *Petite Paroisse* comme
je vous lis toujours—dans un doux recueillement traversé
de frissons pénétrants. Il n'y a pas de manière de faire qui
me contente aussi pleinement que la vôtre; je l'avais
constaté de nouveau justement ces jours-là, en relisant—
chacun pour la troisième fois—*Sapho* et *l'Immortel*.'
(*Selected Letters*, p.179.) ('I have read *Petite Paroisse* as I
always read you—in a state of quiet contemplation, shot
with penetrating shivers. There is no way of doing things
which contents me as fully as yours; I had established
that once more recently while reading—each for the third
time—*Sapho* and *l'Immortel*.') In the spring Daudet comes
to England and writes to ask James to arrange rooms for
himself and his family. Whilst here James acts as general
guide and host and arranges a dinner for Daudet at the
Reform Club.
'The Next Time', *Yellow Book*, July.

1896   'The Figure in the Carpet', *Cosmopolis*, January-February.
'Dumas the Younger' in *Boston Herald*, February. This is
reprinted in *Notes on Novelists*, 1914.
'The Old Things'—the first title for *The Spoils of Poynton*—
appears in *Atlantic Monthly* from April to October.
Zola: *Les Trois Villes. Rome*.
Edmond de Goncourt dies at his home in Champigny on
July 16.

1897   *The Spoils of Poynton*.
'She and He. Recent Documents', *Yellow Book*, January.
This is reprinted in *Notes on Novelists* as 'George Sand'.
What Maisie Knew.
In the December 25 issue of *Literature* James writes a
tribute to Daudet who had died on December 15. James
gives particular praise to Daudet's special skill in representing the visible and sensuous world, in his power to
evoke 'the concrete and the palpable, sensations and
contacts, images, appearances, touches for the eye and
ear.' 'This was a part of that effect of being consummately
done that infallibly attached to anything he attempted;
and the effect came doubtless, in its measure, from his
having so completely accepted and adopted the particular
fact of his spontaneity and sensibility. He let himself
vibrate as he would, and as he had at the same time a
literary instinct of the rarest and acutest, as the artist in

him was exquisitely alive and vigilant, this supreme "doing" inevitably attended his work.'

1898   James writes an introduction for the English translation of Pierre Loti's *Impressions*. In *Literature*, Vol. III, July 23, he writes an article on Prosper Mérimée and in the same issue another article, 'American Letters: The Question of Opportunities' in which he suggests an almost Balzacian theme as a great unexplored region for American fiction: the American 'business-man'.

Zola: 'Lettre à M. Félix Faure, président de la République', *L'Aurore*, January 13. James writes of this: 'one of the most courageous things ever done and an immense honour to our too-puling corporation!' (Edel, IV, pp. 259-60.)

1899   *The Awkward Age.*

For *North American Review* for October James writes 'The Present Literary Situation in France'. Whilst still enunciating strictures on Flaubert's Emma Bovary because too few of her possible relationships have been exhibited, too few human chords have been struck in her nature, he signals out for praise the new work on Flaubert by Émile Faguet.

W. Karénine. *George Sand, sa vie et ses oeuvres*, 3 vols, 1899-1914. James wrote two articles based on this work, the first in 1902 for *North American Review* as 'George Sand, the New Life' and the other in 1914 for *Quarterly Review* as 'George Sand, sa vie et ses oeuvres Vol. III'. Both are reprinted in *Notes on Novelists*, the first as 'George Sand, 1899' and the second as 'George Sand, 1914'.

Zola: *Les Quatres Évangiles. Fécondité.*

Maupassant: *Le Père Milon.*

1900   *The Soft Side.*

1901   *The Sacred Fount.*

Zola: *Les Quatre Évangiles. Travail; La Vérité en marche.*

1902   *The Wings of the Dove.* James provides a 'Critical Introduction' to the English translation of *Madame Bovary* and another to Balzac's *The Two Young Brides* (*Mémoires de deux jeunes mariées*). These both reprinted in *Notes on Novelists* as 'Gustave Flaubert, 1902' and 'Honoré de Balzac, 1902'.

1903   *The Ambassadors.*
The Better Sort.
William Wetmore Story and his Friends.

'Emile Zola' for *Atlantic Monthly* in August, reprinted in *Notes on Novelists.*

Zola: *Les Quatre Evangiles. Vérité.*

1904 *The Golden Bowl.*

1905 *The Question of Our Speech* which includes 'The Lesson of Balzac'.

   English Hours.

1907-09 *The Novels and Tales of Henry James,* the New York Edition.

1913 'Balzac', a review of Emile Faguet's *Balzac* in *The Times Literary Supplement* for June 19. This is reprinted as 'Honoré de Balzac, 1913' in *Notes on Novelists.*

1914 *Notes on Novelists.*

Notes

All references to James's novels are to *The Novels and Tales of Henry James*, 'The New York Edition', 24 volumes, London 1908-9, with two exceptions: *Roderick Hudson* and *The Tragic Muse*. References to these are to the reprints of the first editions edited by Leon Edel, London, 1961 and 1948 respectively. References to *A Small Boy and Others* are to the *Autobiography*, edited by F. W. Dupee, London, 1956. Passages from Flaubert's *Correspondance* are quoted from the Conard edition of the *Oeuvres complètes*, 1926-33.

Abbreviations and Short Titles

CT	*The Complete Tales of Henry James*, 12 volumes, edited by Leon Edel, London, 1962-64
Letters	*The Letters of Henry James*, selected and edited by Percy Lubbock, 2 vols, London, 1920
Notes and Reviews	*Notes and Reviews by Henry James*, with a preface by Pierre De Chaignon La Rose, Cambridge, Mass., 1921
Selected Letters	*Selected Letters of Henry James*, edited by Leon Edel, London, 1956
Art of the Novel	*The Art of the Novel; Critical Prefaces*, introduction by R. P. Blackmur, London, 1934
Literary Reviews and Essays	*Literary Reviews and Essays on American, English and French Literature*, edited by A. Mordell, New York, 1958
House of Fiction	*The House of Fiction: Essays on the Novel*, edited by Leon Edel, London, 1957
Notebooks	*The Notebooks of Henry James*, edited by F. O. Matthiessen and Kenneth B. Murdock, New York, 1947 and 1961

1. THE IDEAL WORLD OF ART

1 For a brief discussion of this general question see introduction to *Ivory Towers and Secret Founts* by Maurice Beebe, New York, 1964.

2 Cornelia Pulsifer Kelley, *The Early Development of Henry James*,

University of Illinois Studies in Language and Literature, Vol. 15, 1930; revised edition Urbana, Illinois, 1965, pp.149-52. Besides the evidence provided by the numerous parallels between the three stories there is a direct reference in 'The Madonna of the Future' to Balzac's earlier tale. One of the characters says: 'I fancy, myself, that if one were to get into his studio, one would find something very like the picture in that tale of Balzac's—a mere mass of incoherent scratches and daubs, a jumble of dead paint.' (*CT*, III, p.28).

3 For drawing my attention to the importance of Balzac's tale I wish to thank Dr Louis Ferguson who let me read his unpublished thesis on James and Balzac. However he and I differ fundamentally in our interpretations of this story and its significance.

4 Balzac, *La Comédie humaine*, Vol. IX, Pléiade edition, Paris, 1950, pp.397-98.

5 For a fuller discussion of the origins and development of the tale see Pierre Laubriet, *Le Chef d'oeuvre inconnu de Balzac*, Paris, 1961.

6 Balzac, op. cit., p.402.

7 Ibid., p.404.

8 Ibid., pp.404-5.

9 When later in Frenhofer's studio she sees Poussin looking at the superb picture he had earlier taken for a Giorgione her jealousy and sense of neglect burst forth. 'Ah! . . . montons. Il ne m'a jamais regardée ainsi.' ('Ah! . . . Let's go up. He has never looked at me in that way.') (Ibid., p.410.)

10 Ibid., p.405.

11 Ibid., p.405.

12 Ibid., p.407.

13 Ibid., p.409.

14 Ibid., p.394.

15 Ibid., p.395.

16 Ibid., p.395.

17 *CT*, III, p.20.

18 Ibid., p.30.

19 Ibid., p.47

2. The Art of the Novel: 'The Costly Charm of Composition'

1 'The Lesson of Balzac', *House of Fiction*, p.66.

2 *Art of the Novel*, p.26.

3 Notice these titles of novels or sections of novels: *Les Mémoires de deux jeunes mariées*, 'Les deux poètes' (*Illusions perdues*), 'Les deux frères' (*La Rabouilleuse*), 'Les deux salons' (*Le Cabinet des Antiques*), 'La Chaste Suzanne et ses deux vieillards' (*La Vieille Fille*).

4 *Art of the Novel*, p.8.

5 *Art of the Novel*, p.18.

6 *Illusions perdues*, ed. Antoine Adam, Paris, 1956, pp.170-71 (all references henceforth are to this edition).

7 Ibid., p.173.

8 Ibid., p.201.

9 Ibid., p.202.

10 *Roderick Hudson*, p.39.

11 Ibid., p.67.

12 *Art of the Novel*, p.133.

13 Ibid., p.135.

14 *CT*, VII, pp.142-3.

15 Ibid. p.144.

16 Ibid., p.181.

17 *Art of the Novel*, p.14.

18 The title also makes reference to a room where the medals of the kingdom are kept. This reference is exploited in various ways by Balzac as Pierre-Georges Castex points out in his edition of *Le Cabinet des*

Antiques, Paris, 1958. All references henceforth are to this edition.
19 Ibid., p.86.
20 Ibid., p.87.
21 Ibid., p.87.
22 Ibid., p.88.
23 Ibid., p.86.
24 Ibid., p.89.
25 *The Wings of the Dove,* Vol. I, p.29.
26 *The Portrait of a Lady,* Vol. II, p.35.
27 Ibid., p.36.
28 Ibid., p.36.
29 Ibid., p.39.
30 Ibid., p.42.
31 Hippolyte Taine, *Nouveaux Essais de critique et d'histoire,* Paris, 1896, pp.69-70.
32 *The Wild Garden,* London, 1963, p.136.
33 *César Birotteau,* ed. Pierre Laubriet, Paris, Garnier, 1964. p.lxxxiii quoted by W. G. Moore, *Modern Language Review,* Vol.LXI, p.136.
34 Preface to the English translation of *Les Mémoires de deux jeunes mariées,* London, 1902, reprinted in Henry James, *Selected Literary Criti-* cism, ed. M. Shapira, London, 1963, p.194.
35 See pp.23-7 in the Garnier edition for the full passage.
36 *Le Cabinet des Antiques,* p.23.
37 Ibid., pp.24-7.
38 Ibid., pp.18 and 19.
39 Ibid., p.21.
40 Ibid., p.40.
41 Ibid., p.40.
42 Ibid., p.48.
43 Ibid., p.38.
44 *The Portrait of a Lady,* Vol. I., p.2.
45 Ibid., p.2.
46 Ibid., p.3.
47 Ibid., p.31.
48 Ibid., p.42.
49 Ibid., p.325-6.
50 *The Portrait of a Lady,* Vol. II, p.100.
51 Ibid., Vol. I, pp.3-4.
52 *The Princess Casamassima,* Vol. II, pp.3-4.
53 Ibid., p.5.
54 Ibid., p.6.
55 Ibid., p.6.
56 Ibid., p.17.
57 Ibid., p.176.
58 Ibid., p.176.

3. James's Evaluation of Flaubert's Achievement

1 Reprinted in *Notes on Novelists,* 1914 and in *The House of Fiction,* 1957. All page references are to this latter edition.
2 Ibid., pp.195-6.
3 *French Poets and Novelists,* p.204.
4 'Pierre Loti' in *Essays in London and Elsewhere,* 1893, p.193.
5 Ibid., p.167.
6 Ibid., pp.167-8.
7 Ibid., pp.182-3.
8 Ibid., p.192.
9 *Notebooks,* p.170.
10 Ibid., pp.171-2.
11 *House of Fiction,* p.198.
12 Ibid., p.199.
13 Ibid., p.199.
14 Ibid., p.200.
15 Ibid., p.198.

4. Flaubert's Influence on James's Technique

1 *House of Fiction,* pp.198-9.
2 *The Tragic Muse,* pp.14 and 15.
3 *The Wings of the Dove,* Vol. I, pp.3-4.

4 Flaubert, *Correspondance*, Vol. III, p.99.

5 A. Thibaudet, *Gustave Flaubert*, Paris, 1935, p.223.

6 Excellent discussions can be found in Thibaudet's *Gustave Flaubert* and Stephen Ullman's *Style in the French Novel*, Oxford, 1964, where further detailed references are given.

7 Thibaudet, op.cit., p.246.

8 I owe this suggestion to an unpublished lecture by Professor Graham Hough.

9 Ibid., Vol. II, p.4.

10 A much fuller and more nuanced discussion of Flaubert's verbs will be found in Thibaudet, op. cit., but the preceding summary is enough for our purposes.

11 Vol. II., p.6. Examples of things that could *not* be said to Milly and Susan Stringham by Densher and Kate, transmitted through Densher's thoughts, can be found on p.16.

12 Ibid., p.12.

5. Two Modes of Possessing: Conquest and Appreciation

1 Within this line comes too the novel that ends, for James, this decade: *The Tragic Muse*, although it is perhaps best discussed in another context—the relation of the artistic life to the pressures and values that stand opposed to it.

2 *Art of the Novel*, p.76.

3 See Lionel Trilling, *The Liberal Imagination*: 'The Princess Casamassima'.

4 *L'Éducation sentimentale*, ed. Édouard Maynial, Paris, 1958, p.179.

5 Ibid., p.198.

6 Ibid., p.52.

7 Ibid., p.141.

8 *The Princess Casamassima*, Vol. II, Chap. 32, pp.168-9.

9 Ibid., Book VI, Chap. 38, p.263.

10 *CT*, XII, pp.256-7.

11 Ibid., p.119; p.121.

6. Henry James and 'L'Art pour l'Art'

1 For the discussion of the movement in France I have found the work of Albert Cassagne, *La Théorie de l'art pour l'art en France chez les derniers romantiques et les premiers réalistes*, Paris, 1906, invaluable. This work is hereafter simply referred to as Cassagne.

2 Perhaps it should be mentioned that to be 'impersonal' is not in itself a sufficient sign for attributing a writer to this group. Mérimée, for example, was 'impersonal' but probably not to be related to these authors in other ways although his example, along with Stendhal's, was of importance to them.

3 Flaubert, *Correspondance*, Vol. V. p.257.

4 Ibid., Vol. III, p.154.

5 Ibid., Vol. III, p.21: letter to Louise Colet, 1852.

6 'The Letters of Delacroix' in *The Painter's Eye*, ed. John L. Sweeney, London, 1956, p.183.

7 *House of Fiction*, p.25.

8 *House of Fiction*, pp.140-1.

9 Ibid., p.29.

10 *Pierre et Jean*, ed. Pierre Cogny, Paris 1959, p.4.

11 Ibid., p.5.

12 *House of Fiction*, p.36.

13 Ibid., p.29.

14 *Pierre et Jean*, p.7.

15 Op.cit., pp.39-40.

16 Cassagne, p.438.

17 Cassagne, p.432.

18 *Selected Letters of Henry James*, ed. Leon Edel, London, 1956, pp.135-6.

19 *House of Fiction*, pp.42-3.

20 Ibid., p.43.

21 Ibid., p.45.

22 Op.cit., p.325.

23 Flaubert, *Correspondance*, Vol. VII, p.163.

24 *Transatlantic Sketches* (1875), pp.56-7. Cf. Flaubert's letter to the Princess Mathilde (1874): 'Les pays sans histoire ne m'intéressent pas, étant plus sensible aux oeuvres de l'Art qu'à celles de la Nature'. ('Countries without history do not interest me, being more sensible to works of art than to those of nature.') *Correspondance*, Vol. VII, p.166.

25 Cornelia P. Kelley in her study *The Early Development of Henry James* (1965, revised edition), points out the importance of Gautier for James's descriptions of Milan Cathedral and the Last Supper, and his general influence on James's descriptive prose at this time. Chapter 9, p.135. For his analysis of Tintoretto, see p.139.

26 *Renée Mauperin*, Chap. 1.

27 Ibid., Chap. 1. A further and more detailed examination of this paragraph and the succeeding ones will be made in Chapter 7.

28 *Manette Salomon*, Chap. 1.

29 *The Ambassadors*, Vol. II, Book XI, Chap. 3, p.247. The movement of the last phrase is specially significant: the climax of emotional intensity is reached with Lambinet —when the scene is a painting and when it is furthest removed from a remembered experience (Tremont Street) or a present one (France). It is France and Tremont Street *because* it is Lambinet: the painting is what gives value to both past and present.

30 Ibid., p.255.

31 *CT*, VI, p.114-5.

32 Ibid., pp.115-6.

33 Ibid., p.116.

34 Ibid., pp.116-7.

35 *The Portrait of a Lady*, Chap. 23, Vol. I, p.354.

36 *The Spoils of Poynton* (*The Novels and Tales*, Vol. X) p.24; p.25.

37 Ibid., p.46.

38 *The Tragic Muse* (reprint of the 1890 text), New York, 1960, p.307.

39 Ibid., pp.309-10.

40 Ibid., p.310.

41 Ibid., p.19.

42 Ibid., pp.99-100.

43 Ibid., p.581.

44 pp.37-8.

45 *Notebooks*, p.58.

46 *CT*, V, p.303.

47 Ibid., p.323.

48 Ibid., p.331.

49 Ibid., p.332.

50 Ibid., pp.332-3.

51 Ibid., p.333.

52 Ibid., p.336.

53 Cassagne, p.220.

54 Ibid., p.220.

55 *Notebooks*, p.87.

56 *Novels and Tales*, Vol. XV, p.19.

57 Ibid., p.41.

58 Ibid., p.9.

59 Ibid., p.11.

60 Ibid., pp.11-12.

61 Ibid., pp.36-7. Compare this with Gautier's remark about Flaubert as reported by Feydeau: 'Il (Flaubert) a eu disait-il la sagesse de ne pas embarrasser sa vie d'une femme légitime ou illégitime, ni d'enfants.' Cassagne, p.220. ('He [Flaubert], he said, had the wisdom not to encumber his life with wife,

legitimate or illegitimate, nor with children.')
62 *Manette Salomon*, Chapter, 36,
63 'The Lesson of the Master', p.66. Compare this with the Goncourts' entry in their *Journal*: 'La pure littérature, le livre qu'un artiste fait pour se satisfaire, me semble un genre bien près de mourir. Je ne vois plus de travailleurs de cette manière que Flaubert et nous.' ('Pure literature, the book which an artist makes for his own satisfaction, seems to me a genre which is almost dead. I see but Flaubert and ourselves as still working in this manner.') Quoted by Cassagne, p.217.
64 Ibid., p.76.
65 Ibid., p.78. Compare Gautier's remark: 'Un artiste est avant tout un homme; il peut refléter dans son oeuvre, soit qu'il les partage, soit qu'il les repousse, les amours, les haines, les passions, les croyances et les préjugés de son temps, à la condition que l'art sacré sera toujours pour lui le but, et non le moyen.' Cassagne, p.459. ('An artist is first of all a man; his work may reflect the loves, hates, passions, beliefs and prejudices of his time, either because he shares them or because he rejects them, but on the condition that for him blessed art is the end and not the means.')
66 *Charles Demailly* is dated Paris, January 1859. First published by Dentu under the title *Les Hommes de lettres* in 1860, it appeared in the second edition, published by Lacroix et Verboekhoven, in 1868 under its present title. James was then twenty-five.
67 *Charles Demailly*, Chapter 36.
68 Ibid., Chapter 36.
69 Ibid., Chapter 36.
70 'At Isella', *CT*, II, p.314.
71 'Venice', *Portraits of Places*, 1883, p.3.
72 *Portrait of a Lady*, Vol. I, p.61.
73 Viola Hopkins, 'Visual Art Devices and Parallels in the Fiction of Henry James', *PMLA*, 1961 in *Modern Judgments: Henry James*, ed. Tony Tanner, London, 1968 p.108.

7. A Little Band of Realists and 'The Ambassadors'

1 *The Ambassadors*, Vol. I, p.195.
2 Ibid., p.195.
3 Ibid., p.195.
4 Ibid., p.196.
5 Ibid., Book II, Chapter 2, pp.96-7.
6 Ibid., Book IV, Chapter 2, pp.169-70.
7 Ibid., Book VI, Chapter 3, p.280.
8 Ibid., p.283.
9 Ibid., Vol. II, p.91.
10 Ibid., Vol. II, p.202.
11 Ibid., Book XII, Chapter 1, Vol. II, p.276.
12 Throughout this section I am greatly indebted to the work of Jacques Dubois, *Romanciers français de l'instantané au XIXème siecle*, Brussels, 1963, for his analysis of the French authors I have used in my comparisons with James.
13 *Partial Portraits*, p.214.
14 *Collected Tales*, Vol III, p.123.
15 *La Comédie humaine*, ed. Marcel Bouteron (Pléiade edition), Paris, 1951, Vol. II, p.1085.
16 *Madame Bovary*, ed. Edouard Maynial, Paris, 1961, p.244.
17 *Renée Mauperin*, Lyon, 1923, p.4 (Chapter I).
18 Ibid., p.203.

19 *Fromont Jeune et Risler Aîné. Oeuvres complètes, Ne Varietur* edition (Paris, 1929), p.271.
20 Op.cit., p.7-8.
21 *The Ambassadors*, Vol. II, p.97.
22 For a discussion of the use of abstract nouns in place of adjectives and the place of abstractions in the style of the Goncourts see Stephen Ullmann, *Style in the French Novel*, Oxford, 1964, pp.121-45.
23 Dubois, op.cit., p.120.
24 Ibid., pp.121-2.
25 *L'Évangéliste*, Ne Varietur Edition, p.64.
26 *The Ambassadors*, Vol. II. pp.13-14.
27 Cf. James's remarks on Daudet's style in his 1883 article: 'It gathers up every patch of colour, every colloquial note, that will help to illustrate, and moves eagerly, lightly, triumphantly along . . . It never rests, never is satisfied, never leaves the idea sitting half-draped . . . it is always panting, straining, fluttering, trying to add more, to produce the effect which shall make the reader see with his eyes, or rather with the marvellous eyes of Alphonse Daudet.' *Partial Portraits*, p.232.
28 *Les Rois en exil*, p.197.
29 *The Ambassadors*, Vol. I, pp. 95-6.
30 For a fuller discussion of this aspect of Daudet and the Goncourts see Dubois, op.cit., p.73.
31 *The Ambassadors*, Vol. II. pp. 200-1.

8. The Culmination: 'The Golden Bowl'

1 *The Golden Bowl*, Vol. I, p.3.
2 Ibid., p.215.
3 Ibid., p.14.
4 Ibid., pp.46-7.
5 Ibid., pp.137-8.
6 Ibid., p.42.
7 *Art of the Novel*, p.38.

Suggested Further Reading

Adams, Percy, G.: 'Young Henry James and the Lesson of His Master Balzac', *Revue de la littérature comparée*, XXXV, pp. 458-67.

Alain, [Emile Chartier]: *Avec Balzac*, Paris, 1937.

Allott, Miriam: 'Symbol and Image in the Later Works of Henry James', *Essays in Criticism* Vol. 3 (1953), pp.321-36.

Bardèche, Maurice: *Balzac romancier*, Paris, 1940.

Beach, Joseph Warren: *The Method of Henry James*, New Haven, 1918.

Beebe, Maurice: *Ivory Towers and Sacred Founts*, New York, 1964; 'The Turned Back of Henry James', *South Atlantic Quarterly*, October 1954, pp.521-39.

Béguin, Albert: *Balzac: lu et relu*, Paris, 1965.

Beuchat, Charles: *Histoire du naturalisme français*, Paris, 1949.

Bewley, Marius: *The Complex Fate*, London, 1952; New York, 1964.

Booth, Wayne, C: *The Rhethoric of Fiction*, Chicago, 1961.

Borgerhoff, Elbert B. O.: '*Réalisme* and Kindred Words: Their Use as Terms of Literary Criticism in the First Half of the Nineteenth Century', *PLMA*, LIII (1938), pp.837-43.

Bouvier, Émile: *La Bataille réaliste*, Paris, 1913.

Bowden, Edwin T.: *The Themes of Henry James*, New Haven, 1956.

Bowen, Ray P.: *The Dramatic Construction of Balzac's Novels*, Eugene, Oregon, 1940.

Brooks, Van Wyck: *The Pilgrimage of Henry James*, London, 1928.

Brunetière, Ferdinand: *Le Roman naturaliste*, Paris, 1882.

Cargill, Oscar: *The Novels of Henry James*, New York, 1961.

Cassagne, Albert: *La Théorie de l'art pour l'art chez les derniers romantiques et les premiers réalistes*, Paris, 1906.

Dargan, E. Preston: 'Studies in Balzac: (III) His General Method', *Modern Philology*, XVII (July 1919), pp.113-24; *Honoré de Balzac, A Force of Nature*, Chicago, 1932.

Dargan, E. Preston, Clair, W. L., et al.: *Studies in Balzac's Realism*, Chicago, 1932.

Dubois, Jacques: *Romanciers français de l'Instantané au XIXème siècle*, Brussells, 1963.

Dumesnil, René: *L'époque réaliste et naturaliste*, Paris, 1945.

Dupee, Frederick Wilcox: *The Question of Henry James*, London, 1945.

Edel, Leon: 'A Letter to the Editor', *American Literature*, XXIV pp.370-72; *Henry James: The Untried Years*, Philadelphia, 1953; London, 1953; *Henry James: The Conquest of London*, Philadelphia, 1962; London, 1962; *Henry James: The Middle Years* Philadelphia, 1962, London, 1963; *Henry James: The Treacherous Years*, Philadelphia, 1969; London, 1969; *Henry James: The Master*, Philadelphia, 1971; London, 1972; 'The Architecture of James's "New York Edition" ', *New England Quarterly*, XXIV, pp. 169-178.

Faguet, Émile: 'De l'influence de Théophile Gautier', *Revue des Deux Mondes*, 1911.

Ferguson, Louis A.: *Henry James and Honoré de Balzac: A Comparative Study in Literary Techniques*, Unpublished dissertation, Fordham University, New York, 1967.

Fernandez, Ramon: 'La méthode de Balzac', in *Messages*, Paris, 1926.

Friedman, Norman: 'Point of View', *PMLA* LXX (1955), pp.1160-84.

Gard, Roger (editor): *Henry James: The Critical Heritage*, London, 1968; New York, 1968.

Garnier, Marie Reine: *Henry James et la France*, Paris, 1927.

Hardy, Barbara: *The Appropriate Form: An Essay on the Novel*, London, 1964; Evanston, Ill., 1971.

Holland, Lawrence: *The Expense of Vision: Essays on the Craft of Henry James*, Princeton, 1964.

Howells, William Dean: 'Mr. Henry James, Jr', *Century*, N.S. III (Nov. 1882);
Criticism and Fiction, London, 1891.

Hunt, Herbert James: *Honoré de Balzac*, London, 1957; Westport, Conn., 1957; *Balzac's Comédie humaine*, London, 1959.

Isle, Walter: *Experiments in Form: Henry James's Novels*, Cambridge, Mass., 1968.

Kelley, Cornelia Pulsifer: *The Early Development of Henry James*, Urbana, Illinois, 1965.

Krook, Dorothea: *The Ordeal of Consciousness in Henry James*, Cambridge, 1962.

Laubriet, Pierre: *L'Intelligence de l'art chez Balzac: d'une esthétique balzacienne*, Paris, 1961.

Leavis, F. R.: *The Great Tradition*, London, 1948; New York, 1963; *Anna Karenina and Other Essays*, London, 1967; New York, 1969.

Leavis, Q. D.: 'A Note on Literary Indebtedness: Dickens, George

Eliot, Henry James.' *Hudson Review*, VIII, pp.423-8.

Levy, Leo Ben: *Versions of Melodrama, a study of the fiction and drama of Henry James, 1865-97*. Berkeley, Calif., 1957.

Lodge, David: *Language of Fiction*, London, 1966; New York, 1967.

Maigron, Louis: *Le Roman historique à l'époque romantique*, Paris, 1898.

Marsan, Jules: *La Bataille romantique*, Paris, 1912-24.

Martin, Harold C. (editor): *Style in Prose Fiction, English Institute Essays, 1958*, New York, 1959.

Martino, Pierre: *Le Naturalisme française 1870-95*, Paris, 1951; *Le roman réaliste sous le second Empire*, Paris, 1913.

Matthiessen, F. O.: *Henry James: The Major Phase*, New York, 1944; 'James and the Plastic Arts', *Kenyon Review*, V (autumn 1943), pp.533-50.

Minter, Elsie G.: *The Image in the Mirror: Henry James and the French Realists*, unpublished dissertation, University of North Carolina, 1962.

Onimus, Jean: 'L'Expression du temps dans le roman contemporain', *Revue de littérature comparée* 1954, pp.299-317.

Pommier, Jean: 'À propos des Emaux et Camées: notes et impressions', *Revue universitaire*, 1943.

Rogers, Samuel: *Balzac and the Novel*, Madison, Wisc., 1953.

Rousset, Jean: *Forme et signification*, Paris, 1964.

Salvan, Albert J.: 'L'essence du réalisme française', *Comparative Literature*, III (1951), pp.218-33.

Seznec, Jean: 'Lettres de Tourguéneff à Henry James', *Comparative Literature*, I (1949), pp.193-209.

Short, R. W.: 'The Sentence Structure of Henry James', *American Literature* XVIII (1946), pp. 71-88.

Stabey, Robert M.: 'Henry James and "The Most Impressive Convention in all History" ', *American Literature*, XXX, pp.89-102.

Starkie, Enid: *From Gautier to Eliot: the influence of France on English Literature*, London, 1962; St. Clair Shores, Mich., 1971.

Steegmuller, Francis: 'Flaubert's Sundays: Maupassant and Henry James', *The Cornhill*, No.974, pp. 124-30.

Stevick, Philip (editor): *The Theory of the Novel*, New York, 1967.

Taine, Hippolyte: *Essais de critique et d'histoire*, Paris, 1858; 'Préface' to *Lettres à une Inconnue* by Prosper Mérimée, Paris, 1874; *Nouveaux Essais de critique et d'histoire*, Paris, 1896.

Tanner, T: *The Reign of Wonder*, Cambridge, 1965; editor: *Henry James: Modern Judgments*, London, 1968; 'The Watcher from the Balcony: Henry James's *The Ambassadors*', *The Critical Quarterly* VIII, No.1 (1966), pp.35-52; 'The Fearful Self: Henry James's *The Portrait of a Lady*', *The Critical Quarterly*, VII, No.3 (1965).

Thibaudet, Albert: *Gustave Flaubert*, Paris, 1935.

Tintner, Adelina R.: 'The Spoils of Henry James', *PMLA*, LXI (1946), pp.239-51.'

Ullmann, Stephen: *Style in the French Novel*, New York, 1957; Oxford, 1964; *Language and Style*, New York, 1964; Oxford, 1964; 'La Transposition dans la poésie de Gautier', *Le Français Moderne*, XV, pp.256-86.

Vial, A.: *Maupassant et l'art du roman*, Paris, 1954; 'Flaubert, émule et disciple émancipé de Balzac', *Revue d'histoire littéraire*, July-September, 1948.

Ward, J. A.: *The Search for Form: Studies in the Structure of James's Fiction*, Chapel Hill, 1967; Oxford, 1967.

Watt, Ian: 'The First Paragraph of *The Ambassadors*: An Explication', *Essays in Criticism*, X, pp.250-74.

Wegelin, Christof: *The Image of Europe in Henry James*, Dallas, Texas, 1958.

Weinberg, Bernard: *French Realism, The Critical Reaction, 1830-70*. New York, 1937.

Wellek, René: 'Henry James's Literary Theory and Criticism', *American Literature*, XXX, pp. 293-321.

Willen, Gerald (editor): *A Casebook on Henry James's 'The Turn of the Screw'*, New York, 1963.

Winters, Yvor: *In Defense of Reason*, Denver, 1947.

Index